TEST VALIDITY

Edited by

Howard Wainer
Henry I. Braun
Educational Testing Service

1988

LAWRENCE ERLBAUM ASSOCIATES, PUBLISHERS
Hillsdale, New Jersey   Hove and London

Lawrence Erlbaum Associates, Inc., Publishers
365 Broadway
Hillsdale, New Jersey 07642

Library of Congress Cataloging-in-Publication Data

Test validity.

  Papers of a conference entitled "Test validity for the
1990's and beyond," held May 28–29, 1986 at the
Educational Testing Service, Princeton, N.J.
  Bibliography: p.
  Includes index.
  1. Examinations—Validity—Congresses. 2. Educational
tests and measurements—Congresses. I. Wainer, Howard.
II. Braun, Henry I., 1949– . III. Educational
Testing Service.
LB3060.7.T47 1988   371.2'6'013   87-8986
ISBN 0-89859-997-0

Printed in the United States of America
10 9 8 7 6 5 4 3 2

To Laurent, Ilana, and Nora,
whose validity needs no testing

Contents

List of Contributors

WILLIAM H. ANGOFF   Distinguished Research Scientist, Educational Testing Service, Princeton, NJ 08541

HENRY I. BRAUN   Director, Statistical and Psychometric Research and Services, Educational Testing Service, Princeton, NJ 08541-0001

LEE J. CRONBACH   16 Laburnum Rd., Atherton, CA 94025

RICHARD P. DURÁN   Department of Education, University of California at Santa Barbara, Santa Barbara, CA 96016

BERT F. GREEN   Department of Psychology, Johns Hopkins University, Charles and 34th Streets, Baltimore, MD 21218

LAWRENCE V. HEDGES   Department of Education, University of Chicago, Chicago, IL 60637

PAUL W. HOLLAND   Director, Research Statistics Group, Educational Testing Service, Princeton, NJ 08541

SAMUEL MESSICK   Vice President, Research, Educational Testing Service, Princeton, NJ 08541

BENGT MUTHÉN   Graduate School of Education, University of California, Los Angeles, CA 90024

JAMES W. PELLEGRINO   Department of Psychology, University of California at Santa Barbara, Santa Barbara, CA 93106

DONALD B. RUBIN   Department of Statistics, Harvard University, Cambridge, MA 02138

FRANK L. SCHMIDT   School of Industrial Relations, Phillips Hall, Room 569, University of Iowa, Iowa City, Iowa 52242

LYNN STEINBERG   Department of Psychology, Indiana University, Psychology Building, Bloomington, IN 47405

ROBERT J. STERNBERG   Department of Psychology, Yale University, Box 11A, Yale Station, New Haven, CN 06520

DOROTHY T. THAYER   Research Statistics Group, Educational Testing Service, Princeton, NJ 08541

DAVID THISSEN   Department of Psychology, University of Kansas, 426 Fraser Hall, Lawrence, KS 66045

HOWARD WAINER   Principal Research Scientist Educational Testing Service, Princeton, NJ 08541

WARREN W. WILLINGHAM   Assistant Vice President, Research, Educational Testing Service, Princeton, NJ 08541

Preface

On May 28–29, 1986, a conference entitled "Test Validity for the 1990s and Beyond" was held at the Educational Testing Service in Princeton, New Jersey. The purpose of this conference was to provide an assessment of the current state of research and practice in test validity and to indicate future directions. With testing expected to undergo significant changes in the years ahead, driven in part by demands of users and in part by advances in technology, we felt it would be useful to bring together some eminent scientists closely involved with test validity and ask them to contribute their views on the subject.

In our opinion, the conference was very successful with a broad range of interests and opinions expressed. This volume is intended to make the conference presentations available to a wider audience.

The chapters contained herein were prepared especially for this volume. The talks given at the conference were based upon the papers but were not necessarily identical to them. At the conference we were fortunate to have Professor Donald B. Rubin to discuss the presentations. An edited transcription of his remarks is appended to Section IV. We decided to include his comments because his wide-ranging remarks often provided both context and generality for the invited contributions.

The volume contains all the proceedings of the conference with one notable exception. One afternoon was devoted to an abbreviated mock trial based on an actual court case that focused on the validity of pre-employment tests used in screening applicants for places in a firefighter academy. Although tests have been increasingly involved in litigation, few of those attending the conference had actually participated in or viewed legal proceedings of this kind. Presenting this trial allowed a close-up view of the nature of the legal argument, as well as contrast between the notions of scientific evidence and those of legal evidence. Posttrial comments by the presiding judge as well as the two attorneys were particularly informative. Although this volume could not include the trial, a videotape of it is available from the editors.

Acknowledgments

We owe thanks to the many individuals who played an important role in bringing the conference and this volume to fruition. Principal funding for the conference was provided by the Air Force Human Resources Laboratory (AFHRL) in San Antonio, Texas [Contract no. F41689-84-D-0002, Subcontract no. S-744-030-001].

Dr. Malcolm Ree, Senior Scientist, was not only instrumental in securing AFHRL support but also provided useful advice on the design of the program. His enthusiasm and commitment to the project is greatly appreciated. Funding for the preparation of the volume was provided by Educational Testing Service. The support of Gregory Anrig, President, Robert Solomon, Executive Vice-President and Ernest Anastasio, (then) Vice President for Research Management were most appreciated. Stanford von Mayrhauser, General Counsel, also provided financial, intellectual, and moral support for this effort. Linda DeLauro, Conference Coordinator, provided administrative support from the inception of the project through to the completion of this book. Without her extraordinary efforts the entire enterprise would surely have foundered.

H. W.
H. I. B.
Princeton, N.J.
July 1987

Introduction

Testing plays a critical role in all our lives. Beyond its formidable presence in our schools, it is widely employed both by government and industry as an aid to making decisions about people. Thus, testing affects us both directly as individuals who are tested and indirectly through its influence on the welfare of the nation. As befits a practice of such importance, the scrutiny of professionals, national policymakers and the courts has become ever more intense. Their concern centers on whether a particular test properly accomplishes its specified goal and whether it does so in a fair and equitable fashion. This is the core of test validity.

More formally, the *Joint technical standards for educational and psychological testing* (APA, AERA, NCME, 1985) states: "Validity is the most important consideration in test evaluation. The concept refers to the appropriateness, meaningfulness and usefulness of *the specific inferences made from test scores.*[1] Test validation is the process of accumulating evidence to support such inferences. A variety of inferences may be made from scores produced by a given test, and there are many ways of accumulating evidence to support any particular inference. Validity, however, is a unitary concept. Although evidence may be accumulated in many ways, validity always refers to the degree to which that evidence supports the inferences that are made from test scores."

Not surprisingly the practice of testing antedates concern with its validity. One of the earliest references to testing is described in *Judges* (12:4–6). It seems

---

[1]Note that it is not the test that has validity, but rather *the inferences* made from the test scores. Thus before we can assess a test's validity, we must know the purposes to which it is to be put.

that the Gileadites developed a short verbal test to uncover the fleeing Ephraimites that were hiding in their midst. The test was one item long. Candidates had to pronounce the word "shibboleth"; Ephraimites apparently pronounced the initial "sh" as "s." Although the consequences of this test were quite severe (the banks of the Jordan were strewn with the bodies of the 42,000 who failed), there is no record of any validity study. Consequently, even though history records all the punished as interlopers, we really do not know how many were Gileadites who spoke with a lisp.[2]

In 1115 B.C., at the beginning of the Chan dynasty, formal testing procedures were instituted for candidates for office. This appears to be the first documented example of a rigorous mental testing program. The Chinese discovered the fundamental tenet of testing; that a relatively small sample of an individual's performance, measured under carefully controlled conditions, could yield an accurate picture of that individual's ability under much broader conditions for a longer period of time. The procedures developed by the Chinese are quite similar to many of the canons of good testing practice used today.[3]

The Chinese system developed over many centuries. By 1370 A.D. it had arrived at a reasonably mature form. A person aspiring to hold public office had to pass three competitive examinations. The first one, given annually and locally, required a day and a night. The passing rate was from 1% to 7%. Those passing were named "budding scholars." The second stage was given every 3 years and was held in each provincial capital. Here all of the "budding scholars" were assembled for three sessions of 3 days and 3 nights each. These examinations were scored with independent readers and the examinees were anonymous. Successful candidates (reported as 1% to 10%) were considered "promoted scholars" and were eligible for the third tier of examinations given the following spring in Peking. In this third set of examinations about 3% passed and became eligible for public office.

Although there is no record of any formal validity studies held as part of the Chinese program, few would doubt that those who succeeded in surmounting the third tier of the rigorous program[4] were highly qualified individuals. Why is it that the results of the biblical test seem obviously questionable, whereas the Chinese program yielded results that no one would question—at least in terms of errors of the first kind?

---

[2]One is reminded of baseball umpire Bill Clem's response when he was asked, "Bill, did you call 'em as you saw 'em? Or did you call 'em as they were?" He answered, "The way I called 'em was the way they were."

[3]The Chinese testing program was used as a model for the British system set up in 1833 to select trainees for the Indian Civil service—the precursor to the British civil service. The success of the British system influenced Senator Charles Sumner of Massachusetts and Representative Thomas Jenckes in developing the examination system they introduced into Congress in 1860. A fascinating description of this is found in Têng (1943) and the interested reader is directed to that source.

[4]There were a number of deaths recorded during the testing process.

The key is the selection ratio. Note that in the Chinese program the overall selection ratio was no greater than about 200 successes per million candidates, and could be as few as 3 per million. Thus the test needed only a very small amount of validity to assure the quality of the final selection.

Modern testing applications usually do not have this extraordinary selection ratio. Instead they are more often like the biblical situation wherein a substantial proportion of candidates will be selected. Consequently, validity becomes a crucial question. The modern shibboleth must be shown to be connected both theoretically and empirically to the criteria of interest.

In the introduction to his classic text on mental testing, Harold Gulliksen pointed out that "During the 1890s several attempts were made to utilize the new methods of measurement of individual differences in order to predict college grades. J. McKeen Cattell and his student, Clark Wissler, tried a large number of psychological tests and correlated them with grades in various subjects at Columbia University; see Cattell (1890), Cattell and Farrand (1896), and Wissler (1901). The correlations between psychological tests and grades were around zero, the highest being .19. A similar attempt by Gilbert (1894) at Yale, produced similarly disappointing results." The validity study provided a clear cautionary note.

Over the last 90 years, as the span of testing has broadened, so too has the notion of test validity. What makes validation research so exciting is not simply that there are always new tests to study. Rather, it is that we are making greater demands of our tests: While asking that they conform to an increasingly stringent set of principles of good practice, we are also asking that they perform more difficult tasks; e.g., predicting performance in complex domains, even when performance levels are not easily quantified. As exciting as the area of test validity is now, it promises to get more so. Rapid advances in cognitive psychology and computer technology will usher in a new generation of tests that may well change not only how we use tests but also how we think about them.

This book addresses some of those changes. It is divided into four sections. The first is concerned with the historical and epistemological bases of validity, as well as current and future issues. Section II, The "Changing Faces of Validity," discusses the potential impact that developments in cognitive psychology and computer technology might have on the makeup and administration of tests. These essays point to changes in the validity criteria as well as methodology of measurement. Section III, "Testing Validity in Specific Subpopulations," examines the questions of validity in the testing of particular groups of individuals. Specifically considered are people with handicaps and members of linguistic minorities. In addition there are two methodological chapters which describe the latest developments in the assessment of differential item functioning. The last section, "Statistical Innovations in Validity Assessment," describes new methods of analysis that allow investigators to look more deeply into the validity question.

We have come a long way in recognizing that we should be seeking not only the best way to separate the Ephraimites from the Gileadites, but also the best way to measure how well we seem to have done so. The contributions to this volume point to new directions for that path.

REFERENCES

American Psychological Association, American Educational Research Association, & National Council on Measurement in Education. (1985). *Standards for educational and psychological testing.* Washington, DC: American Psychological Association.

Cattell, J. M. (1890). Mental tests and measurements. *Mind, 15,* 373–381.

Cattell, J. M., & Ferrand, L. (1896). Physical and mental measurements of the students at Columbia University. *Psychological Review, 3,* 618–648.

Gilbert, J. A. (1894). Researches on the mental and physical development of school children. *Studies Yale Laboratory, 2,* 40–100.

Gulliksen, H. O. (1950). *A theory of mental tests.* New York: Wiley.

Têng, Ssu–yü. (1943). Chinese influence on the Western examination system. *Harvard Journal of Asiatic Studies, 7,* 267–312.

Wissler, C. (1901). The correlation of mental and physical tests. *Psychological Monographs, 3,* (16), 1–62.

HISTORICAL AND EPISTEMOLOGICAL BASES OF VALIDITY

This section opens with the keynote address delivered by Lee J. Cronbach. He argues that validation is best seen as an unending process which ultimately advances most rapidly when it is subject to honest scrutiny from many different viewpoints. While it is impossible to anticipate all the questions that can be asked of a test score and its use, five different perspectives are identified from which these questions can arise. Each perspective places a different burden on the validator. Cronbach counsels both impatience and patience. Impatience with those who mourn for the good old days when validity could be simply described and neatly wrapped up in a few well-designed studies—and patience for the development of an elegant and unassailable theoretical framework for the validation argument.

Subsequently, William Angoff carefully traces the history of the development of the notion of validity, from its operational (and essentially atheoretical) beginnings late in the last century to its present state. It is particularly interesting to watch the evolution of construct validity from a junior member of a troika including criterion validity and content validity, to a coequal status and, finally, to representing "the whole of validity from a scientific point of view." Other types of validation become aspects or strategies in the validation argument. Equally important, Angoff argues, was the realization that it was the interpretation and usage of the test score that was the proper subject of validation. Thus responsibility for validity devolves upon the test user as well as

1

the test developer. Angoff recognizes a sea change in the philosophy underlying this evolution, the effects of which will be felt over many years.

The final chapter in this section, by Samuel J. Messick, presents a unified view of test validity for which empirically grounded construct interpretation is the linchpin. In this view, ''. . . the appropriateness, meaningfulness, and usefulness of score based inferences are inseparable. . . .'' He argues convincingly that proper validation of the use and interpretation of test scores requires both an evidential basis and a consequential basis. While the former refers to empirical appraisals of relationships to other constructs, the latter refers to judgmental appraisals of the value context of implied relationships to various attributes and behaviors. Messick suggests that the profession is not so much in disagreement about the general outlines of a theory of validity but rather how the validation process is to be carried out in practice. He ends with the provocative but quite logical admonition that the notion of validity is itself a construct and should (must?) itself be subject to validation. Indeed another chapter in this volume, authored by Richard Durán, touches exactly on this point.

As we move in the next decade toward new kinds of tests delivered in novel ways, we must as a profession develop meaningful guidelines for practice. The recently published *Standards for educational and psychological testing* are an important step forward. However, they need to be fleshed out by the thoughtful contributions of researchers as well as a well-stocked library of examples that can serve as models to all practitioners.

Chapter 1

Five Perspectives
on Validity Argument

Lee J. Cronbach
Stanford University

Validation was once a priestly mystery, a ritual performed behind the scenes, with the professional elite as witness and judge. Today it is a public spectacle combining the attractions of chess and mud wrestling. Disputes about the appropriateness of tests impose a large responsibility on validators.

Validators meet that responsibility through activities that clarify for a relevant community what a measurement means, and the limitations of each interpretation. The key word is "clarify." Four further comments: "Degree of justification," though not mentioned, is implied in the reference to "limitations." Second, the interpretation may take the form of a description, a prediction, or a recommended decision. Third, a local user's inferences and policies, as well as interpretations that the test producer promulgates, deserve scrutiny. Fourth, the task of validation is *not* to uphold a test, practice, or theory. Ideally, validators will prepare as debaters do. Studying a topic from all angles, a debater grasps the arguments pro and con so well that he or she could speak for either side. Or, shifting the metaphor to legal counselors, so well that they could tell either party what is strong and weak in its position.

The stance of this chapter is, I believe, consistent with the latest test standards (APA, AERA, NCME, 1985) and with recent writings of many scholars. I was especially pleased to find, in Anastasi's just-published (1986) overview of validation, a forceful statement of many of these ideas, and nothing (I think) that runs counter to what I shall say. Not everyone will be happy to find me subordinating traditional positivistic approaches and emphasizing their shortcomings. It is not that the old principles have been overturned; but the old tunes don't sound the same to ears jarred by *Larry P.*, the EEOC, and the Naderites, or by Kuhn and Toulmin.

VALIDATION AS EVALUATION ARGUMENT

A similar crisis of discontent with program evaluation led, in the last 10 years, to a revised conception of the role of research in shaping policy and practice (Cook & Shadish, 1986; Cronbach et al., 1980; and sources cited there). Validation of a test or test use *is* evaluation (Guion, 1980; Messick, 1980), so I propose here to extend to all testing the lessons from program evaluation. What House (1977) has called "the logic of evaluation argument" applies, and I invite you to think of "validity argument" rather than "validation research."

Although the swarm of doctrines and rulings buzzing about us is chaotic, one dominant note is heard. Validation speaks to a diverse and potentially critical audience; therefore, *the argument must link concepts, evidence, social and personal consequences, and values.*

The 30-year-old idea of three types of validity, separate but maybe equal, is an idea whose time has gone. Most validity theorists have been saying that content and criterion validities are no more than strands within a cable of validity argument (Dunnette & Borman, 1979; Guion, 1980; Messick, 1980). A favorable answer to one or two questions can fully support a test only when no one cares enough to raise further questions. Coming to understand what generates test scores and why they relate to antecedents and consequents, and to understand also the context of test use, is what enables the profession to defend against unwarranted criticism or to decide what change is warranted.

Developing an interpretation counts within validation, because confirmation, falsification, and revision intermesh. Especially when an instrument is young, inquiry that clarifies possibilities, anomalies, and boundary conditions—formative evaluation—is worth most. Meehl, in introducing us to construct validation, showed that criticism is able to rebuild as it destroys. (For a comparatively recent statement, see Meehl, 1977). A hypothesis that fails is more likely to be amended than abandoned (Lakatos, 1978). Similarly, adjustment at the margins occurs with a social policy (Braybrooke & Lindblom, 1963) and hence with a plan for test use. The conceptualization or the plan is amended just as much as necessary, in the light of all that has been learned.

I did not say "learned about *this* test." Validation advances on a broad front; what we learn about one test bears on others. Facts about the Law School Aptitude Test, for example, are cited in the literature to make points pertinent to the *class* of aptitude tests, and law school experience is invoked to make general points about the value loadings of selection policies.

"What work is required to validate a test interpretation?" That question, with its hint that we are after a "thumbs up/thumbs down" verdict, I now regard as shortsighted and unanswerable. The usual interpretation has many implications. To determine which ones are somewhat dependable and to define the limits of their applicability could require unlimited time and resources. Nor can supporting research in any amount immunize a theory against a future challenge based on new and credible assumptions. As psychological science generates new concepts, test interpretations will have to be reconsidered. Also, because psychological and educational tests influence who gets what in society, fresh challenges follow shifts in social power or social philosophy. *So validation is never finished.*

Fortunately, humans are willing to regulate their affairs through reasonable argument based on incomplete information. An affirmative argument should make clear and, to the extent possible, persuasive the construction of reality and the value weightings implicit in a test and its application. To be plausible, an argument pro or con must fit with prevailing beliefs and values—or successfully overturn them.

The first talent needed in developing a persuasive argument is that of devil's advocate. It is vital, and hellishly difficult, to become mindful of the many questions that can and should be raised. Questions about tests originate in five perspectives: the functional, the political, the operationist, the economic, and the explanatory. Validators should take seriously questions of all these types.

THE FUNCTIONAL PERSPECTIVE

The literature on validation has concentrated on the truthfulness of test interpretations, but the functionalist is more concerned with worth than truth. In the very earliest discussions of test validity, some writers said that a test is valid if it measures "what it purports to measure." That raised, in a primitive form, a question about truth. Other early writers, saying that a test is valid if it serves the purpose for which it is used, raised a question about worth. Truthfulness is an element in worth, but the two are not tightly linked. I shall illustrate with three challenges arising from the consequences of essentially truthful measurements.

Tests used in the schools ought to encourage sound distribution of instructional and study time. The charge is made again and again that machine-scorable tests emasculate instruction (for example, by giving importance to details of chemistry rather than to its central structure). Many tests have been guilty, so the occasional demonstration that some one objective test is innocent of the charge does not, should not, shift the burden of proof in the next instance from testers to critics (*Association . . . ,* 1978). Recall Frederiksen's (1984) story of the way verbal end-of-course examinations misdirected Navy technical training, whereas hands-on performance tests got instructors to do their proper job. Bloom (1986) spoke similarly about how instruction in a university improved when factual examinations (constructed by eminent psychometricians) were replaced by tests of interpretation skills. The worth of an instructional test lies in its contribution to the learning of students working up to the test, or to next year's quality of instruction.

Tests that honestly report facts may disserve student development and social progress. The Strong interest blank will serve as example. Its Psychologist score identified that career as a good prospect for young persons whose interests matched those typical of established psychologists. This design was inherently conservative, tending to perpetuate the style of the profession. When the profession evolved nonetheless, the original key became patently invalid as a description of psychologists' interests (Cronbach, 1984, p. 477). Similarly, built-in conservatism was what aroused latter-day objections to Strong's blank for women. With its scores for occupations in which women were numerous, the profile seemed to respond directly to typical questions of female counselees. By hinting, however, that the list of scales spanned the range of women's vocational options, the profile reinforced sex stereotypes.

Tests that impinge on the rights and life chances of individuals are inherently disputable. We have come a long way from the naïve testimony given Congress two decades ago to the effect that, if sex life or religion correlates with a criterion, psychologists who ask prospective employees about that are only doing their duty. An example of another sort comes from a California judge who threw out the verbal ability test used to select jurors. Rejecting low scorers tended systematically to exclude members of disadvantaged groups. Representativeness of the jury weighed far heavier on the scales of justice than superior comprehension, said the judge.

The bottom line is that validators have an obligation to review whether a practice has appropriate consequences for individuals and institutions, and especially to guard against adverse consequences (Messick, 1980). You (like Yalow & Popham, 1983) may prefer to exclude reflection on consequences from the meanings of the word *validation*, but you cannot deny the obligation.

THE POLITICAL PERSPECTIVE

Nonprofessionals will do the evaluating of practices unaided, if professionals do not communicate sensibly to them (Kleiman & Faley, 1985). Showing that a test measures reading comprehension is all to the good. Analysis cannot stop there, if a certain score on the test marks off "incompetents" to be penalized (or to benefit from special funding). Whether institutions are treating examinees fairly will be decided by the political-legal process, but the profession ought to improve the basis for that decision. (cf. test standard 6.1 of 1985).

Acceptance or rejection of a practice or theory comes about because a community is persuaded. Even research specialists do not judge a conclusion as it stands alone; they judge its compatibility with a network of prevailing beliefs (Fiske & Shweder, 1986; Lakatos & Musgrave, 1970; Suppe, 1977). Scientific argument and political argument differ in degree rather than kind, science having a longer time horizon, more homogeneous participants, and more formal reasoning. No commentator on evaluation devalues excellence with respect to experimental design, reproducibility, statistical rigor, etc. But we do say that these virtues are purchased at too high a price, when they restrict an inquiry to what can be assessed with greatest certainty.

Validity argument contributes when it develops facts and when it highlights uncertainties of fact or implication. A community *should* be disputatious (Campbell, 1986). Then judgments are more likely to be as sound as present information allows. Informed argument often ought not end in agreement, because substantive findings are equivocal and because participants weigh values differently. Unanimity of beliefs is not required for a political system to reach equilibrium.

Democracy is functioning well when every party learns how a pending decision would affect his or her interests, and feels that the decision process is being suitably sensitive to them. The investigator should canvass all types of stakeholders for candidate questions, then spread resources judiciously over inquiries likely to influence community judgments (Cronbach, 1982; Cronbach et al., 1980). Evaluators should resist pressure to concentrate on what persons in power have specified as *their* chief question. The obvious example of too narrow an inquiry is the validation of employment tests, which used to concentrate on predicting a criterion the employer cared about and neglected to collect facts on what kinds of applicants were most likely to be rejected by the test. A political backlash changed that.

A similar systemic change occurred in education. In Florida, testers and school officials convinced the courts that the test mandated for graduation adequately measured an important kind of competence. But the circuit court in *Debra P.* suspended the test until a further standard could be demonstrably satisfied: The schools had to provide ample opportunity for pupils to learn what the test appraised (Yalow & Popham, 1983). This demand was met by changing schooling in a politically acceptable direction. Perhaps issues of fairness are always resolved by political balancing, however much jurisprudence, philosophy, and factual inquiry try to intellectualize them.

To win acceptance for tests professionals view as fair, effective communication is vital. The student who complains "The exam wasn't fair" almost always goes on to say, "The lessons didn't give us the answers to those questions." Yet for the teacher to anticipate test questions and supply particular answers is not liberal education and not education in problem solving. Response to unfamiliar material must be examined to assess thinking; that was the heart of Bloom's story about university examining. Until educators and testers convince students and the public that, in those very subjects where excellence is most wanted, coping with the problematic is a main objective, valid tests will be howled down as "unfair." Matching tests to the curriculum produces a spurious validity argument, wherever the curricular aim is no higher than to have students reproduce authority's responses to a catechism.

THE OPERATIONIST PERSPECTIVE

Matching test content to a domain of performance is a central idea of operationists. For them, a procedure has validity if it collects an adequate direct sample of behavior of a defined type. Cureton (1951), speaking of criteria, said that the variable to be measured must be defined by specifying "the acts or operations of which it is composed. . . . If the acts observed [adequately represent] . . . the defined series, . . . a set of criterion scores has, by definition, perfect relevance" (pp. 625, 632). Specification, it is agreed, should include, in addition to a content outline, the injunction to the subject, and the instructions to the tester, observer, or scorer, because any change in these could alter what is measured.

Operational language makes clear what class of observing procedures the validity research bears directly upon. In science the function of operational definition is to permit replication of the procedure on the original object or comparable objects. That is also its function in applied testing: to enable us to obtain comparable facts on different persons or groups. We need that, because names of variables are indefinite. "Mastery of the addition facts" is not a subtle concept; still, two test constructors will produce discordant measures when their emphases on speed differ, or when one includes horizontal arrays of numbers and the other does not.

By minimizing interpretation, the operationist temporarily sidesteps most questions of truth and worth. It might seem that the only validity question is whether the instance of the procedure conforms to the definition. But operationism alone cannot establish validity, of test or criterion.

Challenge to the substantive hypotheses built into the definition drags the argument outside operationism. Thus *not* specifying an aspect of the procedure presupposes that a change in that aspect would not alter the scores. A critic advocating a further control proposes a counterhypothesis, and thus raises an empirical question.

On the side of worth, one necessary challenge is whether the variable is overspecified, so that scores are limited by an irrelevancy. Verbal examinations in technical training are the obvious example. The Campbell–Fiske (1959) view that measuring a variable by several methods is a key step in validation directly assaults operationism.

Anyone defining a measuring procedure implies that the variable is relevant to some purpose, and perhaps is by itself sufficient for that purpose. Scrutinizing the fit of an achievement tester's domain definition to the goals of instruction is necessary in the validity argument. When the operationist Ebel said that (1956), he drifted from the clear, flat lake of operationism into the cross-currents of public opinions about the worth of educational goals.

If those interested are persuaded that the measuring instrument matches what they consider important, fine. If not, either the instrument will be rejected, or parties in disagreement will find a political compromise, or a nonoperationist move will be made to justify the claim. The move may be to simple empiricism, a showing that the test correlates with something recognized as important. Or perhaps one tries to demonstrate how the measurement echoes a practically significant causal mechanism. I turn, then, to the empirical.

THE ECONOMIC PERSPECTIVE

In employment testing and almost equally in student selection and guidance, the dominant view of validity has been empirical. Traditional validation puts overwhelming weight on the criterion; and great vulnerability lies therein. A conspicuous feature of many opinions handed down in recent fair employment cases is the judge's criticism of the criterion (Kleiman & Faley, 1985). Improvement of criterion information will always be high among our concerns; I need not dwell on that.

Evaluation of tests as predictors became more explicitly economic following the Taylor–Russell paper of 1939. (See especially Brogden, 1946; Cronbach & Gleser, 1965; Hunter & Schmidt, 1982). The basic idea is to put a dollar value on the quality of personnel decisions. This is now a lively frontier, because there has been progress in estimating dollar values and because sharper questions are being posed (Boudreau, 1983; Murphy, 1986; Reilly & Smither, 1985).

Classification; the Importance of Interactions. A major branch of utility theory stemmed from experience with military classification in World War II. Though vocational guidance and personnel assignment rely on multiscore profiles, validation of profiles was neglected, and is. Efficiency of classification or educational placement is to be evaluated from a difference in regressions. Sorting persons on a test score pays off if the regression slope relating the utility-scaled criterion from the first job to the score is steep, while that from the second job has a gentle slope, or even a negative one. Utility is enhanced, of course, if for another score the steep slope goes with the second job (Brogden, 1951; Cronbach & Snow, 1977, Chap. 2).

The most extensive validation of this type was carried out on the College Board test for placement in English. Its correlations with the criterion are consistently positive. But placement—routing freshmen into remedial rather than regular English courses—requires a further defense. In a search for regression differences, only a modest fraction of the samples showed a pattern indicative of validity (Cronbach, 1985).

The ASVAB profile is supposed to aid in classification. In the technical report, two tables of cross-correlations give information relevant to that aim. Table 1.1a reproduces one set. The validity generalization obvious in its columns, and the high intercorrelations in Table 1.1b, suggest that validity for

TABLE 1.1
Selected Coefficients from the Technical Report
for ASVAB-14[a]

(a) Correlations of ASVAB composite scores with outcomes in
four types of Marine Corps training[b,c]

	Composite			
Course Category	BC	MC	EE	HST
Business and Clerical	.67	.52	.63	.62
Mechanical and Crafts	.57	.64	.63	.63
Electronics and Electrical	.63	.63	.69	.67
Health, Social, Technology	.66	.60	.66	.66

(b) Intercorrelations for composites (and reliabilities)[d]

Composite	BC	MC	EE	HST
BC	(.94)	.71	.86	.86
MC		(.93)	.91	.93
EE			(.94)	.94
HST				(.95)

[a]All data come from persons tested with one or two of forms
8, 9, 10 of ASVAB. These are said to be parallel to form 14.
[b]From Table 46 of Stephenson et al. (1986). They credit the
correlations to Maier and Truss (1984); correlations in a later
report (Maier & Truss, 1985, Tables 11 and C4) depart in minor
ways from those shown here.
[c]The criterion is final school grade. Correlations were corrected to apply to the full range of the youth population, then
averaged across courses in the category. The first row includes
9 courses; numbers for the other rows are 9, 3, and 2. Ns ranged
widely, with 300 persons per course usual.
[d]From the ASVAB Counselor's Manual (1984); Table D2 provides estimated alternate-form reliabilities and Table D7 provides estimated intercorrelations.

assignment is severely limited. In Table 1.2, we estimate the regression differences, which bear more directly on classification. From reworking the available facts, I judge that ASVAB has modest value for assignment; much of the
utility, however, is traceable to sex differences. No reworking of the technical
report can adequately appraise ASVAB's utility for classification. No consideration is given to assignment ratios, utility s.d.'s, or regressions for courses at
various levels within categories. Mostly, the tables and this comment illustrate
how superficial, and how hard to interpret, are validation reports on multiscore
batteries.

We have much to learn about empirical research on placement and classification. We don't know how to translate outcomes in different assignments to a common scale, as we must. For the remedial and regular English courses, a writing sample provided a suitable common criterion. For ASVAB, mapping the criteria from the various courses onto one metric would require tricky judgments. Jaeger (personal communication) has at least identified ways to collect such judgments in the military. Hunter and Schmidt (1982) have made a first brave try at extending their estimation methods to assignment. Others should be criticizing and extending this work. With regard to tests intended for educational ability grouping, we will probably never resolve the common-scale problem. That was the crux in *Larry P.*, because the California curriculum for the retarded did not lead toward several kinds of outcomes sought in the regular curriculum.

Corrections for range restriction are needed, but the available methods are inadequate. We cannot deal properly with the factors apart from the predictors that determine presence in the final sample (Cronbach, 1982, Chap. 6; Murnane, Newstead, & Olsen, 1985; Muthén & Jöreskog, 1983). The corrections that went into Table 1.1a are dubious because they neglect the fact that males opt for different military assignments than females. Finally, statistical power is a grave problem in assessing slope differences; that follows from the well-known Schmidt–Hunter argument about sample size (see Schmidt et al., 1985; see also Cronbach & Snow, 1977, pp. 45–47, 55–61).

TABLE 1.2
A Preliminary Look at the Utility of ASVAB for Classification

Estimated semistandardized regression coefficients:
criterion difference regressed onto difference
between the corresponding predictor composites[a,b]

Course Category	BC	MC	EE	HST
Business and Clerical		.29[c]	.19[c]	.09[c]
Mechanical and Crafts			.16	.19[c]
Electronics and Electrical				.06[d]
Health, Social, Technology				

[a]The upper-right cell, for example, is the regression coefficient for the difference between standardized criterion scores in BC and HST, predicted from the standardized difference between composites BC and HST.

[b]Each criterion, and each predictor *difference*, is assigned an s.d. of 1.00 in its validation sample. I calculated these coeficients from values in 1(a) and 1(b).

[c]The sex difference for this predictor exceeds 1.0 s.d.

[d]The reliability of this predictor difference I estimate to be near .35. All other difference reliabilities appear to be about .75; several drop to about .60 within sexes. (The information on reliability of differences in the manual's Tables 33–37 is seriously in error.)

Judgments Needed in Extrapolating.   Program evaluators have been discussing how evidence collected in one natural situation enables us to reason about a
different one. The key seems to be qualitative understanding (Cronbach, 1982).
Predictive validation is usually described as purely empirical, a comparison of
forecasts with later events. Extrapolation, however, relies on constructs. We
predict on the basis of experience judged relevant to the future situation. Young
people seeking guidance consider occupations for which the counselor has no
tabulated direct experience; experience that is conceptually related has to be
used. And where experience has been tabulated, a counselor or other caseworker
must choose between recommending the action that has worked best on the
average and an amended plan that recognizes special features of the case in hand.
The choice can be rationalized only through notions about the causal influence of
such features.

A pertinent paper by Meehl (1957) carries the title, "When shall we use our
heads instead of the formula?" That title, unfortunately, obscures the fact that
clinicians and employment psychologists must use their heads in *deciding
whether* to use the formula. Although a certain kind of test has worked well in
some class of situations, users cannot logically apply that generalization until
they check the fit of the next instance to the class where experience accumulated.
Beyond that, they may have to assess whether a court will be persuaded that the
particular features of this case did not matter.

That is the only thought I offer on validity generalization. The recent 100-
page debate among eight specialists is exhaustive (Sackett, Tenopyr, Schmitt, &
Kahn, 1985; Schmidt, Pearlman, Hunter, & Hirsh, 1985). Both sides agreed that
a general ability test valid for one job and employer has a strong probability of
being valid in other settings; disagreement, about the probative value of prior
probabilities, remains.

THE EXPLANATORY PERSPECTIVE

Now, a few comments on the search for explanations. Much has been learned
since 1955 about the difficulties of building and validating explanations; I can
extract only a few key points from fuller discussions, and provide references
(Cook & Campbell, 1979; Cronbach, in press; Fiske & Shweder, 1986; Meehl,
1978, 1979).

Running through the literature on construct validation are two conflicting
recommendations for inquiry: a strong program and a weak program. The weak
program is sheer exploratory empiricism; any correlation of the test score with
another variable is welcomed. The specific standards on construct validity of
1954 and 1966 said little more than "The more information the test developer
provides, the better." This advice trivializes the idea of strenuous inquiry into
the soundness of a proposed explanation. Still, the weak program has some
merit.

Casting about for facts is a route toward alternative interpretations and toward improved testing technique. In developing test interpretations, many methods have had heuristic value, ranging from exploratory factor analysis to case studies of persons with extreme scores. Having subjects work through the items orally, with a good deal of free association, is almost always instructive. Any type of inquiry, then, that seems likely to sharpen interpretative questions or to suggest explanations should be welcome.

The 1974 and 1985 *Standards* implicitly adopt the strong program, though their procedural recommendations are too brief to be definite. The strong program, spelled out in 1955 (Cronbach & Meehl) and restated in 1982 by Meehl and Golden, calls for making one's theoretical ideas as explicit as possible, then devising deliberate challenges. Popper taught us that an explanation gains credibility chiefly from falsification attempts that fail. Human nature being what it is, validation-through-challenge is more likely to be the contribution of a rival scientist than of the proponent of the interpretation (Lakatos, 1978, p. 3).

The construct validation rationale applies to all use of general terms describing behavior or situations. A well-trained investigator records what was done to a sample on a stated date and what was observed by what means, then derives various numbers. To that point, interpretation is minimal and ordinarily no question of validity arises. At most, a critic can wish that a different study had been made. Questions of construct validity become pertinent the moment a finding is put into words. (On this, see especially Cook & Campbell, 1979, p. 38). The following fairly typical sentence from a journal abstract illustrates the usual quick escalation to construct language: "Insecurely attached infants showed a trend toward earlier self-recognition. . . ." (Lewis, Brooks–Gunn, & Jaskir, 1985). That sentence is pitched at a quasitheoretical level. I have already spoken of the need to use judgment—that is, a cognitive construction of the present situation—in deciding where a generalization applies. With regard to the statement about infants, the would-be applier is better off than usual, because 25 specialists have published a penetrating and multifaceted argument about the interpretation of the Strange Situation Test whose validity the abstract takes for granted (Lamb, Thompson, Gardner, Charnow, & Estes [and discussants], 1984).

Construct validation is often mistakenly conceived to be an attempt to prove that some one trait label matches a test score. Clinicians have long known that a score can be reached in many ways, hence measures different variables in different persons. What variable an ability test measures is significantly affected by a person's style or process of test taking. French's classic factor-analytic evidence (1965) is now supplemented by experimental analysis of cognition that illustrates highly sophisticated construct validation. (See, for example, remarks of Cooper and Regan [1982] and Estes [1982] at pages 151ff. and 207 of Sternberg, 1982).

Validation cannot proceed along all lines at once. Strong construct validation is best guided by the phrase "plausible rival hypotheses." The phrase dates back to a 1957 paper on validity by Campbell, and takes on added meaning in his subsequent writings. The advice is not merely to be on the lookout for cases your hypothesis does not fit. The advice is to find, either in the relevant community of concerned persons or in your own devilish imagination, an alternative explanation of the accumulated findings; then to devise a study where the alternatives lead to disparate predictions. Concentrating on plausible rivals is especially important in validation because persons unfriendly to a test interpretation are likely to use a rival hypothesis as ammunition. Proponents' prior checks on the rival hypothesis provide a potent defensive weapon—or warn them to pick a line of retreat.

The positivists' distinction between theory and observation can no longer be sustained (Meehl, 1986; Suppe, 1977), and there is no hope of developing in the short run the "nomological networks" we once grandly envisioned (Cronbach, 1986). The pace of natural science should teach us patience. Chemists had to struggle through 60 years of confusion to move from a commitment to the *idea* of atomic theory (which Dalton's Law of Definite Proportions warranted) to a theory sturdy enough to sustain Mendeleev's table (Glymour, 1980).

Our best strategy is probably the contextualism suggested by McGuire (1983), among others. In brief, one offers a generalization and then tries to locate the boundaries within which it holds. As that structure ultimately becomes clumsy, someone will integrate most of the information into a more graceful one. For scientists, this is a reminder that knowledge evolves slowly and indirectly, that one can be prideful about contributing to the advance without the hubris of insisting that one has the "correct" theory. For practical testers, this warns that an instructive program of construct validation—strong or weak—is unlikely to reach the closure needed to defend a test that already is under fire.

THE KEY TO PROGRESS

This was scheduled as one of three "keynote speeches." So, what is my keynote? Can it be anything but "blood, toil, tears, and sweat"? Yes, there is a better text from another Englishman—no less exigent, but upbeat. Validation "is doing your damnedest with your mind—no holds barred." Eddington, as you know, said that about science. Validators should indeed do what the detached scientist would do, as best they can within the constraints usually imposed by a short time horizon. In validation, a vigorous, questing intellect has further importance for analyzing the values and rights embodied in—or sacrificed to—a testing program, and also for appreciating the beliefs and wants of members of the community that will arbitrate the validity argument.

Fortunately, validators are also a community. That enables members to divide up the investigative and educative burden according to their talents, motives, and political ideals. Validation will progress in proportion as we collectively do our damnedest—no holds barred—with our minds and our hearts.

REFERENCES

American Psychological Association, American Educational Research Association, & National Council on Measurement in Education. (1985). *Standards for educational and psychological testing*. Washington, DC: Author.

Anastasi, A. (1986). Evolving concepts of test validation. *Annual Review of Psychology, 37*, 1–15.

Association Against Discrimination v. City of Bridgeport, 454 F. Suppl. 751. (D. Conn. 1978).

Bloom, B. S. (1986). Ralph Tyler's impact on evaluation theory and practice. *Journal of Thought, 21*, 36–46.

Boudreau, J. W. (1983). Economic considerations in estimating the utility of human resource productivity improvement programs. *Personnel Psychology, 36*, 551–576.

Braybrooke, D., & Lindblom, C. E. (1963). *A strategy of decision: Policy evaluation as a social process*. New York: Free Press.

Brogden, H. E. (1946). On the interpretation of the correlation coefficient as a measure of predictive efficiency. *Journal of Educational Psychology, 37*, 65–76.

Brogden, H. E. (1951). Increased efficiency of selection resulting from replacement of a single predictor with several differential predictors. *Educational and Psychological Measurement, 11*, 173–196.

Campbell, D. T. (1957). Factors relevant to the validity of experiments in social settings. *Psychological Bulletin, 54*, 297–312.

Campbell, D. T. (1986). Science's social system of validity-enhancing collective belief change and the problems of the social sciences. In D. W. Fiske & R. A. Shweder (Eds.), *Metatheory in social science: Pluralities and subjectivities* (pp. 108–135). Chicago: University of Chicago Press.

Campbell, D. T., & Fiske, D. W. (1959). Convergent and discriminant validity in the multitrait-multimethod matrix. *Psychological Bulletin, 56*, 81–105.

Cook, T. D., & Campbell, D. T. (1979). *Quasi-experimentation: Design and analysis issues for field settings*. Chicago: Rand–McNally.

Cook, T. D., & Shadish, Jr., W. R. (1986). Program evaluation: The worldly science. *Annual Review of Psychology, 37*, 193–232.

Cooper, L. A., & Regan, D. T. (1982). *Attention, perception, and intelligence* (pp. 123–169). New York: Cambridge University Press.

Counselor's Manual for the Armed Services Vocational Aptitude Battery Form 14 (1984). Washington, DC: Department of Defense.

Cronbach, L. J. (1982). *Designing evaluations of educational and social programs*. San Francisco: Jossey–Bass.

Cronbach, L. J. (1984). *Essentials of psychological testing* (4th ed.). New York: Harper & Row.

Cronbach, L. J. (1985). College Board Scholastic Aptitude Test and Test of Standard Written English. In J. V. Mitchell, Jr. (Ed.), *The ninth mental measurements yearbook* (Vol. 1, pp. 363–364). Lincoln: University of Nebraska.

Cronbach, L. J. (1986). Social inquiry by and for Earthlings. In D. W. Fiske & R. A. Shweder (Eds.), *Metatheory in social science: Pluralities and subjectivities* (pp. 83–107). Chicago: University of Chicago Press.

Cronbach, L. J. (in press). Construct validation after thirty years. In R. E. Linn (Ed.), *Intelligence: Measurement, theory, and public policy*. Urbana: University of Illinois Press.

Cronbach, L. J., Ambron, S. R., Dornbusch, S. M., Hess, R. D., Hornik, R. C., Phillips, D. C., Walker, D. F., & Weiner, S. S. (1980). *Toward reform in program evaluation*. San Francisco: Jossey–Bass.

Cronbach, L. J., & Gleser, G. C. (1965). *Psychological tests and personnel decisions* (2nd. ed.). Urbana: University of Illinois Press.

Cronbach, L. J., & Meehl, P. E. (1955). Construct validity in psychological tests. *Psychological Bulletin, 52,* 281–302.

Cronbach, L. J., & Snow, R. E. (1977). Aptitudes and instructional methods: A handbook for research on aptitude-treatment interactions. New York: Irvington.

Cureton, E. E. (1951). Validity. In E. F. Lindquist (Ed.), *Educational measurement.* Washington, DC: American Council on Education.

Dunnette, M. D., & Borman, W. C. (1979). Personnel selection and classification. *Annual Review of Psychology, 30,* 477–525.

Ebel, R. L. (1956). Obtaining and reporting evidence on content validity. *Educational and Psychological Measurement, 16,* 269–282.

Estes, W. K. (1982). Learning, memory, and intelligence. In R. J. Sternberg (Ed.), *Handbook of Human Intelligence* (pp. 170–224). Cambridge, England: Cambridge University Press.

Fiske, D. W., & Shweder, R. A. (Eds.). (1986). *Metatheory in social science: Pluralities and subjectivities.* Chicago: University of Chicago Press.

Frederiksen, N. (1984). The real test bias: Influences of testing on teaching and learning. *American Psychologist, 39,* 193–202.

French, J. W. (1965). The relationship of problem-solving styles to the factor composition of tests. *Educational and Psychological Measurement, 25,* 9–28.

Glymour, C. (1980). *Theory and evidence.* Princeton, NJ: Princeton University Press.

Guion, R. M. (1980). On trinitarian conceptions of validity. *Professional Psychology, 11,* 385–398.

House, E. R. (1977). *The logic of evaluation argument.* Los Angeles: Center for the Study of Evaluation.

Hunter, J. E., & Schmidt, F. L. (1982). Fitting people to jobs: The impact of personnel selection on national productivity. In M. D. Dunnette & E. A. Fleishman (Eds.), *Human capability assessment.* Hillsdale, NJ: Lawrence Erlbaum Associates.

Kleiman, L. S., & Faley, R. H. (1985). The implications of professional and legal guidelines for court decisions involving criterion-related validity: A review and analysis. *Personnel Psychology, 38,* 803–833.

Lakatos, I. (1978). *The methodology of scientific research programmes.* Cambridge, England: Cambridge University Press.

Lakatos, I., & Musgrave, A. (1970). *Criticism and the growth of knowledge.* Cambridge, England: Cambridge University Press.

Lamb, M. C., Thompson, R. A., Gardner, W. P., Charnow, E. L., & Estes, D. [and discussants]. (1984). Security of infant attachment as assessed in the "strange situation": Its study and biological interpretation. *Behavioral and Brain Sciences, 7,* 127–171.

Lewis, M. C., Brooks–Gunn, J., & Jaskir, J. (1985). Individual differences in visual self-recognition as a function of mother–infant attachment relationship. *Developmental Psychology, 21,* 1181–1187.

McGuire, W. J. (1983). A contextualist theory of knowledge. In L. Berkowitz (Ed.), *Advances in experimental social psychology.* Orlando, FL: Academic Press.

Maier, M. H., & Truss, A. R. (1984). *Validity of the occupational and academic composites for the Armed Services Vocational Aptitude Battery Form 14, in Marine Corps Training Courses.* Alexandria, VA: Center for Naval Analyses.

Maier, M. H., & Truss, A. R. (1985). *Validity of the Armed Services Vocational Aptitude Battery Forms 8, 9, and 10 with applications to Forms 11, 12, 13, and 14.* Alexandria, VA: Center for Naval Analyses.

Meehl, P. E. (1957). When shall we use our heads instead of the formula? *Journal of Counseling Psychology, 4,* 268–273.

Meehl, P. E. (1977). Specific etiology and other forms of strong influence. *Journal of Medicine & Philosophy, 2,* 33–53.

Meehl, P. E. (1978). Theoretical risks and tabular asterisks: Sir Karl, Sir Ronald, and the slow progress of soft psychology. *Journal of Clinical & Consulting Psychology, 46,* 806–834.

Meehl, P. E. (1979). A funny thing happened on the way to the latent entities. *Journal of Personality Assessment, 43,* 564–577.

Meehl, P. E. (1986). What social scientists don't understand. In D. W. Fiske & R. A. Shweder (Eds.), *Metatheory in social science: Pluralities and subjectivities* (pp. 315–338). Chicago: University of Chicago Press.

Meehl, P. E., & Golden, R. E. (1982). Taxometric methods. In P. C. Kendall & J. N. Butcher (Eds.), *Handbook of research methods in clinical psychology.* New York: Wiley.

Messick, S. (1980). Test validation and the ethics of assessment. *American Psychologist, 35,* 1012–1027.

Murnane, R. J., Newstead, S., & Olsen, R. J. (1985). Comparing public and private schools: The puzzling role of selectivity bias. *Journal of Business and Economic Statistics, 3,* 23–35.

Murphy, K. R. (1986). When your top choice turns you down: Effect of rejected offers on the utility of selection tests. *Psychological Bulletin, 99,* 133–138.

Muthén, B., & Jöreskog, K. G. (1983). Selectivity problems in quasi-experimental studies. *Evaluation Review, 7,* 139–174.

Reilly, R. R., & Smither, J. W. (1985). An examination of two alternative techniques to estimate the standard deviation of job performance in dollars. *Journal of Applied Psychology, 70,* 651–661.

Sackett, P. R., Tenopyr, M. L., Schmitt, N., & Kahn, J. (1985). Commentary on forty questions about validity generalization and meta-analysis. *Personnel Psychology, 38,* 697–798.

Schmidt, F. L., Pearlman, K., Hunter, J. E., & Hirsh, H. R. (1985). Forty questions about validity generalization and meta-analysis. *Personnel Psychology, 38,* 697–798.

Stephenson, J. D., Mathews, J. J., Welsh, J. R., Ree, M. J., & Earles, J. A. (1986). *Technical supplement to the Counselor's Manual for the Armed Services Vocational Aptitude Battery Form-14.* North Chicago, IL: U.S. Military Entrance Processing Command.

Sternberg, R. J. (Ed.). (1982). *Handbook on human intelligence.* New York: Cambridge University Press.

Suppe, F. (Ed.). (1977). *The structure of scientific theories* (2nd ed.). Urbana: University of Illinois Press.

Taylor, H. C., & Russell, J. T. (1939). The relationship of validity coefficients to the practical effectiveness of tests in selection. *Journal of Applied Psychology, 23,* 565–578.

Yalow, E. S., & Popham, W. J. (1983). Content validity at the crossroads. *Educational Researcher, 12*(8), 10–15.

Chapter 2

Validity: An Evolving Concept

William H. Angoff
Educational Testing Service

Conceptions of validity have changed several times in the last 35 years, but one conception, that validity itself is pre-eminent among the various psychometric concepts, remains constant. Validity has always been regarded as the most fundamental and important in psychometrics. It is therefore curious that serious work in clarifying the concept did not begin in earnest until the profession was 50 years old. Since then it has occupied the frequent and continuing attention of some of the prominent people in this field.

Not that it had been entirely ignored prior to that time. Before 1950 or so, it was generally understood that it was incumbent on anyone who proposed to offer a test for an announced purpose, or on anyone who proposed to use a test for an announced purpose, to demonstrate that the test was in fact useful for that purpose. This requirement, known as test validity, was defined in the following traditional formula: "The validity of a test is the extent to which"—or, in Garrett's words, "the fidelity with which"—"it measures what it purports to measure" (Garrett 1937, p. 324; 1947, p. 394).

CONCEPTIONS OF VALIDITY

Although different writers chose to define validity in slightly different language, the language, and the work dictated by that language in studying the validity of tests at that time, was characteristically pragmatic and empirical, even atheoretical, and validity data were generally developed to justify a claim that a test was useful for some particular purpose. When the use of the test was explicitly intended for selection, it was expected that the claimant would demonstrate its predictive vaildity in the form of a correlation between the test scores and the later behavior it was expected to predict.

Consistent with other writers at that time, Bingham defined validity in purely operational terms, as simply the correlation of scores on a test with "some other objective measure of that which the test is used to measure" (Bingham, 1937, p. 214). Guilford defined validity similarly: "In a very general sense, a test is valid for anything with which it correlates" (Guilford, 1946, p. 429). He also defined it (1942) as the quality of a test that made it an efficient forecaster of future behavior, and further extended his definition to say that the validity of a test as a measure of a factor is indicated by its correlation with that factor. Guilford also emphasized, as other writers did, that, unlike reliability, validity is not a general characteristic of a test, but specific to a particular purpose. Thus, a test could be highly valid for one purpose, but not at all valid for other purposes.

Lindquist's 1942 book on elementary statistics defines validity in the traditional way, but, like Bingham's, carries the definition a step further by suggesting that it is the correlation between the fallible and infallible measure of a trait. Clearly, this definition comes close to defining the trait in question in purely operational terms as simply that which the test measures. The view was also that, assuming the criterion to be perfectly reliable and the test to be perfectly representative of the criterion, the maximum validity of the (fallible) test would have to be the correlation of the observed test scores with true scores on the test itself—which classical test theory would show to be the square root of the reliability. It was this notion that led to the rule, frequently expressed for some time thereafter, that the square root of the test reliability provides the upper limit for validity.

Cureton's (1950) chapter in the first edition of *Educational measurement* also defines validity as the correlation of observed scores on the test with true scores on the criterion. He distinguished the test's *validity* from the test's *predictive power* by defining the latter as the correlation between observed scores on the test with observed scores on the criterion. And he distinguished both of these from what he called *relevance,* which is the correlation between true scores on both predictor and criterion.

But it was the use of validity in its predictive sense that dominated the scene. The most dramatic and extensive use of tests in prediction was the administration of the Air Force Aviation Psychology Program (Flanagan, 1948) in which a battery of 21 pencil-and-paper and performance tests was used for predicting the criterion of pass or fail in the primary phase of training as bombardier, navigator, or pilot. Validation of the battery was continually monitored on successive samples by observing the correlation of the weighted composite of scores, expressed as stanines, against the pass–fail criterion observed several weeks later. This selection program was a clear example of the application of the predictive validity concept, in which the value of the battery stood or fell on its observed correlation with the criterion. Research in the program went on continually, and it was of chief interest then to know whether a newly proposed test would be a useful addition to the battery. The criterion of usefulness was uncomplicated: It was simply whether the inclusion of the test would add to the existing multiple correlation, and if so, by how much. Paul Horst, a senior officer in the program, had developed an algorithm which provided an estimate of the contribution to the multiple R, given the validity of the existing battery, the validity of the proposed test, and the correlation of the test with the battery.

During this period another type of criterion-related validity, concurrent validity, was introduced and referred to as a separate type of validity in its own right (see APA, AERA, NCME, 1954; pp. 13, 14). Concurrent validity was one which also called for the correlation of test against criterion; but here the predictor scores and the criterion scores were observed at the same point in time. Typically, concurrent validity data were taken as evidence that a newly proposed test, or a brief version of an existing test, was measuring a given trait if it correlated strongly with another test already acknowledged to be a measure of that trait. Although this type of "validation" was not considered definitive, it was felt to be essential if its author proposed it as a measure of a trait, especially one for which there was already an accepted measure. The concern was, as Truman Kelley (1927, p. 64) expressed it, that it was a fallacy to think that two tests bearing the same name were necessarily measuring the same trait. This, he said, has been referred to as the "jingle fallacy." Correspondingly, he suggested, there is the "jangle fallacy," the fallacy that two tests that bore different names necessarily measured different traits. What he urged was simply that evidence was needed to support both types of claims. One important line of evidence was the correlation of the test with an existing, acceptable measure of the trait in question.

Concurrent validity was, and still is, held to be useful for predictive purposes if it could be demonstrated, or argued convincingly, that scores on the test would not change systematically during the period between the time when the test *might* have been given as an actual predictor and the time when criterion data would normally become available. In effect, concurrent validity data were, and are, a reasonable substitute for predictive validity data if the regressions of criterion scores on test scores are the same for the situations in which the tests are given at the two different points in time relative to the criterion scores.

Anastasi (1976, p. 105) held that the logical distinction between predictive and concurrent validity is not based on time, but on the objectives of the testing. In her thinking, concurrent validity justifies the use of tests in identifying and classifying individuals into groups that are to be kept conceptually separate for purposes of differential decision and treatment, as in clinical and educational diagnosis.

The view was held during the 1940s and even earlier, as it is held today in the context of ordinary prediction, that the behavior of chief interest was the criterion behavior, and that it was left to the test author to develop a test, or to the user to find a test, that would predict that behavior. Whether or not the test performance measured psychological or educational constructs of interest as we define them today was of less importance than the fact that they correlated across the span of time. True, there was some acknowledgment, as in Cureton's (1950) chapter, that there existed a more nearly ultimate criterion and that the measure being used was a convenient and useful behavioral surrogate for that criterion. Nevertheless, the day-to-day emphasis was on the behavioral criterion and efforts were expended in developing a measure that would be most reliable and least biased. In this connection there was a new recognition in the last half of the 1940s, following World War II, that many of the criteria used in formal prediction programs were highly inadequate. Accordingly, a search was initiated for techniques for developing improved criteria. It was in this spirit that Jenkins's (1946) analysis was written, outlining the faults of existing criteria, even giving some attention to the possible invalidity of the criteria themselves. It was also in this spirit that Flanagan (1954) developed the critical incident technique, and in this spirit that the staff at the Personnel Research Section of the Adjutant General's Office (Sisson, 1948) developed the forced-choice technique for rating subordinates in a work situation.

Consistent with the empirical orientation and the emphasis on predictive validity that prevailed at the time, there was a strong tendency to think of criteria in strictly behavioral terms, rather than in terms of psychological traits or processes. Rulon (1948) and Anastasi (1950), for example, tended to exert a behavioral influence, and although Anastasi's position appears to be more moderate today (Anastasi, 1982), she still insists on the need for behavioral definitions. At the time, though, she dismissed the notion of "psychological processes" and argued that they "fall outside the domain of scientific inquiry" (1950, p. 77). Test scores, she said, should not be taken to be "measures of hypostasized and unverifiable 'abilities'" (1950, p. 77). "Nor should the terminology of factor analysis mislead us into the belief that anything external to the tested behavior has been identified. The discovery of a "factor" means simply that certain relationships exist between tested behavior samples" (1950, p. 75).

Leaving aside the tests used for prediction and diagnosis, there is a class of tests, principally achievement and proficiency tests, used, for example, for retrospective evaluation—including the more recently discussed criterion-referenced tests, on which minimum competency and mastery cut-scores are determined—that some writers, Rulon (1946), for example, felt required no validity justification. Rulon's view was that tests of chemistry, arithmetic, penmanship, and sewing, for example, tests that are administered to measure the status of an individual's acquired knowledges and skills, are their own criterion. Such tests, he claimed, if they are exhaustive, fall in the class of "obviously valid" tests; no external criterion is needed. In such instances the demand for a determination of validity is satisfied by a review of the test by subject-matter experts and a verification that its content represents a satisfactory sampling of the domain—an exercise in content validity.

The weakness in this conception is that a test composed of a limited number of items could be thought to exhaust or even to sample the subject matter adequately. The fact is that only rarely do the items of a test exhaust the universe, and even when they do, the instances are likely to be trivial. Nor are test items normally drawn randomly from some universe of items. Typically, they are written to represent, but not in any precise statistical sense, the various important domains, objectives, and goals deemed to be important. There may have been a time when the items of the test were thought to be a sample of the universe of items in the general domain of the test. But this conception seems not to have been widely accepted. Items are typically written, not often drawn from a pool. The items conform to only some selected objectives of the total subject matter, not all; they are written to elicit only some types of processes and responses; they appear in particular formats and are written to conform to only some item types; and they are further selected to represent only certain particular levels and ranges of difficulty and to satisfy only certain minimum levels of discriminating power. But even if the sampling requirement for items is abandoned, as Loevinger (1957) quite properly argued must be done, care must be taken at the very least to represent the subject matter elements of the domain, the psychological processes of interest, and the educational objectives (such as those outlined by Bloom and his associates, 1956).

Accordingly, the objectives and the curricular domain governing the construction of one chemistry test, for example, are not necessarily the same as those governing the construction of another chemistry test. Even a job sample test is understood to represent only a sampling of the possible tasks of which the job might conceivably consist. It would remain, then, for the publisher or user to specify the domain in detail and to show that the items of the test are indeed representative of the domain, but representative in relation to the number and perceived importance of the elements of the domain. Just as importantly, the publisher or user would have to show that they do not represent any irrelevant elements which could only serve to render the score interpretations ambiguous. Similarly for the representation of process categories. In any case, the notion that the test items must represent properly the domain of interest—and *only* the domain of interest—was paramount, and remains so today. From this point of view, then, it is clear that aptitude and personality tests cannot easily satisfy the demands of content validity, if they can satisfy those demands at all, since the domain cannot be adequately described.

Another kind of validity notion that enjoyed some currency during the 1940s was that of "face validity," the *appearance* of validity. Although face validity was discussed in some detail by Mosier (1947), it seems not to have been treated elsewhere with much technical interest. Mosier himself suggested that, because of its inherent ambiguity, any serious consideration of face validity should be abandoned. Recently, Nevo (1985) argued that the concept of face validity is in fact useful and reliably judged, and should be reported regularly. It remains to be seen whether there will be a response to Nevo's defense of it. There is, however, longstanding and even recent acknowledgement, (e.g., Anastasi, 1982, p. 136), that tests should be constructed to be face valid, that it is important, for example, that the language and contexts of test items be expressed in ways that would *look* valid and be acceptable to the test taker and to the public generally. This means that the items of an arithmetic test for carpenters, for example, should be couched in language and tasks appropriate to their work, that the contexts of verbal items for barely literate adults should be adult contexts, etc. But generally speaking, the effort to make a test face valid was, and probably is today, regarded as a concession, albeit an important one, to gain acceptability rather than a serious psychometric effort. Superficial judgments of the validity of a test made solely on the basis of its appearance can easily be very wrong.

During the 1940s and earlier the need for validity studies and for valid tests was clearly recognized, but the burden of establishing validity appeared to be placed chiefly, if not entirely, on the shoulders of the test publisher and was regarded as an exercise simply in demonstrating the "proof of the pudding," as it were, to be carried out in support of the claim that the test was indeed "measuring what it purports to measure." True, there was some acknowledgment, as in an article by Rulon (1946, p. 290), that a preferred definition of validity was "whether the test does the work it is *employed* to do" (emphasis added), a definition also subscribed to by Cureton (1950, p. 621). This rewording implied to them that validity is the responsibility of the user. But not until later did it come to be more fully understood that one does not validate a test, nor even the scores yielded by the test, but the interpretations and inferences that the user draws from the test scores, and the decisions and actions that flow from those inferences. This new emphasis confirms that validity is now taken to be the user's responsibility. It is also of some interest to note that, while the earlier Standards for educational and psychological tests, APA, AERA, NCME, 1954, 1966 and 1974, are entitled in such a way as to impose requirements on the tests, the latest Standards, APA, AERA, NCME, 1985, are called "Standards for Educational and Psychological *Testing*" (emphasis added), implying not only that the test is at issue but that the rest of the testing situation is also at issue. This represents a significant modification. What is also significant in the change from "test" to "testing" is a confirmation of Rulon's and Cureton's view, that the person who conducts the testing and the person who uses the scores are responsible for supplying evidence for the validity of the testing (i.e., for the validity of the interpretation of the results of the testing).

At the same time it is clear that the test constructor is not relieved of responsibility. All four sets of Standards make repeated reference to the publisher's manual for the test and the kinds of data and interpretations that the publisher is expected to provide for the benefit of the user in making interpretations from scores. Moreover, it is maintained today that validation is a continuing, indeed, unending process, as Messick (1980, p. 1019) describes it, that begins early in the test development process itself. As Anastasi (1986, p. 3) also points out, "Validity is . . . built into the test from the outset rather than being limited to the last stages of the test development, as in traditional criterion-related validation."

During the 1940s and early 1950s validity was thought to be of several types. The 1954 Standards (actually, "Recommendations") classified them into four: content validity, predictive validity, concurrent validity, and construct validity, the last, a new type. Although it must be conceded that the 1954 Standards also referred to them as *aspects* of validity, it seems clear that the authors had in mind that they were indeed *types*. The 1966 and 1974 Standards combined concurrent with predictive validity and referred to the two as a class, called "criterion-related validity," reducing the number of types to three. In essence, then, validity was represented, even well into the 1970s as a three-categoried concept and taken by publishers and users alike to mean that tests could be validated by any one or more of the three general procedures. This view prompted Guion (1980, p. 386) to describe the three "types" of validity as "something of a holy trinity representing three different roads to psychometric salvation." But this was only a temporary way station in the development of the concept. To continue with Guion's metaphor, it may be said that the more recent view, in which construct validity comprises all of validity, holds that these three types are now to be regarded in a monotheistic mode as the three aspects of a unitary psychometric divinity.

Actually, in the 1940s, before construct validity became a conceptual force to be reckoned with, different writers classified the different types of validity differently. As indicated earlier, Guilford (1946) spoke of it as consisting of two types: factorial (i.e., the loading of a particular factor on the test in question) and practical (i.e., criterion-related). Cronbach (1949), writing at about the same time, also spoke then of validity as being supported by two types of analysis. But he classified them into logical, or judgmental, analysis and empirical analysis. Anastasi (1954) listed face validity, content validity, factorial validity, and empirical validity, the last of these including, but not restricted to, criterion-related validity. Her most recent edition of *Psychological testing* (1982) continues to list face validity, but makes it clear that this is not validity in the technical sense but only in the sense of a superficial appearance of validity.

CONSTRUCT VALIDITY

It was no coincidence that the 1954 Standards listed construct validity for the first time as one of the four types. Lee Cronbach was the chairman of the committee chosen to develop the Standards and Paul Meehl was a member of the committee, and the seminal Cronbach–Meehl (1955) article on construct validity, relying heavily on ideas Meehl brought from philosophy of science, appeared in the literature the very next year. In construct validity, a major innovation in the conception of validity. and already perceived as the most fundamental and embracing of all the types of validity, Cronbach and Meehl maintained that we examine the psychological trait, or construct, presumed to be measured by the test and we cause a continuing, research interplay to take place between the scores earned on the test and the theory underlying the construct. In this way the theoretical conception of the construct in question dictates the nature of the data that are collected to validate the scores on the test and used to interpret the results of the testing. In turn, the data resulting from the test administration are used to validate, reject, or revise the theory itself. Viewed this way, we see that all data that flow from the theory, including concurrent and predictive data—but not exclusively so—are useful for construct validity. Indeed, virtually all properly collected data are legitimately validity data, including ethnic and sex distributions—group data, generally—internal correlation matrices among items and among subtests, factor studies, correlations with various types of external criteria, data showing long-term longitudinal change, data showing change over occasions as found in both experimental and observational (i.e., uncontrolled) studies, and finally, data resulting from studies of content analyses. In this general sense, Gulliksen's (1950) conception of intrinsic validity, in which one theorizes the existence of similar (or, alternatively, dissimilar) constructs and examines the data of several measures for the appearance of expected patterns of correlations, falls clearly in the domain of construct validation efforts.

From the forgoing, we can see that construct validity as conceived by Cronbach and Meehl cannot be expressed in a single coefficient. Construct validation is a process, not a procedure; and it requires many lines of evidence, not all of them quantitative. Moreover, simple rationalizing or theorizing about the nature of a construct is not to be regarded as construct validation; "[a]n admissible psychological construct must be behavior- [and data-] relevant" (Cronbach & Meehl, 1955, p. 291). And finally, all measures that are taken to be behavioral expressions of the construct, including criteria and tests alike, are expected to yield data consistent with the theory of the construct.

The concept of construct validity moved a significant step forward a few years following the publication by Cronbach and Meehl with the appearance of an article by Campbell and Fiske (1959), in which these authors offered a conceptual and an empirical test for construct validation. In its conceptual form the test of validity bore a close resemblance to Gulliksen's (1950) intrinsic validity: Any given measure of a construct should show strong relationships with other measures of the same construct, but weak relationships with measures of other constructs. Empirically, the strategy called for the intercorrelation of the scores on two or more different methods of measuring two or more different constructs. One would ordinarily expect, with such data, that the correlations among different methods of measuring the same construct (i.e., convergent validity) to be clearly higher than the correlations among different constructs that are measured by the same method (i.e., discriminant validity). For further verification, both of these sets of correlations should be higher than the correlations between different constructs measured by different methods, and lower than the reliability of a given method of measuring a given construct. "Method" may be defined in any convenient, but reasonable, way. Multiple-choice tests, free-answer tests, questionnaires, and ratings might be taken as different methods. Different item types of a multiple-choice sort (synonyms items, reading comprehension items, sentence completion items, etc.) might also be considered examples of different methods. Different levels of correlations, however, would have to be anticipated for methods that are less clearly similar.

In effect, discriminant validity is a necessary test of construct validity, perhaps even a stronger test in this sense than is convergent validity, because it implies a challenge from a plausible rival hypothesis. As Messick (1975, p. 956) pointed out, "If repeated challenges from a variety of plausible rival hypotheses can be systematically discounted, then the original interpretation becomes more firmly grounded." Nor is construct validation necessarily limited to correlation analysis. Indeed, "the most sensitive and soundest evidence is likely to come from experimental studies of groups receiving different instructional treatments or of tests administered under different conditions of motivation and strategy" (Messick, 1975, p. 959).

Messick (1975) also furthered the view that content validity was in fact not validity at all in the sense shared by the other types, or aspects. of construct validity. "Content validity," it is recalled, "is evaluated by showing how well the content of the test samples the class of situations or subject matter about which conclusions are to be drawn" (APA, AERA, NCME, 1954, page 13; APA, AERA, NCME, 1966, p. 12; Cronbach, 1971, p. 444; Messick, 1975, p. 959). It is a blueprint for the test development process, and it is later evaluated and attested to as a result of the judgments made by competent reviewers. Unlike the other conceptions of validity, "content validity gives every appearance of being a fixed property of the *test* . . . rather than being a property of test *responses*" (Messick. 1975, p. 959). This is its chief distinction, and to Messick, its chief limitation. Without response data it yields no empirical evidence of convergent validity and sheds no light on the factors, ambient or otherwise, that cause examinees to respond the way they do.

Cronbach's (1969) illustration of the dictated spelling test is apt here: The test per se contains items designed for oral administration. The responses, however, as, for example, in the case of deaf children, could easily be affected by factors having nothing whatever to do with the ability for which the test is designed; and this would never be known from the test items themselves, only from the response data and from interviews with the children. Successful performances on such a test, available only from the response data, might permit reasonable inferences, but inferences from the items alone necessarily remain equivocal. "The major problem here," Messick contends, "is that content validity . . . is focused on test *forms* rather than test *scores,* upon *instruments* rather than *measurements''* (1975, p. 960); and it is only the scores and the measurements that provide evidence for interpretation. ''We would be much better off conceptually to use labels more descriptive of the character and intent of [content validity], such as content relevance [i.e., domain specification] and content coverage [i.e., domain representativeness] . . .'' (Messick, 1980, p. 1014) rather than to use the label content validity.

At about the same time (the latter 1970s) the view, as originally offered by Loevinger (1957), became more generally accepted that ''since predictive, concurrent, and content validities are all essentially ad hoc, construct validity is the whole of validity from a scientific point of view (Loevinger, 1957, p. 636). This was the conclusion reached also by Messick (1975), Tenopyr (1977), and Guion (1977) and was probably expressed most comprehensively by Messick: ''[C]onstruct validity is indeed the unifying concept of validity that integrates criterion and content considerations into a common framework for testing rational hypotheses about theoretically relevant relationships'' (1980, p. 1015).

If construct validity becomes the overarching term for validity generally representing the ''evidential basis of test interpretation'' (Messick, 1980, p. 1019), what becomes of the terms content validity, predictive validity and concurrent validity? As already indicated, in Messick's classification, ''content validity'' becomes ''content relevance'' and ''content coverage,'' and ''predictive'' and ''concurrent'' validity became, respectively, ''predictive utility'' and ''diagnostic utility'' (Messick, 1980, Table 1, p. 1015). Where concurrent validity is used to justify the use of a substitute test of the same construct, it may be referred to as ''substitutability.''

Here may be a task worthy of a taxonomist. It is suggested at this point that some of the several ''validities'' Messick (1980, p. 1015) enumerates—convergent and discriminant validity, predictive and concurrent validity, factorial validity, and so on—should be considered data collection and data analysis *strategies,* used for testing the conceptual connections between measurement and construct. In other contexts, some validity concepts, like predictive validity, have the clear utilitarian value of testing the use of a practical decision rule. Still others—population validity, ecological validity, task validity, and temporal validity, for example—refer to research efforts in which the variation in validity coefficients across different populations, situations, tasks, and points in time are often found to be attributed in large part to small sample size, criterion unreliability, and variations in the dispersions of the samples. Studies of these effects, which have been referred to recently as yielding evidence of validity generalization (Schmidt & Hunter, 1977, for example), provide extremely important data and theory that have value not only in testing and modifying the construct, but in the strictly utilitarian sense of extending the contexts in which a predictor may be usefully applied.

These developments, following the initial article by Cronbach and Meehl

(1955) have clearly had a profound effect on our view of the general validation process, and beyond that, to the process of scientific verification and modification generally. We have had the benefit of Messick's (1975, 1980, 1981a, 1981b) clarifications into areas that go far beyond the narrow conceptions of validity that characterized the first half of the century, into questions of meaning, values, and ethics and their implications for future work in educational and psychological measurement. These notions would have been quite foreign to us 35 years ago.

SUMMARY

Several changes in emphasis and orientation toward validity are seen to have taken place in the last 35 years. The most significant of these is the articulation by Cronbach and Meehl (1955) and later by Cronbach alone (1969, 1971) of the concept of construct validity, a mutual verification of the measuring instrument and the theory of the construct it is meant to measure. More accurately, it reflects a verification of the inferences and interpretations to be drawn from the test scores and a corresponding modification (if so indicated) of the instrument and/or the theory underlying the construct. Another change is that one does not validate the test in the purely pragmatic sense that prevailed in earlier years; one involves the instrument in a continuing investigation of the properties of the construct, beginning in the early stages of test development. Yet another is that since all validation may be subsumed under construct validation, the study of validity may consist of more than one of several research strategies; criterion-related validation, for example, is only one such strategy.

A second major change in emphasis, closely related to the conception of construct validity, is that there has been a new recognition of that which is to be validated. The earlier view was that it was the test whose validity was being sought, and then, in a specific sense and context. But the question tended to be highly applied: "How well will the test work in this setting?" In the course of these passing decades it has become clear that it was the subject's responses to the test, even more, the inferences and interpretations to be drawn from those responses, that were to be validated. Thus, the responsibility for the validation falls to a considerable degree to the user, or perhaps more generally, to the person willing to claim that certain inferences may be validly drawn from the test scores. Consistent with this change there is an active effort under way even now of a committee appointed by APA (the Test User Qualification Working Group), whose charge it is ultimately to define the minimum qualifications of those who administer and interpret test scores. In this connection and for some time now along with other activities, there has been increasing attention being given to the matter of codifying the rules for defining proper uses and misuses of tests. Even the title of the most recent *Technical Standards for Educational and Psychologi-*

cal Testing (APA, AERA, NCME, 1985) has been made to reflect the fact that the administration and interpretation of test scores, as well as the tests themselves, are subjected to scrutiny. At the same time, there has been no corresponding relinquishment of the demands on the test developer; the Standards continue to direct their attention to the responsibilities and obligations of those who construct the tests.

Third, as it became clear that it was not the test, but the inferences drawn from the test scores that were on trial, it also followed that the theory that dictated the inferences was also on trial. Accordingly, the view was enunciated that there had to be a continual mutual research interplay between the data provided by the instrument and the theory within which the instrument was developed, in a process in which each served to test and modify the other.

As a consequence of the foregoing, all data yielded by the administration of a test could serve as legitimate evidence of validity—not only predictive data, but correlational studies generally, factorial studies, studies of differences with respect to groups, situations, tasks, and times, observational studies of change, and studies of experimentally induced change.

This active interest in a new conception of validity has also signaled a more pervasive philosophical change, from the purely pragmatic and empirical orientation that characterized psychometrics in the first half of the 1900s to a new and growing interest in psychometric and psychological theory. A simple count of the number of articles on the theory and meaning of validity that have appeared in the literature before and after 1950 attests to the change. Anastasi (1986) maintains that the emphasis on pure empiricism in the early decades of this century arose as a revolt against the excessive armchair theorizing that preceded it. The present emphasis appears to signify a return, but to a more moderate position, in which theory again becomes respectable, but only when stated in the form of testable hypotheses. What is most encouraging is that we find this renewed dependence on data-based theory also discernible outside the psychometric area—for example, in clinical psychological and health fields that have traditionally paid little heed to the contributions of psychometrics (Anastasi, 1985, p. xxv). More than likely, this new emphasis will remain with us for some time to come.

REFERENCES

American Psychological Association, American Educational Research Association, & National Council on Measurement Used in Education. (1954). Technical recommendations for psychological tests and diagnostic techniques. *Psychological Bulletin, 51*(2, Pt. 2) (Supplement).

American Psychological Association, American Educational Research Association, and National Council on Measurement in Education (1966). *Standards for educational and psychological tests and manuals.* Washington, DC: American Psychological Association.

American Psychological Association, American Educational Research Association, and National Council on Measurement in Education (1974). *Standards for educational and psychological tests.* Washington, DC: American Psychological Association.

American Psychological Association, American Educational Research Association, and National Council on Measurement in Education (1985). *Standards for educational and psychological testing.* Washington, DC: American Psychological Association.

Anastasi, A. (1950). The concept of validity in the interpretation of test scores. *Educational and Psychological Measurement, 10,* 67–78.

Anastasi, A. (1954). *Psychological testing.* New York: Macmillan.

Anastasi, A. (1976). *Psychological testing.* New York: Macmillan.

Anastasi, A. (1982). *Psychological testing.* New York: Macmillan.

Anastasi, A. (1985). Mental measurement: Some emerging trends. *Ninth mental measurements yearbook.* Lincoln, NB: Buros Institute of Mental Measurement, pp. xxiii–xxix.

Anastasi, A. (1986). Evolving concepts of test validation. *Annual Reviews of Psychology, 37,* 1–15.

Bingham, W. V. (1937). *Aptitudes and aptitude testing.* New York: Harper.

Bloom, B. S., Engelhart, M. D., Furst, E. J., Hill, W. H., & Krathwohl, D. R. (1956). *Taxonomy of educational objectives, Handbook I: Cognitive domain.* New York: Longmans, Green.

Campbell, D. T. & Fiske, D. W. (1959). Convergent and discriminant validation by the multitrait-multimethod matrix. *Psychological Bulletin, 56,* 81–105.

Cronbach, L. J. (1949). *Essentials of psychological testing.* New York: Harper.

Cronbach, L. J. (1969). Validation of educational measures. *Proceedings of the 1969 Invitational Conference on Testing Problems.* Princeton, NJ: Educational Testing Service, 35–52.

Cronbach, L. J. (1971). Test validation. In R. L. Thorndike (Ed.), *Educational measurement* (2nd ed.). Washington, DC: American Council on Education, pp. 443–507.

Cronbach, L. J., & Meehl, P. E. (1955). Construct validity in psychological tests. *Psychological Bulletin, 52,* 281–302.

Cureton, E. E. (1950). Validity: In E. F. Lindquist (Ed.), *Educational measurement* (pp. 621–694). Washington, DC: American Council in Education.

Flanagan, J. C. (1948). *The aviation psychology program in the Army Air Forces.* Washington, DC: U. S. Government Printing Office.

Flanagan, J. C. (1954). The critical incident technique. *Psychological Bulletin, 51,* 327–358.

Garrett, H. E. (1937). *Statistics in psychology and education.* New York: Longmans, Green.

Garrett, H. E. (1947). *Statistics in psychology and education.* New York: Longmans, Green.

Guilford, J. P. (1942). *Fundamental statistics in psychology and education.* New York: McGraw–Hill.

Guilford, J. P. (1946). New standards for test evaluation. *Educational & Psychological Measurement, 6,* 427–438.

Guion, R. M. (1977). Content validity—The source of my discontent. *Applied Psychological Measurement, 1,* 1–10.

————. (1980). On trinitarian doctrines of validity. *Professional Psychology, 11,* 385–398.

Gulliksen, H. (1950). Intrinsic validity. *American Psychologist, 5,* 511–517.

Jenkins, J. G. (1946). Validity for what? *Journal of Consulting Psychology, 10,* 93–98.

Kelley, T. L. (1927). *Interpretation of educational measurements.* Yonkers-on-Hudson, NY: World Book Company.

Lindquist, E. F. (1942). *A first course in statistics.* New York: Houghton Mifflin.

Loevinger, J. (1957). Objective tests as instruments of psychological theory. *Psychological Reports, 3,* 635–694 (Monograph Suppl. 9).

Messick, S. (1975). The standard problem: Meaning and values in measurement and evaluation. *American Psychologist, 30,* 955–966.

Messick, S. (1980). Test validity and the ethics of assessment. *American Psychologist, 35,* 1012–1027.

Messick, S. (1981a). Constructs and their vicissitudes in educational and psychological measurement. *Psychological Bulletin, 89,* 575–588.

Messick, S. (1981b). Evidence and ethics in the evaluation of tests. *Educational Researcher, 10,* 9–20.

Mosier, C. I. (1947). A critical examination of the concepts of face validity. *Educational and Psychological Measurement, 7,* 191–205.

Nevo, B. (1985). Face validity revisited. *Journal of Educational Measurement, 22,* 287–293.

Rulon, P. J. (1946). On the validity of educational tests. *Harvard Educational Review, 16,* 290–296.

Rulon, P. J. (1948). The criterion. *Proceedings of the 1948 Invitational Conference on Testing Problems.* Princeton, NJ: Educational Testing Service, pp. 32–34.

Schmidt, F. L., & Hunter, J. E. (1977). Development of a general solution to the problem of validity generalization. *Journal of Applied Psychology, 62,* 529–540.

Sisson, E. D. (1948). Force choice—The new Army rating. *Personnel Psychology, 1,* 365–381.

Tenopyr, M. L. (1977). Content-construct confusion. *Personnel Psychology, 30,* 47–54.

Chapter 3

The Once and Future Issues of Validity: Assessing the Meaning and Consequences of Measurement

Samuel Messick
Educational Testing Service

Over the next decade or two, computer and audiovisual technology will dramatically change the way individuals learn as well as the way they work. Technology will also have a profound impact on the ways in which knowledge, aptitudes, competencies, and personal qualities are assessed and even conceptualized. Along with rapid technological change to new and more varied interactive delivery systems in education and the workplace, there will come a heightened individuality in learning and thinking as well as an increased premium on adaptive learning, restructuring skills, and flexibility in modes of thinking and performance. There will also come a heightened emphasis on individuality in assessment with a premium on the adaptive measurement, perhaps even the dynamic measurement, of knowledge structures, skill complexes, personal strategies, and styles as they interact in performance and as they develop with instruction and experience. But although the modes and methods of measurement may change, the basic maxims of measurement, and especially of validity, will likely retain their essential character.

The key validity issues in future assessment are the same as they have always been, although we continue to have difficulty in discerning and articulating them and in agreeing on what is or ought to be construed as validity. The key validity issues are the interpretability, relevance, and utility of scores, the import or value implications of scores as a basis for action, and the functional worth of scores in terms of social consequences of their use. These manifold aspects or thrusts of validity have been integrated in the following unified view: Validity is an overall evaluative judgment, founded on empirical evidence and theoretical rationales, of the *adequacy* and *appropriateness* of *inferences* and *actions* based on test scores (Messick, 1980, 1981b). As such, validity is an inductive summary of both the adequacy of existing evidence for and the appropriateness of potential consequences of test interpretation and use.

The difficulty and disagreement alluded to earlier occurs not so much at the theoretical level of validity as an evolving concept, although there is contention enough at this level, to be sure. This is especially true in regard to the explicit subsuming of values and consequences in the unified validity concept, as is intended by the foregoing use of the term "appropriateness." In a sense, the unified view is a return to origins because the words "validity" and "value" have the same root meaning (Kaplan, 1964). Rather, the disagreement is more forcefully, though indirectly, revealed by the persistent disjunction between validity conception and validation practice.

TENSION BETWEEN IDEAL PRINCIPLES
AND REAL-WORLD PRACTICES

From the perspective of a unified view of validity, the 1985 *Standards for Educational and Psychological Testing* (American Psychological Association, 1985) enunciates sound validity principles but with sufficient qualification to permit considerable variation in practice. Much of this variation, stemming from appropriate allowance for professional judgment, is highly desirable. But the same allowance for professional judgment that facilitates flexibility in test validation also permits a perpetuation of less desirable uses of the past.

To quote the *Standards* specifically, "Validity . . . refers to the appropriateness, meaningfulness, and usefulness of the specific inferences made from test scores. Test validation is the process of accumulating evidence to support such inferences [p. 9]." Although not elaborated upon and possibly not intended, the explicit use of the term "appropriateness" here provides an uneasy foothold for appraising value implications and social consequences of score interpretation and use under this official rubric of validity.

Standards goes on to state:

A variety of inferences may be made from scores produced by a given test, and there are many ways of accumulating evidence to support any particular inference. Validity, however, is a unitary concept. Although evidence may be accumulated in many ways, validity always refers to the degree to which evidence supports the inferences that are made from the scores. The inferences regarding specific uses of the test are validated, not the test itself. . . . An ideal validation includes several types of evidence, which span all three of the traditional categories [of content-related, criterion-related, and construct-related evidence]. . . . Professional judgment should guide the decisions regarding the forms of evidence that are most necessary and feasible in light of the intended uses of the test and likely alternatives to testing. (p. 9)

The very first validity standard promulgated requires evidence for the major types of inferences entailed in the specific test uses recommended, along with a rationale supporting the particular mix of evidence presented. However, the accompanying comment may give the gain away, for it states that "Whether one or more kinds of validity evidence are appropriate is a function of the particular question being asked and of the context and extent of previous evidence" (p. 13). This comment is cogent under circumstances in which, for example, knowledge and skills important in job performance are identified by content-related evidence and then assessed by tests of that knowledge and skill deemed to be construct valid on the basis of prior results. But the comment also leaves the door open for an interpretation that there exist circumstances under which only one kind of validity evidence—be it content-related, for example, or criterion-related—may be adequate and fitting for a particular applied purpose. This selective reliance on one kind of validity evidence, when it occurs, is tantamount to reliance on one kind of validity as the whole of validity, regardless of how discredited such overgeneralization may have become and of how much lip service is paid to validity as a unitary concept (Guion, 1980; Messick, 1980).

The heart of the unified view of validity is that appropriateness, meaningfulness, and usefulness of score-based inferences are inseparable and that the unifying force is empirically grounded construct interpretation. Thus, from the perspective of validity as a unified concept, all educational and psychological measurement should be construct-referenced because construct interpretation undergirds all score-based inferences—not just those related to interpretive meaningfulness but also the content- and criterion-related inferences specific to applied decisions and actions based on test scores. As a consequence, although construct-related evidence may not be the whole of validity, there can be no validity without it. That is, there is no way to judge responsibly the appropriateness, meaningfulness, and usefulness of score inferences in the absence of evidence as to what the scores mean.

When stated baldly, exclusive reliance on only one kind of validity evidence (as, in the past, on only one kind of so-called validity) is unlikely to be seriously endorsed for long. Who would maintain as a *general* proposition, for example, that validity is solely good criterion prediction? Or, validity is representative coverage of relevant content? Or, validity is the attainment of intended functional consequences with minimal or tolerable adverse side-effects? Or, validity is trustworthy score interpretation? Although the latter formulation is more generally supportable, it too needs to be buttressed in many testing applications by evidence for the relevance of the construct to the particular applied purpose and for the utility of the measure in the applied setting (Guion, 1976; Messick, 1980). Or, validity is all of the foregoing? And if that is the case, how can it be made tangible in testing practice?

Rather than make one or another of these general claims, many testing practitioners instead argue for restrictive or selective reliance on one kind of validity evidence depending on the purpose of the testing. For example, many test users might advocate reliance on content-related evidence for educational achievement and job-sample tests used in certification, while for tests used in educational or occupational selection, they might advocate reliance on criterion-related evidence. But what about educational achievement or job-sample tests used in selection? And how does restrictive reliance on one kind of validity evidence jibe with the clear endorsement in the 1985 *Testing Standards* of validity as a unitary concept?

A pessimist might view the current state of testing practice as blatant hypocrisy, because of the inconsistency between expressed principles of unified validity on the one hand and widespread behavior of selective reliance on limited kinds of validity evidence on the other. But as an optimist, and I hope not a Pollyanna, I lean toward James March's (1972) analysis of hypocrisy as a transitional state. In March's words, "A bad man with good intentions may be a man experimenting with the possibility of becoming good. Somehow it seems to me more sensible to encourage the experimentation than to insult it" (p. 426). So enough of polemics, at least for a time. Let us turn instead to a more dispassionate and detailed examination of score-based inferences that may be sustained by content-, criterion-, and construct-related evidence as well as evidence related to the consequences of the testing. Perhaps cogent rationales for the centrality of construct-based inferences will help accelerate the time of transition from fragmented to unified validation practice.

Criterion-Predictor Relationships

The key inference that is sustainable from a statistically significant criterion-related validity study is that there is a dependable relationship in the particular setting between the predictor test or tests and the criterion measure. The inference that the practitioner wishes to make, however, is that the test should be used for selection. To reach this conclusion, additional evidence is required bearing on the content relevance and construct meaning of both the predictor and the criterion and on the potential social consequences of the particular selection use.

Indeed, since some provisional understanding or hypotheses about the nature of the criterion domain probably influenced the choice of the predictor test in the first place, the forthcoming criterion-related evidence contributes to the joint construct validation of both the criterion and the predictor (Guion, 1976; Smith, 1976). The more systematic and empirically grounded that the construct understanding of the criterion domain is, the more a rational foundation is afforded for forecasting likely predictive relationships. For example, job analysis might be employed to delineate important task requirements in the criterion domain, leading to both the development of pertinent criterion measures and the selection or construction of predictor tests judged to match the task requirements in some sense. But the empirical consistency of measures based on these rational or logical judgments must still be evaluated. That is, the meaning of the criterion measures and of criterion–predictor relationships must still be appraised, which suggests that the whole question of the validity of the job analysis itself has empirical substance.

Criterion measures must be evaluated like all measures in terms of their reliability, relevance to the applied purpose, construct meaning, and adequacy, especially in regard to completeness and to possible contamination by irrelevant variance (Smith, 1976). What if a measure of docility significantly improves the prediction of freshman grades at a particular college? Should it be used in selection, or should the criterion be scrutinized and refined? What if the incremental predictor were a measure of "flexibility versus rigidity?" What if the direction of prediction favored admission of rigid students? What if entrance to a military academy were at issue, or a medical school? What if the scores had been interpreted instead as measures not of "flexibility versus rigidity" but of "confusion versus control?" What if the best predictors of grades in performance training were reading comprehension tests? Should they be heavily weighted in selection, or should the verbal end-of-course examinations be replaced or supplemented with hands-on performance tests (Frederiksen, 1984; Messick, 1981a)? These are intrinsic validity questions and they cannot be answered by demonstrating significant criterion–predictor relationships alone (Gulliksen, 1950). In addition, one needs evidence addressing the meaning of the criterion and predictor measures, especially concerning the extent and nature of contamination by irrelevant variance. Nor should the value implications of test interpretation or the potential social consequences of the proposed test use be ignored in making the overall validity judgment (Cronbach, 1980; Messick, 1980).

Given satisfactory answers to these questions of construct meaning and irrelevant variance for both the predictor and the criterion, the issue of predictive utility can be broached. That is, the size of the criterion–predictor relationship can be appraised in relation to base rates, selection ratios, and both the benefits and the costs of selection to estimate the likely utility of the predictor in the applied setting (Brogden, 1946; Cronbach & Gleser, 1965; Curtis & Alf, 1969; Hunter, Schmidt, & Rauschenberger, 1977).

Moreover, implicit in the rational, construct-based approach to hypothesized predictive relationships, there is also a rational basis for judging the relevance of the test to the criterion domain. Thus, the issue of the job- or domain-relatedness of the test can be meaningfully addressed, even when criterion-related empirical verification is infeasible because of small samples, for instance, or inadequate variance or unreliable or otherwise questionable criterion measures (Guion, 1974, 1976). In such cases, the defense of the predictor rests on a combination of construct validity evidence and the rational justification for basing the predictive hypothesis on the selected construct. The case becomes stronger if the predicted relationship has been verified empirically in other similar settings. Thus, while selective reliance on only one kind of validity evidence is to be avoided, foregoing of one kind of validity evidence when infeasible may be defended if heavy reliance can be placed on the other types of evidence, especially construct-related evidence and a construct-based rationale for the plausibility of the unverified empirical relationships.

Conjunction of Content- and Construct-Related Evidence

The key inference sustainable from content-related evidence is that the content of the items or tasks included on a test is representative of the content of some defined domain about which inferences are to be drawn or predictions made. The inference that the practitioner wishes to make, however, is that "the behaviors demonstrated in testing constitute a representative sample of behaviors to be exhibited in a desired performance domain" (p. 28), as stated in the 1974 *Standards* (American Psychological Association), or that the processes employed in test performance are a representative sample of the processes employed in domain performance, as emphasized by Lennon (1956). Inferences regarding behaviors require evidence of response or performance consistency and not just judgments of content, while inferences regarding processes require construct-related evidence (Cronbach, 1971; Loevinger, 1957).

Typically, content-related inferences are inseparable from construct-related inferences. What is judged to be relevant and representative of the domain is not the surface content of test items or tasks but the knowledge, skill, or other pertinent attributes measured by the items or tasks. There is an implied two-step rationale: First, relevant knowledge and skill important in domain performance are delineated by means, for example, of job- or task-analysis; second, construct-valid measures of the important knowledge and skill are selected or developed. Test items and tasks are deemed relevant and representative because they are construct-valid measures of relevant and representative domain knowledge and skill.

In practice, content-related evidence usually takes the form of consensual informed judgments about the representative coverage of content in a test and about its relevance to a particular behavioral domain of interest. But this is evidence about the content of the test instrument and not evidence to support inferences from individuals' test scores, which are not even addressed in typical considerations of content. Thus, in a fundamental sense, content-related evidence does not qualify as validity evidence at all, although such content considerations clearly do and should influence the nature of score inferences supported by other evidence (Messick, 1975). Yalow and Popham (1983) describe this state of affairs as an implicit inference waiting to be made. They claim that "content validity resides in a test and once the test is taken, that validity makes available an inference about the examinee's status on the performance domain of interest"

(p. 11). But this inference relies on evidence of response consistency and score meaning and not on content coverage alone.

If the test tasks are a direct sample of domain tasks as in a job-sample test, limited content-based inferences may be sustained about high scorers but not low scorers and only then if the strict behavioral language of task description is adhered to. Otherwise, constructs are apt to be invoked and construct validity evidence required (Cronbach, 1971). Thus, one might infer that high scorers possess suitable skills to perform domain tasks successfully because they repeatedly succeeded on representative test tasks. But even here the inferences implicitly rely on conceptions of test and domain meaning, because these inferences are threatened by context effects (such as an evaluative atmosphere) that influence the test but not the job, at least not in the same way, or by situational factors (such as interpersonal attraction) that influence the job but not the test (Guion, 1977; Messick, 1981a).

And what of low scorers on these purported job- or domain-sample tests? The caution could not be colder on this point. In terms of content-related evidence, all that can be claimed is that low scorers did not perform the tasks successfully, they did not demonstrate domain or test competence or skill (Cronbach, 1971). But there is no basis for interpreting low scores as reflective of incompetence or lack of skill. To do that requires evidence to discount such plausible rival interpretations of low test performance as anxiety, inattention, low motivation, fatigue, limited English proficiency, or certain sensory handicaps. And evidence discounting plausible rival hypotheses is the hallmark of construct validation (Messick, 1980).

Thus, even under the best of direct domain sampling conditions where test tasks and domain tasks are viewed as members of the same behavioral class, content considerations are only one-directional in import—what bearing content per se has on validity at best holds for high scores but not for low scores (Messick, 1981b). Ironically, even with respect to these straightforward job-sample and domain-sample tests, the need for construct-related evidence is pervasive and fundamental. This is so because, except for simple domains that might be strictly operationally defined, the notion of a domain or behavioral class is a construct. The notion is of a class of behaviors all of which change in the same or related ways as a function of stimulus contingencies or that share or are organized by common processes (Messick, 1983). In other words, to claim that a body of information or tasks is a domain or behavior class is a hypothesis, which may ultimately be rejected on the basis of evidence (Shapere, 1977).

Consequential Basis of Validity

Judging whether a test does the job it is employed to do (Cureton, 1951), that is, whether it serves its intended function or purpose, requires evaluation of the intended and unintended social consequences of test interpretation and use. Thus, appraisal of the functional worth of the testing in terms of social values contributes to a consequential basis of test validity (Messick, 1980). For example, the occurrence of sex or ethnic differences in score distributions might lead to adverse impact if the test were used in selection, which would directly reflect on the functional worth of the selection testing. Whether the adverse impact is attributable to construct-relevant or construct-irrelevant test variance or to criterion-related or criterion-unrelated test variance are key validity issues in appraising functional worth and in justifying test use. Or, as another instance, the use in educational achievement tests of structured response formats such as multiple-choice (as opposed to contructed responses) might lead to increased emphasis on memory and analysis in teaching and learning at the expense of divergent production and synthesis. This is an example of what Frederiksen (1984) called "the real test bias"; and test bias, of course, is ultimately a question of validity—or rather, of invalidity (Shepard, 1982).

There are few prescriptions for how to proceed here because there is no guarantee that at any point in time we will identify all of the critical social consequences of the testing, especially those unintended side-effects that are remote from the expressed testing aims. One recommendation is to contrast the potential social consequences of the proposed testing with those of alternative procedures and even of procedures antagonistic to testing, such as *not* testing at all (Ebel, 1964). The intent of these contrasts is to draw attention to vulnerabilities in the proposed test interpretation and use, thereby exposing tacit value assumptions to open examination and debate (Churchman, 1971; Messick, 1980).

And once again, the construct meaning of measures plays a central role. Just as the construct meaning of the test provided a rational basis for hypothesizing predictive relationships to criteria, construct meaning also provides a rational basis for hypothesizing potential outcomes and for anticipating possible side-effects. Thus, evidence of construct meaning is not only essential for evaluating the import of testing consequences, it also helps determine where to look for testing consequences.

Construct Interpretation as Unifying Force

Pervasive throughout this treatment of content- and criterion-related evidence and of the consequential basis of test validity is the central and unifying role played by the construct meaning of test scores. It would appear that construct-related evidence undergirds not only construct-based inferences but content- and criterion-based inferences as well. After all, constructs are the medium of exchange of ideas in scientific and social discourse, and their essential role in measurement gives a means of making or maintaining contact with those ideas or of embodying them in quantitative terms (Messick, 1981a).

Despite this pervasiveness and centrality, however, the applied testing field seems reluctant to highlight construct validity evidence, perhaps because the process of construct validation seems complicated and vague. But the appearance of complexity and vagueness stems from its enormous flexibility and generality. Test validation in the construct framework is integrated with hypothesis testing and with all of the philosophical and empirical means by which scientific theories are evaluated. Thus, construct validation embraces all of the statistical, experimental, rational, and rhetorical methods of marshaling evidence to support the inference that observed consistency in test performance has circumscribed meaning. With respect to the generality of the process, the development of evidence to support an inferential leap from an observed consistency to a construct or theory that accounts for that consistency is a generic concern of all science.

Another reason for trepidation in pursuing construct validation is that the process has been described as a never-ending one, as the ever-expanding development of a mosaic of research evidence where at any moment new findings or new credible assumptions may dictate a change in construct interpretation, theory, or measurement (Messick, 1980). But just because a process is never-ending does not mean that it should not have a beginning. And a good beginning, at the least, is to attempt to discount plausible hypotheses about construct-irrelevant variance in the test. For example, a plausible rival hypothesis for a subject-matter achievement test is that it might, by virtue of its vocabulary level, be in part a reading comprehension test in disguise. Or for a reading comprehension test, that it might be merely a measure of recall or recognition or of feature matching between the question and the passage. Or for a general knowledge test, that it might be partly a measure of common sense or of reasoning about the multiple-choice distractors, answerable perhaps without even perusing the question stem. Or for a reasoning test, that it might instead or in part be a measure of knowledge. A variety of correlational, experimental, or logical approaches could be undertaken to render such rival hypotheses much less plausible (Cronbach, 1971; Messick, in press).

EVIDENTIAL AND CONSEQUENTIAL BASES
OF VALIDITY

The process of construct interpretation inevitably places test scores in both a theoretical context of implied relationships to other constructs and a value context of implied relationships to good and bad, to desirable and undesirable attributes and behaviors. Empirical appraisals of the former substantive relationships contribute to an *evidential basis for test interpretation,* that is, to construct validity. Judgmental appraisals of the latter value implications provide a *consequential basis for test interpretation.*

The process of test use inevitably places test scores in both a theoretical context of implied relevance and utility and a value context of implied means and ends. Empirical appraisals of the former issues of relevance and utility, along with construct validity, contribute to an *evidential basis for test use*. Judgmental appraisals of the ends a proposed test use might lead to, that is, of the potential social consequences of a proposed use and of the actual consequences of the applied testing, provide a *consequential basis for test use* (Messick, 1981b).

Four Facets of Validity

Test validity, as an overall evaluative judgment of the adequacy and appropriateness of inferences and actions based on test scores, thus rests on four bases. These are (1) an inductive summary of convergent and discriminant evidence that the test scores have a plausible meaning or construct interpretation, (2) an appraisal of the value implications of the test interpretation, (3) a rationale and evidence for the relevance of the construct and the utility of the scores in particular applications, and (4) an appraisal of the potential social consequences of the proposed use and of the actual consequences when used.

Putting these four bases together, we see that test validity can be represented in terms of two interconnected facets linking the source of the justification— either evidential or consequential—to the function or outcome of the testing, either interpretation or use. This crossing of basis and function provides a unified view of test validity, as portrayed in Fig. 3.1 (Messick, 1980).

	Test Interpretation	Test Use
Evidential Basis	Construct Validity	Construct Validity + Relevance/Utility
Consequential Basis	Value Implications	Social Consequences

FIG. 3.1.   Facets of test validity.

Local Value Contexts and the Ethics of Test Use

Although the value implications of test interpretation and the potential social consequences of proposed test use derive largely from the test's construct meaning and its evidential basis, there are other more political and situational sources of social values bearing on testing that often assume equal or greater importance (Messick, 1984). Critical value implications frequently emerge when the test is placed in the particular social context of an applied setting. As a further complication, these context-specific value implications may differ, depending on whether the test use applies to selection, guidance, training, certification, or other social functions. Because the test user is in the best position to evaluate these specific value implications, a heavy ethical burden thereby falls on the user.

The test user is also in the best position to evaluate the meaning of individual scores under local circumstances, that is, to appraise the construct interpretation of individual scores and the extent to which their intended meaning may have been eroded by contaminating influences. Although the delineation of possible influences that might contaminate test scores from the standpoint of a proposed construct interpretation is part of construct validation, the test user's task in this instance is not construct validation but to recognize which of the possible contaminants are operating in his or her particular situation (Cronbach, 1969, 1971). Thus, the test user bears not only a heavy ethical burden but a heavy interpretive burden. And that interpretation entails responsibility for its value consequences. But the test user cannot be the sole arbiter of the ethics of assessment, because the *value* of measurement is as much a scientific and professional issue as the *meaning* of measurement (Messick, 1981b). This is the main reason why the testing profession in its formal conception and implementation of validity and validation should address values and consequences as well as utility and meaning.

KEYNOTE FOR FUTURE VALIDITY

I noted earlier that validity is an inductive summary of both the existing evidence for and the potential consequences of test interpretation and use. As an inductive summary, validity is itself clearly a construct and subject to construct validation. That is, validity must obey the same principles it is designed to reveal. And in the last analysis, these principles are those of science. Since science moves patiently and inexorably except for sporadic bursts of restructuring, I conjectured at the outset that the maxims of measurement and especially of validity would likely retain their essential character over the next several decades. And if a radical restructuring of the validity concept does occur, these same scientific principles of rationality and evidence will be used to evaluate its validity.

I once had a dear friend, now long deceased, who was fond of proclaiming that "science *is* measurement" (Siegel, 1964). This insight had a profound effect on his research and teaching, as it might for all of us. The inverse— measurement is science—is not necessarily the case. But from the perspective of construct validation and the unified view of validity, the claim is that it *is* or ought to be the case. Moreover, the practical use of measurements for decision making and action is or ought to be *applied* science, recognizing that applied science always occurs in a political context. Indeed, social and political forces are sometimes so salient that we may need a new discipline to deal explicitly with the politics of applied science, which is what the field of program evaluation shows signs of becoming (Cronbach, 1982; Cronbach & Associates, 1980). But if measurement is science and the use of measurements is applied (political) science, the justification and defense of measurement and its validity is and may always be a rhetorical art.

ACKNOWLEDGMENTS

This chapter is based on a paper presented at the conference on Test Validity for the 1990s and Beyond, jointly sponsored by the Air Force Human Resources Laboratory and Educational Testing Service, at Princeton, N.J., May 1986.

REFERENCES

American Psychological Association, American Educational Research Association, & National Council on Measurement in Education. (1974). *Standards for educational and psychological tests*. Washington, DC: American Psychological Association.

American Psychological Association, American Educational Research Association & National Council on Measurement in Education. (1985). *Standards for educational and psychological testing*. Washington, DC: American Psychological Association.

Brogden, H. E. (1946). On the interpretation of the correlation coefficient as a measure of predictive efficiency. *Journal of Educational Psychology, 37,* 65–76.

Churchman, C. W. (1971). *The design of inquiring systems: Basic concepts of systems and organization*. New York: Basic Books.

Cronbach, L. J. (1969). Validation of educational measures. *Proceedings of the 1969 Invitational Conference on Testing Problems: Toward a theory of achievement measurement*. Princeton, NJ: Educational Testing Service.

Cronbach, L. J. (1971). Test validity. In R. L. Thorndike (Ed.), *Educational measurement*. Washington, DC: American Council on Education.

Cronbach, L. J. (1980). Validity on parole: How can we go straight? *New directions for testing and measurement—Measuring achievement over a decade—Proceedings of the 1979 ETS Invitational Conference*. San Francisco: Jossey–Bass.

Cronbach, L. J. (1982). *Designing evaluations of educational and social programs*. San Francisco: Jossey–Bass.

Cronbach, L. J., & Associates. (1980). *Toward reform of program evaluation*. San Francisco: Jossey–Bass.

Cronbach, L. J., & Gleser, G. C. (1965). *Psychological tests and personnel decisions* (2nd ed.). Urbana: University of Illinois Press.

Cureton, E. E. (1951). Validity. In E. F. Lindquist (Ed.), *Educational measurement* (1st ed.). Washington, DC: American Council on Education.

Curtis, E. W., & Alf, E. F. (1969). Validity, predictive efficiency, and practical significance of selection tests. *Journal of Applied Psychology, 53,* 327–337.

Ebel, R. L. (1964). The social consequences of educational testing. *Proceedings of the 1963 Invitational Conference on Testing Problems*. Princeton, NJ: Educational Testing Service.

Frederiksen, N. (1984). The real test bias: Influences of testing on teaching and learning. *American Psychologist, 39,* 193–202.

Guion, R. M. (1974). Open a window: Validities and values in psychological measurement. *American Psychologist, 29,* 287–296.

Guion, R. M. (1976). Recruiting, selection, and job placement. In M. D. Dunnette (Ed.), *Handbook of industrial and organizational psychology*. Chicago: Rand–McNally.

Guion, R. M. (1977). Content validity—The source of my discontent. *Applied Psychological Measurement, 1,* 1–10.

Guion, R. M. (1980). On trinitarian doctrines of validity. *Professional Psychology, 11,* 385–398.

Gulliksen, H. (1950). Intrinsic validity. *American Psychologist, 5,* 511–517.

Hunter, J. E., Schmidt, F. L., & Rauschenberger, J. M. (1977). Fairness of psychological tests:

Implications of four definitions of selection utility and minority hiring. *Journal of Applied Psychology, 62,* 245–260.

Kaplan, A. (1964). *The conduct of inquiry: Methodology for behavioral sciences.* San Francisco: Chandler.

Lennon, R. T. (1956). Assumptions underlying the use of content validity. *Educational and Psychological Measurement, 16,* 294–304.

Loevinger, J. (1957). Objective tests as instruments of psychological theory. *Psychological Reports, 3,* 635–694 (Monograph Suppl. 9).

March, J. G. (1972). Model bias in social action. *Review of Educational Research, 42,* 413–429.

Messick, S. (1975). The standard problem: Meaning and values in measurement and evaluation. *American Psychologist, 30,* 955–966.

Messick, S. (1980). Test validity and the ethics of assessment. *American Psychologist, 35,* 1012–1027.

Messick, S. (1981a). Constructs and their vicissitudes in educational and psychological measurement. *Psychological Bulletin, 89,* 575–588.

Messick, S. (1981b). Evidence and ethics in the evaluation of tests. Educational Researcher, 10, 9–20.

Messick, S. (1983). Assessment of children. In W. Kessen (Ed.), *Handbook of child psychology: Vol. 1. History, theories and methods* (4th ed.). New York: Wiley.

Messick, S. (1984). The psychology of educational measurement. *Journal of Educational Measurement, 21,* 215–237.

Messick, S. (in press). Validity. In R. L. Linn (Ed.), *Educational measurement* (3rd ed.). New York: Macmillan.

Shapere, D. (1977). Scientific theories and their domains. In F. Suppe (Ed.), *The structure of scientific theories* (2nd ed.). Urbana: University of Illinois Press.

Shepard, L. A. (1982). Definitions of bias. In R. A. Berk (Ed.), *Handbook of methods for detecting test bias.* Baltimore: Johns Hopkins University Press.

Siegel, A. E. (1964). Sidney Siegel: A memoir. In S. Messick & A. H. Brayfield (Eds.), *Decision and choice: Contributions of Sidney Siegel.* New York: McGraw–Hill.

Smith, P. C. (1976). Behaviors, results, and organizational effectiveness: The problem of criteria. In M. D. Dunnette (Ed.), *Handbook of industrial and organizational psychology.* Chicago: Rand–McNally.

Yalow, E. S., & Popham, W. J. (1983). Content validity at the crossroads. *Educational Researcher, 12*(8), 10–14.

THE CHANGING FACES OF VALIDITY

The chapters in Section I clearly show how the epistemological bases of testing have matured since their beginnings decades ago. Many of the changes observed involved making explicit some of the structures that were previously implicit in the test. Moreover, newer cultural concerns surfaced, manifesting themselves in a greater sensitivity to the wide diversity of the environments and backgrounds inherent in a multicultural society.

Scientific research in cognitive psychology and related areas has developed quite apart from any formal concern with testing. Nevertheless this research can have a profound effect upon the theory and practice of testing. In the first chapter in this section, James Pellegrino provides a general discussion of the relationship between the developments in cognitive psychology and questions of test validity. The second, by Robert Sternberg, is more specific, proposing a general framework to measure intelligence. He expresses clearly a triarchic view of intelligence which is different both in tone and character from factor analytical (Guilford, 1967) treatments. The conceptions of intelligence gleaned from factor analytical approaches has been the subject of heated debate for decades (besides Guilford, see Burt, 1940; Gould, 1981; & Thurstone, 1924). Sternberg's ideas are more strongly based upon contemporary theories of cognition and less on the sometimes Byzantine methodology of factor analysis.

Parallel to the advances made in scientific psychology have been enormous strides in the technology for administering test.

Chief among these is the availability of inexpensive high-speed computing. This allows the presentation of new kinds of items, the measurement of other characteristics besides "right or wrong" (i.e., response latency), and the possibility of adapting the test "on the fly" to better measure the individual examinee. The third chapter in this section, by Bert Green, discusses the problems and promises of computerized adaptive testing. He also presents data which, in the instance studied, show that the initial implementations of computerized adaptive testing are fulfilling these promises.

REFERENCES

Burt, C. (1940). *The factors of the mind*. London: University of London Press.
Gould, S. J. (1981). *The mismeasure of man*. New York: Norton.
Guilford, J. P. (1967). *The nature of human intelligence*. New York: McGraw–Hill.
Thurstone, L. L. (1924). *The nature of intelligence*. London: Kegan, Paul.

Chapter 4

Mental Models
and Mental Tests

James W. Pellegrino
University of California, Santa Barbara

INTRODUCTION AND BACKGROUND

The primary goal of this chapter is to describe some of the ways that research in cognitive science can contribute to resolution of difficult issues involving test development and validation. The intent is to illustrate how such research would help address some past, present, and future concerns about test validity.

It is useful to begin with a brief overview of the general nature of research in cognitive science since this establishes a context for the substantive points of this chapter. Theory and research that falls under the rather broad rubric of cognitive science is concerned with specifying the roles of various mental structures, processes, strategies, and representations, and their respective interactions, in the performance of cognitive tasks. A very general and somewhat loose theoretical framework is used as the background for specifying these constructs for particular domains of cognition and performance. Examples range from children's counting behaviors, to solving geometry problems, to summarizing a text, to planning a route through a city, to solving analogy or paragraph comprehension items. Each instance involves delineating the details of a theory of the knowledge and processes involved in solving problems. Such a theory of cognitive components yields a theory of problem types and their mappings to components. These theories permit the design of sets of items and tasks which can be used to validate the theoretical constructs. Systematic, theory-based variations in problem characteristics constitute the basis for hypothesis testing, with very specific predictions derived about patterns of performance over the set of problems. Different sets of predictions correspond to different theories and models of task performance.

Most recently, the emphasis in this type of research has been on using within subjects designs for theory validation. Response characteristics for individual items, such as latency, accuracy and error types, form the basis for validating the theory and models of the cognitive constructs proposed. In addition, there has been a general movement toward combining both nomothetic and ideographic research. A goal is to specify detailed theories and models of performance capable of accounting for the data produced by a single individual over a set of items or tasks. Generalizability and further validation of the theory is established by demonstrating similar applicability of the theory's predictions to the performance patterns exhibited by other individuals, typically those of the same age. The explanatory power of the theory and its construct validity can be further tested by demonstrating applicability to the performances of individuals at a wide range of ages.

A superficial analogy can be drawn between what is done under the heading of cognitive science research and what is done in developing and validating mental tests. In the latter case, the interest is in validating a theory of the constructs involved in different tests. Items are selected to construct such a test, with data then collected on the performance of an individual over a series of different tests. Rather than the item being the unit of analysis, the test composed of a set of items becomes the unit. Nevertheless, the primary concern is the performance pattern over tests given some theory about the constructs represented by the tests. This is very much like validation of the constructs specified within a cognitive science theory. Unfortunately, the analogy now breaks down since not only are the constructs different, but most importantly, the pattern can only be understood and used to validate the original hypotheses about constructs by simultaneously examining the performance patterns exhibited by other individuals on these same tests.

From an admittedly naïve perspective on issues of test validity, it seems that many general concerns and problems regarding test validity emanate from the basic problem of interpreting the meaning of a single person's score on a single test, as well as the further problem of interpreting the meaning of a pattern of scores over a series of tests in the absence of data provided simultaneously by others. The problem of interpreting a single score on a single problem is also present in the cognitive science effort. What differs is the ability to draw conclusions by looking at the pattern of responses within an individual over a set of problems. Whether those inferences are relevant to issues of individual differences is another matter entirely.

It would appear that we have two different levels of analysis in the traditional test development and validation approach and the cognitive science approach. By combining them and considering their complementary properties we may find ways to approach many of the validity issues that have existed for years. In the remainder of this chapter I explore how research in cognitive science relates to traditional issues of test validation. Specifically, I want to show how the research of the last decade on the assessment of human performance within a cognitive science, information-processing framework can contribute to resolving concerns about the validity of tests during and beyond the next decade.

The presentation is organized in terms of three topics. In each section I have tried to strike a balance between briefly reviewing what cognitive science research has contributed to addressing that topic and how it can further contribute to resolving scientific and practical issues of test validity. The sections are loosely structured and tied to three issues of validity: (1) *construct validity,* (2) *criterion validity,* and (3) *practical validity.*

CONSTRUCT VALIDITY

For a considerable period of time it has been argued that construct validation of aptitude and achievement tests should be of central concern (e.g., Messick, 1975). It has also been recognized that approaches to construct validation using correlational and factor analytical procedures are limited and have a certain circularity (e.g., Sternberg, 1979). One problem is that the constructs assumed to be represented by particular tests have to do with specific and general traits that can only be verified by correlational patterns of tests with each other. Thus, the construct validity of a test is defined in reference to a trait theory of aptitude and both are defined by correlational patterns among tests. Furthermore, the nature of the construct remains very general and lacks specification relative to the dynamics of human cognition (e.g., McNemar, 1964).

Cognitive researchers have provided some resolution of this problem by engaging in information-processing analyses of the performances required to solve the individual items found on a wide variety of tests associated with major aptitude constructs. This research, which is only a decade old at this point, has tried to answer the question of what is tested by intelligence and aptitude tests, but from a cognitive science perspective of the human mind.

The details of what has been done are clearly beyond the scope of this chapter and are well documented elsewhere (e.g., Sternberg, 1985a,b). The essential features, however, are those described earlier as characteristic of cognitive science theory and research. The only difference is that the problems focused on are those drawn from aptitude and achievement tests or are very similar to such problems. In many cases the theory generation and empirical validation regarding component processes, strategies, representations, and knowledge required for problem solution actually starts with the types of items typically found on tests. However, it seldom stops there, and for a very good reason. The limited set of items found on most tests represents a sampling from a large and complex universe of problem characteristics. Those characteristics can be related to a theory of processing but tests seldom contain a sufficiently well-structured and representative sample to permit theory testing and validation of the type described earlier in which one is interested in performance patterns exhibited over problems. Thus, the researcher is left to design a theoretically more useful problem set so that effective hypothesis testing and validation can occur. Once this aspect of experimental and test design has been accomplished then both nomothetic and ideographic approaches to data collection and hypothesis testing can be pursued.

This basic approach has now been applied to a very wide range of performances representing the world of aptitude and achievement testing. It includes many of the major aptitude constructs and tests in use for the past 50 years. The list includes analogies, series completion problems, classification items, figural matrix problems, linear, categorical and conditional syllogisms, perceptual comparison items, spatial relations and visualization problems, vocabulary items, paragraph comprehension tasks, algebra equations, mathematics word problems, and mechanical comprehension items. In virtually every one of the preceding cases we now have reasonably well-defined analyses of the knowledge, processes, strategies and representations involved in solving items. We also have theories of how items differ relative to these processes and data on how individuals differ in their performances on these items relative to these theories and models of cognition. By no means do we have all the issues nailed down but an impressive amount of theoretical and empirical information has been accumulated in the last decade (see Sternberg, 1985a,b).

What does all this mean relative to issues of construct validity both for the present and the future? I would claim that cognitive scientists have been engaged wittingly and unwittingly in a process of construct validation but of a type different from the typical psychometric approach. In many ways this body of research on the cognitive components of performance on aptitude and achievement tests has provided an independent method of explaining some of the typical correlational patterns obtained in validation studies. For example, tasks that consistently load on a major factor, such as induction, require similar processes, strategies, and representations for problem solution (Goldman & Pellegrino, 1984; Pellegrino, 1985). An explanation for typical validity results is not necessarily in terms of aptitude constructs but in terms of constructs about the nature of human thought, particularly its dynamics and limits. It must be noted, however, that we have a way to go within cognitive science to validate all of its various constructs. Individual differences data can play an important role in this process (see e.g., Pellegrino & Kail, 1982).

With respect to the future of testing, it is not sufficient to note complacently that an independent process of construct validation has generally supported the results of 80 years of psychometric theory and test development. In fact I believe that such a conclusion is wrong. It is wrong because it ignores the fact that cognitive science research has emphasized the need for two things with regard to mental tests. First, we need to focus on a different type and level of constructs if we want to understand the meaning of test scores and use tests effectively. Second, the latter can only come about by applying these theories of cognitive constructs to the design and interpretation of new tests.

These issues are not new and they have been discussed at some length by others (e.g., Bejar, 1983, 1985; Embretson, 1983, 1985a, 1986). The issues of concern can be illustrated by using Embretson's argument for the separation of two issues in construct validation research, namely construct representation and nomothetic span. "Construct representation refers to the processes, strategies, and knowledge stores that are involved in item responses. . . . Construct representation is understood when the various components, metacomponents, strategies and knowledge stores that are involved in solving psychometric items are explained," (Embretson, 1985a, p. 196). The cognitive science research I have alluded to represents pursuit of this issue in construct validity research. In contrast, nomothetic span refers to the "utility of the test as a measure of individual differences." (p. 196) The two issues of construct representation and nomothetic span are essential for addressing issues of test design and validation in the future.

Perhaps the best way to see the application of these issues and the relevance of research in cognitive science is to consider them with regard to present and future tests. If we focus on tests currently in use we have the situation where nomothetic span is already known but construct representation remains to be determined. Cognitive components analyses of the characteristics of the items can be done to see which ones are represented in the item set and how they relate to item difficulty. By doing this over a series of tests or item samples we can begin to understand the cognitive factors involved in a test and why various tests or item samples may be more or less correlated with each other and vary in nomothetic span (Embretson, 1986). It seems that this work is particularly appropriate in the context of analyzing existing item banks, selection procedures, and validity coefficients in current and proposed implementations of computerized adaptive tests (see e.g., Embretson, 1986).

A more exciting possibility is that of designing tests so that the item sets systematically reflect the characteristics deemed relevant from cognitive science theories of performance. There have been a number of recent arguments that it is time to move test design from the position of being an art to that of being a science (e.g., Bejar, 1985; Embretson, 1985b, Glaser, 1985). How we do this depends on the availability of theories of the processes and knowledge required to solve problems and their mappings to the characteristics of the problems to be solved. I would argue that an agenda for testing is to begin the systematic process of test design based upon the results of cognitive science research. In this way we can attempt to control construct representation while then pursuing issues of nomothetic span but in a more principled and theory-based manner. I see no reason why test design and validation research could not move to a point where systematic hypotheses about performance patterns over problems within and across tests are evaluated as part of the normal validation process.

If we were to begin this process right now it would take us well into the next decade to consider the results and incorporate them into large-scale testing programs such as the administration of the SAT, GRE, or ASVAB. I believe that we are presently in a position to design many different types of items using cognitive science theories and research results. As mentioned earlier, we can begin doing this for many standard tests and problem types such as analogies, series, syllogisms, vocabulary, paragraph comprehension, spatial relations, visualization, computation and word problem items (see e.g., Hunt & Pellegrino, 1985; Hunt, Pellegrino, Abate, Alderton. Farr, Frick, & McDonald, 1986). What we most certainly gain is information regarding construct representation. Thus, we would be able to state quite clearly what is being assessed by reference to a dynamically oriented theory of cognition without resorting to constructs only validated through individual difference patterns. What we may lose or change is nomothetic span. There is no guarantee that better designed tests from the perspective of construct representation will be better measures of individual differences. This remains to be determined.

In summary, I do not see how we can effectively pursue issues of construct validity without some principled applications of cognitive theory in the design and validation of tests. It has taken the last 10 years to make progress with regard to cognitive task analyses of intellectual behaviors and it will take a least a decade more to apply and refine such procedures for practical testing purposes.

CRITERION VALIDITY

I have already indicated that new tests based on cognitive science approaches to test design may not lead to improvements in criterion validity even though they should have better construct validity relative to current cognitive theory. A few years ago Earl Hunt made this point more forcefully.

> The cognitive science view may lead to the development of new tests that are more firmly linked to a theory of cognition than are present tests. Such tests are yet to be written. There is no compelling reason to believe that new tests will be better predictors of those criteria that are predicted by today's tests. After all the present tests are the results of an extensive search for instruments that meet the pragmatic criterion of prediction. Theoretically based tests may expand the range of cognitive functions that are evaluated and certainly should make better contact with our theories of cognition. Theoretical interpretation alone is not a sufficient reason for using a test. A test that is used to make social decisions must meet traditional psychometric criteria for reliability and validity. No small effort will be required to construct tests that meet both theoretical and pragmatic standards. The effort is justified, for our methods of assessing cognition ought to flow from our theories about the process of thinking. (Hunt, 1983, p. 146)

The problem of criterion or predictive validity is another longstanding issue that also bears some consideration relative to developments in cognitive science. At a very simple level, the argument about the utility of cognitive science research with respect to construct validation of the test domains serving as predictors is also applicable to construct validation of the criterion domains and performances to be predicted. I do not see how we can improve predictive validity by unilaterally understanding and then improving the construct validity of only one side of the regression equation. In fact, it seems that the more we understand about the meaning of the performances we assess the less likely we will be to predict or want to try to predict performances which lack a similar theoretical analysis and understanding.

A first step is to apply the same framework of theoretical and empirical analysis to the criterion performances serving as the targets of prediction. In this way we can begin to explain existing predictive validity in terms of concepts drawn from a common theory of cognition focusing on mental structures, processes, representations, and knowledge. This is currently feasible in the area of aptitude–achievement relationships since several aptitude and achievement measures can be and have been analyzed in a cognitive science framework (see e.g., Sternberg, 1985a,b).

If we apply cognitive science approaches to the analysis of important criteria to be predicted then we can also make progress in developing new criterion performance measures that have improved construct validity. This is most easily accomplished with respect to academic achievement criteria which are often expressed in terms of performance on standardized tests. Other criteria, such as school grades, are of a much coarser nature and so long as they are maintained as important criteria there may be relatively little that can be done. In those cases where the criterion is reasonably well defined and subject to an analysis within a cognitive science framework then we can address issues of improving criterion validity by designing tests that are psychologically closer to the criteria being predicted.

All of the foregoing is predicated on the same basic assumption developed earlier in this chapter, namely that issues of validity in testing flow from a deeper theoretical understanding and analysis of the constructs represented in the test and the manner in which they are represented. This is true for tests of aptitude and achievement as well as other criteria of social significance. The constructs of concern, however, must flow from a theory of the processes and dynamics of cognition and tests designed to represent those constructs specifically.

In addition to providing a basis for analyzing the criteria to be predicted and developing tests with greater construct representation, cognitive science research can further contribute to research on criterion validity by broadening the scope of criteria to be predicted and specifying how the various performances are different relative to a theory of cognition. In this regard there are differences between academic achievement criteria, technical and high performance skills, everyday practical skills and tacit knowledge. Only recently have we come to understand better some of the differences between these criteria by engaging in detailed analyses of the cognitive competencies exhibited by experts and novices in different task domains (see e.g., Chi, Glaser, & Rees, 1982; Glaser, 1985). What I am suggesting is that we can only improve criterion validity when we understand the criterion better from the same theoretical perspective as that used to understand the predictor.

Furthermore, we can then engage in a systematic process of design to improve construct representation in both the criterion and the predictor. This should help achieve two goals: simultaneously increasing both construct validity and criterion validity.

Increasing the range of predictors and/or criteria will not automatically solve the problems of criterion validity. However, better theoretical analyses of both, with resultant better test designs for their assessment, can increase the probability of enhanced predictive validity.

PRACTICAL VALIDITY

In considering both construct and criterion validity I have focused on two traditional areas of test validity. What I have argued thus far is that a cognitive science framework for analyzing and developing tests and selecting criteria can help alleviate two recurrent test validity issues. There is a very interesting and important by-product of adopting this approach to test analysis, test design, and construct validation. I will refer to this as practical validity from the point of view of instructional diagnosis and prescription.

The argument has been made in the past by Messick (1980) and others (e.g., Glaser, 1985) that issues of test validity need to take into account the purposes of testing and the use of test information. It has also been asserted that the information derived from current tests is frequently outside the domain of instruction and/or irrelevant to instructional decision making. It is difficult to argue that tests have practical validity for the types of decision making that go on daily in normal instructional settings. Furthermore aptitude and achievement testing behave as periodic summative evaluations rather than repetitive and integrated formative evaluations embedded within the normal instructional process. Finally, the argument is often made that they seldom provide diagnostic and prescriptive information for instructional decision making, given the normative evaluation procedures. This argument is less powerful for criterion referenced assessment but nonetheless still appropriate given the nature of the information typically provided to student and teacher.

How do we bypass some of these problems given procedures for test design derived from cognitive science research? One answer is to refer back to my very early description of cognitive science approaches to analyzing the processes, strategies, and knowledge involved in solving problems. Not only does one need a cognitive theory of knowledge and processes but also how they are specified relative to problem characteristics. The item set then becomes the basis for testing hypotheses and inferring the mental models and representations used by individuals in solving problems. The validation and inferences, however, are not based on the solution of a single problem or the aggregate score over a problem set but the pattern of performances over groups of items within a test. The pattern of scores or performance measures on items matters as much as (if not more than) the total test score. In cognitive science research these results provide the basis for internal validation of the theory or model of task performance. This can be done at the aggregate group level or at the level of individual examinees.

This brings me back to my earlier point about using tests in ways that are currently not possible. By increasing construct validity and representativeness we set the stage for developing diagnostic tests which have substantial practical utility for diagnosis and prescription.

All of this is based upon a more general cognitive science concept, that of an abstract representation of a situation, what is frequently referred to as a mental model. There are really two mental models that we wish to consider. One is the mental model of the learner or examinee relative to some domain of knowledge and performance. The examinee's mental model consists of the organized knowledge and processes that pertain to some area such as mathematics, story comprehension, physics problem solving, or analogy solution. The mental model is a hypothetical representation of what is known, how it is known, that is to say, the format and organization and how it governs performance. What we want is a good working model of the mental model of the person being examined. The way to infer it is by presenting systematic sets of problems and examining performance patterns to see if we can infer the structure of what is known. A good teacher engages in this process and thereby creates his or her mental model of the student's mental model. The teacher then refines his or her model as a result of gathering further systematic evidence. Instruction can then be prescriptive and geared to modifying hypothesized misconceptions or other problems in the student's mental model. The goal of a test should be to elucidate the examinee's mental model of the content tested. This constitutes a practical form of diagnosis which can then be used for the purpose of instructional prescriptions. Current designs for intelligent tutoring systems incorporate these concepts (e.g., Anderson, 1985).

The concept of mental models has been applied in cognitive science to several substantive domains of knowledge and performance. Examples include complex procedural math skills, such as multicolumn addition or subtraction, physics concepts and laws, physical systems; devices such as electronic circuits and troubleshooting; computational devices such as calculators, and computer hardware; and software interactions such as text editors, programming languages, and operating systems.

If our goal is to develop theory-based tests with greater construct, criterion, and practical validity then we can make progress with regard to meeting all three goals by attempting to follow a cognitive science approach of drawing inferences based upon patterns of responses emitted by a single individual over well-conceived sets of problems in a given domain. As mentioned earlier, this can be approximated in certain domains of achievement such as mathematics, text comprehension, and scientific reasoning. Perhaps two of the best known examples of this approach to testing are the work on multicolumn subtraction by Brown, Burton, and Van Lehn, and Siegler's research on children's reasoning in various logical tasks such as balance scales (Brown & Burton, 1978; Brown & Van Lehn, 1980; Siegler 1978; Siegler & Klahr, 1982; Van Lehn, 1983).

Some of this research could now be converted into sets of test problems with well-developed scoring schemes that provide diagnostic information to a teacher. This includes a child's understanding and misunderstanding of components of the algorithm to perform subtraction or the child's representation of the problem features and combination rules to be used in integrating information in proportional reasoning problems. Similar types of information can be provided about performance on problems drawn from aptitude tests. The virtue is that diagnostic information can be provided about what an individual knows, what she or he is doing in solving problems, and how efficiently it is being done. This is not the same as the information provided by a criterion-referenced test since the latter only tells which objectives of instruction have and have not been met. The very important and subtle difference is that embedded in this cognitive science research is a theory of correct performance with derived theories of errors and misconceptions in mental models of tasks and knowledge domains.

Developing tests and testing procedures which have the three properties of improved construct, criterion, and practical validity is an important part of the agenda for test development and test validity in the next several decades. Research in cognitive science does not provide all the answers but this perspective provides some valuable theoretical and analytical tools at a very different level from traditional psychometric approaches.

REFERENCES

Anderson, J. R. (1985). *Tutoring of mathematics skills*. Presentation at ONR-NPS meeting on Mathematical Reasoning and Basic Mathematical Skills, December, San Diego, CA.

Bejar, I. I. (1983). *Achievement testing*. Beverly Hills, CA: Sage.

Bejar, I. I. (1985). Speculations on the future of test design. In S. E. Embretson (Ed.), *Test design: Developments in psychology and psychometrics* (pp. 279–294). New York: Academic Press.

Brown, J. S., & Burton, R. R. (1978). Diagnostic models for procedural bugs in basic mathematics. *Cognitive Science, 2,* 155–192.

Brown, J. S., & Van Lehn, K. (1980). Repair theory: A generative theory of bugs in procedural skills. *Cognitive Science, 4,* 379–426.

Chi, M. T. H., Glaser, R., & Rees, E. (1982). Expertise in problem solving. In R. J. Sternberg (Ed.), *Advances in the psychology of human intelligence* (Vol. 1, pp. 7–75). Hillsdale, NJ: Lawrence Erlbaum Association.

Embretson, S. E. (1983). Construct validity: Construct representation and nomothetic span. *Psychological Bulletin, 93,* 179–197.

Embretson, S. E. (1985a). Multicomponent latent trait models for test design. In S. E. Embretson (Ed.), *Test design: Developments in psychology and psychometrics* (pp. 195–218). New York: Academic Press.

Embretson, S. E. (1985b). Introduction to the problem of test design. In S. E. Embretson (Ed.), *Test design: Developments in psychology and psychometrics* (pp. 3–17). New York: Academic Press.

Embretson, S. E. (1986). *Component latent trait models as an information processing approach to testing.* Paper presented at the annual meeting of the American Educational Research Association, April, San Francisco.

Glaser, R. (1985). *The integration of instruction and testing.* Paper presented at the ETS Conference on the Redesign of Testing for the 21st Century, December, New York.

Goldman, S. R., & Pellegrino, J. W. (1984). Deductions about induction: Analyses of developmental and individual differences. In R. J. Sternberg (Ed.), *Advances in the psychology of human intelligence* (Vol. 2, pp. 149–197). Hillsdale, NJ: Lawrence Erlbaum Associates.

Hunt, E. B. (1983). On the nature of intelligence. *Science, 219,* 141–146.

Hunt, E. B., & Pellegrino, J. W. (1985). Using interactive computing to expand intelligence testing: A critique and prospectus. *Intelligence, 9,* 207–236.

Hunt, E. B., Pellegrino, J. W., Abate, R., Alderton, D., Farr, S., Frick, R., & McDonald, T. (1986). *Computer controlled testing of spatial-visual ability.* NPRDC Final Report, Seattle, WA: University of Washington, March.

McNemar, Q. (1964). Lost: Our intelligence? Why? *American Psychologist, 19,* 871–882.

Messick, S. (1975). The standard problem: Meaning and values in measurement and evaluation. *American Psychologist, 30,* 955–966.

Messick, S. (1980). Test validity and the ethics of assessment. *American Psychologist, 35,* 1012–1027.

Pellegrino, J. W. (1985). Inductive reasoning ability. In R. J. Sternberg (Ed.), *Human abilities: An information processing approach* (pp. 195–225). New York: W. H. Freeman.

Pellegrino, J. W., & Kail, R. (1982). Process analyses of spatial aptitude. In R. J. Sternberg (Ed.), *Advances in the psychology of human intelligence* (Vol. 1, pp. 311–365). Hillsdale, NJ: Lawrence Erlbaum Associates.

Siegler, R. S. (1978). The origins of scientific reasoning. In R. S. Siegler (Ed.), *Children's thinking: What develops?* (pp. 109–149). Hillsdale, NJ: Lawrence Erlbaum Associates.

Siegler, R. S., & Klahr, D. (1982). When do children learn? The relationship between existing knowledge and the acquisition of new knowledge. In R. Glaser (Ed.), *Advances in instructional psychology* (Vol. 2, pp. 121–211). Hillsdale, NJ: Lawrence Erlbaum Associates.

Sternberg, R. J. (1979). *The construct validity of aptitude tests: An information processing assessment.* Paper presented at an ETS Conference on Construct Validation, October, Princeton, NJ.

Sternberg, R. J. (Ed.), (1985a). *Human abilities: An information processing approach.* New York: W. H. Freeman.

Sternberg, R. J. (1985b). Cognitive approaches to intelligence. In B. B. Wolman (Ed.), *Handbook of intelligence* (pp. 59–118). New York: Wiley.

Van Lehn, K. (1983). Bugs are not enough: Empirical studies of bugs, impasses and repairs in procedural skills. *Journal of Mathematical Behavior, 3*(2), 3–71.

Chapter 5

GENECES: A Rationale
for the Construct Validation
of Theories and Tests of Intelligence

Robert J. Sternberg
Yale University

After many years of almost incredible stability in theories and tests of intelligence—at least as stability is measured by the standards of development in science—extraordinary instability has finally hit the field of intelligence. The field needed this instability, because until the early 1970s, its movement was so slow as to lead some to believe that it had become stagnant (see, e.g., Hunt, Frost, & Lunneborg, 1973; Sternberg, 1977). But the field is anything but stagnant now. Instead of having a disturbing paucity of new theories and kinds of tests to evaluate, the field is now being inundated with new theories and tests. Within just the last 3 years, three major new theories of intelligence have been proposed—those of Gardner (1983), Sternberg (1984, 1985a), and Baron (1985). Each of these investigators is developing tests that are based upon his theory, and moreover, within this time period, a major new test has been proposed, the Kaufman Assessment Battery for Children (K–ABC) (Kaufman & Kaufman, 1983) that, although not based on a new theory, nevertheless represents a major departure from traditional intelligence tests.

At this point in time, a major challenge for researchers and test developers is to figure out how these and other new theories and tests are conceptually interrelated. Sternberg (1985b) has made one attempt to do this through the analysis of the conceptual models underlying and generating various theories and tests of intelligence. But another major challenge is to figure out how to go about evaluating these various theories and tests. In particular, if, as Sternberg's (1985b) article claims, the theories and tests deal with somewhat different aspects of intelligence, and deal with them in somewhat different ways, how can we decide just how useful the theories and tests are? For example, are they dealing with important aspects of intelligence or with unimportant aspects of intelligence? Indeed, are they all even dealing with intelligence at all? The purpose of this chapter is to address these questions, and to propose a new framework—GENECES—for the construct validation of theories and tests of intelligence.

The chapter is divided into three main parts. First, I present the GENECES framework. Then I apply it to some existing theories and tests. Finally, I summarize the main points of the chapter, and draw some conclusions.

THE GENECES FRAMEWORK

The framework proposed here is an expansion of that of Sternberg (1985a), and places constraints upon theories of intelligence beyond those of abilities required to adapt to, select, and shape environments. The criteria are very basic ones, and yet make it clear that in an important sense, not all intellectual abilities or theories of such abilities are equal. The criteria are summarized in Table 5.1.

GENECES is an acronym for *GE*nerality and *NECES*sity. The idea is that it is possible to generate a taxonomy of intellectual abilities on the basis of answers to two fundamental questions:

1. Is the ability *general* across the range of tasks that is required of an individual to adapt to, select, or shape environments?
2. Is the ability *necessary* for performance of tasks that involve adaptation to, selection, and shaping of environments?

Note that the two criteria proposed here pertain to *use* of the abilities in task performance, not to *identification* of the abilities, as is the case with Gardner's (1983) criteria. Thus, investigators are free to identify intellectual abilities through whatever analytical method they choose. The GENECES framework does not evaluate such methods, and hence does not imply that some methods are better than others. Rather, alternative methods can be useful for identifying the full range of abilities.

Generality

Traditionally, both psychometric and information-processing theorists of intelligence have been concerned with the issue of generality of mental abilities. The reason for this concern is straightforward: The more general an identified mental ability is, the more central that ability is viewed as being to intelligence because of its pervasion of large numbers of tasks. Executive abilities, such as planning, monitoring, and evaluating problem solving, and certain nonexecutive abilities, such as making inferences and applying inferences to new tasks and situations, appear to be quite general across a wide variety of tasks and situations (see

TABLE 5.1
The GENECES Framework for Intellectual Abilities

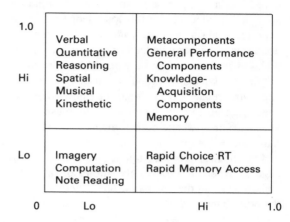

	1.0		

NECESSITY:
Proportion of Tasks to
which Ability is Applied in
which it is Necessary
	Hi	Verbal
		Quantitative
		Reasoning
		Spatial
		Musical
		Kinesthetic
			Metacomponents
			General Performance
			  Components
			Knowledge-
			  Acquisition
			  Components
			Memory

	Lo	Imagery Computation Note Reading	Rapid Choice RT Rapid Memory Access
	0	Lo Hi	1.0

GENERALITY:
Proportion of Tasks Requiring Adaptation,
Selection, or Shaping to which Ability is
Applied

Campione & Brown, 1979; Sternberg, 1985a). There are relatively few problems that can be solved without some degree of planning, monitoring, evaluating, inferencing, and applying of inferences. Clearly, generality is a graded or continuous criterion rather than a stepwise, discrete one: Abilities occupy graded levels of generality.

Researchers have used somewhat different methods for assessing generality of abilities. Psychometricians have relied largely on factor analysis and percentages of variance accounted for by various factors. Factors accounting for more variance in a data set are more general, and tests with higher loadings on a general factor are considered to tap abilities that are more general. Information-processing psychologists have relied largely upon mathematical and computer modeling of task performance: The more tasks in which a given component of information processing appears, the more general the component is considered to be (see, e.g., Sternberg & Gardner, 1982, 1983).

Regardless of methodology, the goal of both kinds of psychologists is the same—to identify abilities of some degree of domain generality. In recent years, psychologists interested in human cognition have been placing increasingly greater emphasis on domain-specific knowledge and abilities (e.g., Chi, Glaser, & Rees, 1982), and in an argument that emphasizes the importance of domain generality, something must be said with respect to the recent emphasis on domain specificity.

First, there is no real inconsistency between the emphasis proposed here on domain-general abilities and the emphasis elsewhere on domain-specific knowledge. Clearly, expertise in any particular field requires a great deal of domain-specific knowledge, and this knowledge will be a large part of what enables an expert to deal successfully with his or her domain of expertise. At the same time, domain-specific knowledge is clearly not a sufficient condition for expertise: We all know people who are very knowledgable about a given field, but are unable to put this knowledge to productive use. They may be unable to analyze the knowledge, interrelate and integrate the knowledge, access the knowledge when it is needed, or go beyond the information to use it in a creative way. Indeed, there is nothing more pathetic than someone who is a walking store of inert and essentially useless information. Studies such as those of Chase and Simon (1973) and of Larkin, McDermott, Simon, and Simon (1980) on the importance of knowledge to expertise are actually studies of the joint (a) possession and (b) use of knowledge. On the one hand, one cannot use knowledge one does not have. On the other hand, static or inert knowledge is of little value to the expert in plying his or her trade. We deceive ourselves if we believe that filling heads with facts or even patterns is the royal road to expertise, or to intelligence.

Intelligence resides in the *learning* and *use* of knowledge, not in the knowledge itself. The expert has become an expert by virtue of his being able to learn and use large bodies of knowledge, not by virtue of the knowledge itself. Indeed, equating knowledge with expertise puts forth a rather trivial conception of expertise. Are our best scientists, writers, artists, or business managers merely people who have crammed their heads with bunches of facts? Is expertise truly best measurable by multiple-choice tests of acquired knowledge? Is intelligence truly best measured in this way? The answer to these questions must be no.

Second, consider the ever more recent emphasis on domain-specific abilities, manifested in Gardner's (1983) theory. Clearly, expertise in any given field of endeavor will require domain-specific abilities as well as domain-specific knowledge. But we need to distinguish carefully between two separate and rather different constructs: domain-specific abilities and domain-specific manifestations of more general abilities. I would contend that theorists, such as Gardner (1983), have given far too much emphasis to the former, and in some cases, have confused the latter with the former.

Consider an executive ability such as the ability to plan a strategy to solve problems. Some people certainly appear to be better planners than others. But are we to believe that the ability to plan (or the more molecular components of information processing it requires in particular tasks or situations) is really N abilities, with each ability independent of the other and specific to a given domain? Is there a separate verbal-planning ability, quantitative-planning ability, spatial-planning ability, and so on? Might it not be more plausible, and much more parsimonious, to suggest that the ability is rather general, but that its manifestation is constrained by domain-specific knowledge? One cannot plan in a domain about which one knows little or nothing. A good planner in designing psychology experiments could not be a good planner in designing physics experiments if he or she did not have substantial knowledge about physics, and the ability to bring this knowledge to bear upon the design of physics experiments. Moreover, even with this planning ability, the psychologist might not succeed in the alternative field of endeavor without the high-level quantitative and abstract reasoning abilities necessary to succeed in physics. These abilities would be necessary for good planning, but they would not be the planning abilities themselves. These abilities are separate although interactive with planning ability. The interaction of various abilities in various fields of endeavor, and the interaction of these abilities with domain-specific knowledge, might well give the epiphenomenal appearance of many domain-specific abilities.

Again, it is important to distinguish between domain-specific abilities and specific instantiations of more general abilities and domain-specific knowledge. Consider, for example, the finding of Ceci and Liker (1986) regarding expertise in predicting outcomes of horse races. In particular, these investigators found that expert handicappers using complex models of handicapping often have unimpressive IQs: Are planning and implementing strategies for predicting outcomes of horse races specific to that domain, and if so, just how many domains are there? Indeed, then what is a domain, and how many thousands or even tens of thousands of them might there be? What is left for the scientific theory of intelligence, or even its possibility?

Rather than positing a separate planning ability for each of Gardner's seven domains, or for the thousands of domains that might arise out of analyses of the specificity of Ceci and Liker's, one might conceive of the problem in a more parsimonious way. A variety of constraints operate upon the effectiveness of intelligence in a given domain—domain-specific knowledge, interest in a given domain, values regarding how problems in that domain should be handled, motivation to excel in a given domain, interactions of these various constraints, and, of course, domain-specific abilities. But what appear to be domain-specific abilities may actually be artifacts of complex interactions of constructs other than abilities. Intelligence-test scores are every bit as susceptible to these constraints as are performances of other kinds. People who are poorly educated, who are not socialized into a test-taking frame of mind, who do not care about doing well on the tests, or who do not work well under time pressure, among other things, are not going to do well on standard intelligence tests. These are just some of the reasons for a broader conception of how to test intelligence (Sternberg, 1985a). Moreover, there is a difference between the ability to perform well in abstract, formal kinds of situations, and the ability to apply what abilities one has to real-world contexts (Sternberg, 1985a). Thus, tasks such as Ceci and Liker's may argue not for myriad domain-specific abilities, but for a broader conception of how abilities that may be fairly general are constrained in their operations in domain-specific contexts.

Necessity

We tend to confound necessity and generality of abilities in our thinking, but they are not the same. An ability may be general, but nevertheless optional in its utilization in some of the tasks to which it may be applied. Moreover, the ability may be general, but not necessary for adaptation, selection, and shaping, in general. Necessity and generality are logically, although probably not psychologically, independent. For example, Hunt (1978) has shown that speed of access to lexical information is general to a wide range of tasks. If one views the ability as that of whether or not the required information is actually accessed (an accuracy criterion), then the ability is certainly necessary to the range of tasks that Hunt analyzes. But the error rate in the Posner–Mitchell (1967) task, and in the other tasks Hunt uses, is extremely low. If one views the ability as *speed* of lexical access, then the ability must be seen in another light: Rapid lexical access is not necessary to performance of any of the tasks that Hunt uses. Even the slowest of performers can reach high levels of accuracy. Similarly, choice decision making is necessary in a wide variety of intellectual tasks, but very rapid choice reaction time is not.

The present contention is that necessity forms a second criterion for identifying important intellectual abilities and tasks that measure these abilities. The question one asks is whether a given ability is necessary for adaptation to, selection of, and shaping of environments. If an ability is necessary for the performance of large numbers of tasks, it is more important to intelligent performance than it is if it can be bypassed.

Necessity of an ability for task performance can be assessed by componential analysis of individual subject data. Componential analysis (Sternberg, 1977, 1985a) enables one to determine the components and strategies a person uses in task performance. By modeling each individual's data separately, it becomes possible to determine the extent to which people do or do not differ in their components and strategies of task performance. Differences, of course, suggest optionality of the components or strategies. In linear syllogisms tasks, for example, Sternberg and Weil (1980) found that there is an option in the selection of a linguistic versus a spatial strategy, and that there is a further option of selecting a strategy that combines both linguistic and spatial elements. MacLeod, Hunt, and Mathews (1978) have found the same in their analyses of the sentence–picture comparison task. Other tasks, such as analogies, can also be solved in multiple ways, but certain components of processing, such as the inferential one, seem necessary for correct solution of most analogy items (Mulholland, Pellegrino, & Glaser, 1980; Sternberg, 1977).

Consider, however, spatial ability. Although the use of this ability is certainly not general across the whole range of tasks one might use to measure intelligence, it can be involved in a fairly large number and variety of tasks, such as mental rotation (Shepard & Metzler, 1971), sentence–picture comparison (MacLeod, Hunt, & Mathews, 1978), and cube comparison (Just & Carpenter, 1985).

66

Yet, every one of these tasks can be performed verbally, and, in fact, is performed verbally by at least some of the individuals confronting the task. In contrast, relatively few verbal tasks can be performed spatially. For example, vocabulary and reading generally do not lend themselves to spatial strategies. And indeed, whereas spatial tasks often tend to show mixed loadings on spatial and verbal factors, verbal tasks generally do not, except in cases where the verbal material is used merely as a vehicle for manipulation of abstract mental arrays of symbols. In these cases, the verbal meaning of the words is peripheral or incidental to task performance. For example, in linear syllogisms such as "John is taller than Mary, Mary is taller than Susan. Who is tallest?" the formal task requirements are not changed either by using different names (e.g., Harry, Cindy, Jane) or a different adjective (e.g., faster). Tasks such as linear syllogisms are not even intended to measure the verbal factor, whereas the spatial visualization tests are certainly intended to measure a spatial visualization factor.

I am not arguing that abilities that are unnecessary in most or even all of the tasks in which they are used are thereby not measures of intelligence. I would argue, however, that the greater the optionality of an ability in intelligent thinking, the less central that ability ought to be in our conceptualization of intelligence.

Combining the Criteria

Carrying the GENECES framework to its logical conclusion, the abilities that should be most central to our conceptualization and measurement of intelligence ought to be those that are general to a broad range of tasks and that are necessary to the performance of at least a substantial proportion of the tasks to which they are general. If an ability is both quite general and necessary in a broad range of tasks that somehow assess adaptation to, shaping of, and selection of environments, the ability is one to be reckoned with.

APPLICATION OF THE GENECES FRAMEWORK TO CURRENT THEORIES AND TESTS

How do current theories and tests fare when the GENECES framework is applied to them? Consider some of the main ones.

Gardner's Theory of Multiple Intelligences

Gardner (1983) has proposed a theory, mentioned earlier, of multiple intelligences, according to which intelligence should be understood in terms of roughly seven distinct and independent multiple abilities: linguistic, logical/mathematical, spatial, bodily/kinesthetic, musical, interpersonal, and intrapersonal. The question here is not whether this (or any other) theory is valid as a theory, but the extent to which it meets the GENECES criteria for a theory of intelligence. In this respect, the theory is something of a mixed bag.

The linguistic, logical/mathematical, interpersonal, and intrapersonal intelligences would seem to fare well by the GENECES criteria. Although none of them is wholly general, they certainly are widely involved in intellectual functioning. Moreover, it would be difficult to function in the complete or near-complete absence of any of these abilities. Spatial ability is probably a bit more dispensable in our culture, although there are cultures in which it would probably be indispensable, for example, the culture of the Puluwat (Gladwin, 1970), in which navigation with minimal cues requires some form of highly developed large-scale spatial mapping ability.

Musical ability seems to be much more questionable as an intelligence. For the large majority of people—in our culture and others—musical ability is required for few, if any, of the tasks we perform that require adaptation to, selection of, and shaping of environments. Clearly, this would not be the case for musicians, but specialized skills are required in every occupation, and one would scarcely want to catalog every specialized skill required in every occupation and call it an intelligence. Moreover, musical ability is clearly not necessary: A person could be tone deaf, utterly unable to read music, or insensitive to music, and yet adapt to real world environments extremely successfully. Indeed, few people would even be aware that the person was lacking in musical talent. Certainly, no one would wish to label the individual as mentally retarded. If one were to compare this state of affairs with the absence or near-absence of verbal ability, one would encounter an utterly different situation. People would recognize a nonverbal individual at once, and that individual would have extreme difficulty coping in any but the least demanding of environments, such as in an institution for the retarded. People would have little hesitation in labeling the nonverbal adult as mentally retarded. Moreover, this generalization is not limited to the North American culture. Throughout the world, verbal ability is simply much more general in its usage, and necessary in its implementation, than is musical ability.

Similarly, bodily/kinesthetic ability would seem to fare poorly in meeting the GENECES criteria. Helen Keller was multiply handicapped, but would anyone have wished to refer to her as mentally retarded? In contrast, there are many athletes (some of them at my own institution) who are excellent ball players, but one would scarcely want to label them as excellent in their level of intelligence. At the same time, some of the biggest klutzes might well be labeled as being at the genius level in intelligence. This is not to say that intelligence is not required in athletics, or in music, for that matter. To the contrary, a good athlete will require some of the abilities that fare better by the GENECES criteria—linguistic and spatial ability, perhaps—in order to excel at his or her game. But the brute strength of the batter ought to be distinguished from ability to plan where to hit the ball so as to maximize the chances of, say, getting a home run. Intelligence is involved in bodily/kinesthetic activities, but it does not inhere in the bodily/kinesthetic activity itself, but rather in the cognitive activity that backs up this bodily/kinesthetic activity.

Sternberg's Triarchic Theory of Intelligence

Sternberg (1985a) has proposed a triarchic theory of intelligence, also mentioned earlier, according to which intelligence should be understood in terms of the relation of intelligence to the internal world of the individual, to the external world of the individual, and to experience. There are three subtheories in the theory as a whole, with each subtheory dealing with one of these interrelations. The first, componential subtheory, specifies three kinds of processes: metacomponents, or executive planning, monitoring, and evaluation processes; performance components, or nonexecutive implementation processes; and knowledge-acquisition components, or nonexecutive learning processes. These three kinds of mental processes are applied, in a contextual subtheory, to the external world through the functions of adaptation to, selection of, and shaping of real world environments. And the processes are particularly relevant to intelligence at two levels of experience: coping with relative novelty, and automatizing information processing.

The triarchic theory fares rather well by the GENECES criteria. Consider each part of the theory in turn: the componential, then contextual, then experiential subtheory.

According to Sternberg (1985a), the general factor in intelligence is largely traceable to individual differences in metacomponential abilities—in the abilities to plan, monitor, and evaluate one's problem solving. He makes this claim, in part, on the basis of the generality and necessity of the metacomponents in intellectual functioning. Regardless of the problem, problem solving requires one to define the problem to be solved, to select a strategy for solving it, to allocate attentional resources, and so on. Of course, the exact nature of the problem may vary from one problem to the next. But the fundamental metacomponential processes probably do not vary, and moreover, they are for the most part not optional. One cannot solve a problem until it is defined, until some kind of strategy is in place, and so on.

Sternberg and Gardner (1982) further argued for the centrality of certain performance components to psychometric g (which may not be quite the same thing as any g that exists when this construct is viewed in terms of a broader range of tasks of everyday life). These components include encoding, inferring of relations, mapping of relations between relations, applying relations, and response. At least, these components are common to inductive reasoning tasks, which are themselves quite common in everyday life. As Sternberg (1979, 1985a) has pointed out, performance components differ widely in their generality. Some are general, but others apply only to classes of tasks, and still others only to specific tasks. From the standpoint of the theory of intelligence, the most interesting ones are the general and class ones.

In the triarchic theory, the knowledge-acquisition components include selective encoding—deciding what information is relevant for a given purpose; selective combination—putting that information together; and selective comparison—relating new to old information. These components, too, would seem to be quite general and even necessary for most tasks. People are almost constantly barraged by stimulus inputs, and must somehow decide which ones they should attend to, how the inputs can be integrated, and how the inputs relate to what they know. To the extent that learning is going on almost constantly, even if, sometimes, at a low level, knowledge-acquisition components fare well by the GENECES criteria.

The GENECES criteria specify that generality and necessity extend over those tasks that require adaptation to, selection of, and shaping of environments, and hence it is not surprising that the contextual functions of adaptation, selection, and shaping fit the criteria—by definition.

Finally, coping with novelty and automatizing information processing would also seem to be quite general in intellectual functioning, and also necessary. We are almost constantly confronting novelty in some degree, and were we totally unable to cope with it, we would have to be institutionalized so as to guarantee a wholly predictable setting. Similarly, automatization is ongoing. Someone who was truly unable to automatize would be unable to read, write, speak, walk, and do any of the things that makes for survival in everyday life.

If the triarchic theory does well by the GENECES criteria, it is perhaps because it was constructed, in part, on the basis of a knitting of past and present theories of intelligence such that it would include within its purview those aspects of past and present theories that were common to the demands of everyday life. Skills like planning in problem solving, learning, and coping with novelty via the components of intelligence seem to be of a different order, say, than a domain such as musical ability. In the first place, of course, they are process-rather than domain-based. But of equal importance is their indispensability to everyday intelligent functioning, something that simply cannot be said of musical and certain others of Gardner's intelligences.

Baron's Theory of Rationality and Intelligence

Baron (1985), like others, essentially used the generality criterion to define intelligence. He views intelligence in terms of the repertoire of cognitive skills that makes for effectiveness, regardless of the environment a person is in. He believes that rational thinking is an important and central element of this effectiveness, and hence of intelligence.

I am less enamored than is Baron of the role of rational thinking in intelligence, because although I believe his definition of intelligence is on the right track (although it deals only with generality and not with necessity), I also believe that he substantially overemphasizes the role of rational thinking in intelligence. The problem is that in most life problems and decisions, it is not clear what constitutes a rational solution or choice, except, perhaps, after the fact. It would be nice if we could go through life following prescriptive models, but how often is there a prescription etched in stone, merely waiting to be used? Most of the time, it is difficult even to trust the experts in a given area (whether they be doctors, lawyers, teachers,). Moreover, much of intelligent functioning would seem to be largely intuitive, and not very susceptible to rational processing. Intuitive thinking would seem not so much to be irrational as arational: Rationality just doesn't apply. Moreover, it is possible to be rational but quite unintelligent if the premises from which one is preceding are erroneous. Some of the worst decision making in our own government, for example, has been made by rational men and women using false presuppositions.

My argument, then, is that although Baron's definition of intelligence in the abstract is on the right track, he is probably not on the right track in assigning as important a role as he does to rational thinking in intelligence, and in excluding other kinds of thinking in which rationality does not apply in any clear way. Although Baron tries, by distinguishing among normative, prescriptive, and descriptive models, to circumvent the problem of talking about an ideal rather than actual world, the theory nevertheless at times seems to apply to a world in which there is much less uncertainty and more stability than the world in which we live.

Hunt's and Jensen's Speed of Processing Theories

Hunt (1978, 1980) and Jensen (1982) have emphasized the role of speed of information processing in intelligence. In the case of Hunt, the emphasis is on speed of lexical retrieval. In the case of Jensen, the emphasis is on choice reaction time. In both cases, however, speed of mental functioning as measured by reaction time is the critical dependent variable. A basic idea underlying these notions is that we are constantly barraged by information, and the more information we can pick up and digest per given unit of time, the smarter we are likely to be, and become.

Clearly, accurate intake of information is reasonably important for learning and information processing, in general, as noted by Eysenck (1982). Were we to distort informational inputs too regularly, we would be left with a substantial amount of misinformation, much of which would eventually lead us astray. It is not clear, however, that sheer speed of information processing is quite as generally required. As noted by Sternberg (1985a), whereas there are some tasks where fast performance is a prerequisite, there are also some tasks in which slow performance is preferable or even prerequisite. Obviously, an extremely slow information processor would be at a severe disadvantage in most aspects of life. In the normal range of speeds, the disadvantages may be quite a bit more modest.

The research of Jensen (1982), Hunt (1978), and many others indicates that

there is a modest to moderate correlation between speed of information processing and psychometrically measured intelligence, although for some components
of intelligence, slower rather than faster processing is actually associated with
superior psychometric scores (Sternberg, 1985a). But the correlations favoring a
positive relation between speed and psychometric test scores have been obtained
within the range of tasks that tend to favor fast processing. On some tasks, such
as insight tasks, where more pondering may be necessary, the correlation can go
the opposite way (Sternberg & Davidson, 1982). Thus, whereas fast processing
may be necessary in comprehending a rapidly paced lecture, slower processing
may be necessary in solving a difficult insight problem.

   If the neural oscillation model of Jensen (1982), according to which intelligence depends on speed of neural conduction, is correct, then presumably rapid
processing speed is both quite general and at least desirable, although not necessary, for task performance. To date, however, there seems to be no direct
evidence to support the model, plausible though it might seem to some. Jensen
and others have relied on indirect evidence from reaction-time experiments in
which the link between the neural oscillation model and the empirical data is
rather distant.

The Kaufman Assessment Battery for Children

Kaufman and Kaufman's Assessment Battery for Children (K–ABC, 1983) has
two primary scales of intelligence: a simultaneous processing scale and a sequential processing scale. The test, based upon the Luria–Das model of intelligence,
seeks to relate intelligence to neural functioning, as does Jensen's model, except
that here, the focus is upon kinds of processing rather than sheer speed of
processing. Simultaneous processing is parallel and tends to apply to complex
spatial organization tasks; sequential processing is serial and tends to apply to
rote learning and memory tasks.

   From the standpoint of the GENECES criterion, it is not clear that the K–
ABC represents a step forward rather than backward for the measurement of
intelligence. The rote memorization abilities that are an important component of
functioning on the sequential-processing scales would not seem to be very generally used by children or adults—at least in today's world—although they are
helpful, say, in studying for final exams. Certainly, there would seem to be
something of a misplacement of emphasis when one of two scales essentially taps
rote memorization. The scales used to measure simultaneous processing put a
heavy load on spatial and perceptual abilities, which fare better by the GEN-
ECES criteria. Oddly enough, verbal abilities are scarcely measured at all by the
intelligence scales. Rather, they are placed in an achievement scale. As a result,
highly verbal children with lesser memory and spatial abilities will come out
looking like "overachievers," with relatively lower intelligence than achievement scores. Yet, verbal abilities are probably more universally required, and

necessary for adaptation, than are rote memory and spatial abilities, at least in many, although certainly not all, environmental settings. The balance of skills measurement between the two intelligence scales, and the balance between the intelligence and achievement scales, does not seem to be right, either according to other theories or according to the GENECES criteria.

The Scholastic Aptitude Test and Graduate Record Examination

Although the Scholastic Aptitude Test (SAT) and Graduate Record Examination (GRE) are not billed as intelligence tests, and although they are not scored via an IQ, SAT and GRE scores are highly correlated with IQ, and the content of the SAT and GRE is similar to that of a conventional intelligence test. Hence, I consider the tests here. The SAT has two sections, a verbal and a quantitative one. The GRE has three sections: verbal, quantitative, and analytic.

To the extent that the universe of environmental performance is the school, the SAT and GRE seem to fare quite well, both in terms of correlations with school grades and in terms of the GENECES criteria. The verbal and quantitative skills measured by the SAT are required throughout most of the school curriculum, and are necessary for good grades in this curriculum. The addition of an analytical section to the GRE is a nice touch because of the importance of such abilities in schooling and particularly in higher education.

Tests such as the SAT and GRE, and conventional intelligence tests as well, face a fundamental problem when prediction moves beyond the realm of schooling. The tests seem to lack items that measure social or practical abilities (see Gardner, 1983; Sternberg, 1985a). In the case of the SAT and GRE, the names of the tests specifically restrict their domains. But this is not the case for "intelligence" tests. But even the SAT and GRE fall down in the measurement of another set of essential abilities, namely, synthetic thinking abilities, which are necessary in the performance of certain life tasks, and even scholarly tasks of the higher orders. It is one thing to be able to criticize and analyze ideas, and conventional tests seem to measure these abilities well. But it is another to come up with good ideas of one's own, and the tests do not seem well to measure these synthetic abilities. Some might prefer to separate these synthetic abilities from intellectual ones, and call them "creativity" instead. But it is hard to believe that we would want to label someone as "intelligent" who never had a good idea of his or her own. Good ideas are a necessary part of so many life pursuits, even some fairly mundane ones (see Scribner, 1984), that the ability to produce them would seem to be an important part of intelligence. Some of the newer theories, such as those of Gardner (1983) and Sternberg (1985a), reflect this emphasis, although Baron's (1985) theory seems, if anything, to move in the opposite direction, emphasizing rational and hence analytical thinking.

CONCLUSIONS

How, then, do current theories and tests stock up if one applies the GENECES criteria to them? Theories that emphasize executive control processes in intelligence do quite well (e.g., Campione & Brown, 1979; Sternberg, 1985a), especially because these theories also emphasize general performance and knowledge-acquisition components. Standard information-processing and psychometric theories (e.g., Hunt, 1978; Jensen, 1982; Thurstone, 1938) do not fare quite as well, because they generally do not meet the necessity criterion. Gardner's (1983) recent theory of multiple intelligences turns in a mixed performance, with some abilities faring well on the GENECES criteria and others, not. Baron's (1985) recent theory of rationality and intelligence does not do well on either of the GENECES criteria: The kind of rational, deductive thinking of which he writes is not very general across a broad range of intellectual tasks, nor is it necessary to performance of those tasks in which it could be used. Baron's model is probably more of a competence model than a performance model, in any case.

Most existing intelligence tests measure something of a potpourri of skills, including but not limited to those skills that are both general and necessary in those tasks to which they generalize. Virtually all of these tests require some amount of executive processing, but I believe this load could be increased, and that if it were, it would make for better tests of intelligence (see also Sternberg, 1985a). My own forthcoming test of intelligence, which will be based upon the triarchic theory, explicitly seeks to increase metacomponential load.

To conclude, I have proposed in this chapter a framework—GENECES—for evaluating the centrality of mental abilities to human intelligence. This centrality is a function of the extent to which a given ability meets either or both of two criteria—generality and necessity. Although they may not be ultimate criteria, taken together, these two criteria provide a useful basis for evaluating tasks and theories.

REFERENCES

Baron, J. (1985). *Rationality and intelligence*. New York: Cambridge University Press.
Campione, J. C., & Brown, A. L. (1979). Toward a theory of intelligence: Contributions from research with retarded children. In R. J. Sternberg & D. K. Detterman (Eds.), *Human intelligence: Perspectives on its theory and measurement* (pp. 139–164). Norwood, NJ: Ablex.
Ceci, S. J., & Liker, J. (1986). Academic and nonacademic intelligence: an experimental separation. In R. J. Sternberg & R. K. Wagner (Eds.), *Practical intelligence: Nature and origins of competence in the everyday world* (pp. 119–142). New York: Cambridge University Press.
Chase, W. G., & Simon, H. A. (1973). The mind's eye in chess. In W. G. Chase (Ed.), *Visual information processing*. New York: Academic Press.
Chi, M. T. H., Glaser, R., & Rees, E. (1982). Expertise in problem solving. In R. J. Sternberg

(Ed.), *Advances in the psychology of human intelligence* (Vol. 1, pp. 7–75). Hillsdale, NJ: Lawrence Erlbaum Associates.

Eysenck, H. J. (Ed.) (1982). *A model for intelligence.* Berlin: Springer–Verlag.

Gardner, H. (1983). *Frames of mind: The theory of multiple intelligences.* New York: Basic Books.

Gladwin, T. (1970). *East is a big bird.* Cambridge, MA: Harvard University Press.

Hunt, E. B. (1978). Mechanics of verbal ability. *Psychological Review, 85,* 109–130.

Hunt, E. B. (1980). Intelligence as an information-processing concept. *British Journal of Psychology, 71,* 449–474.

Hunt, E. B., Frost, N., & Lunneborg, C. (1973). Individual differences in cognition: A new approach to intelligence. In G. Bower (Ed.), *The psychology of learning and motivation* (Vol. 7, pp. 87–122). New York: Academic Press.

Jensen, A. R. (1982). The chronometry of intelligence. In R. J. Sternberg (Ed.), *Advances in the psychology of human intelligence* (Vol. 1, pp. 255–310). Hillsdale, NJ: Lawrence Erlbaum Associates.

Just, M., & Carpenter, P. (1985). Cognitive coordinate systems: Accounts of mental rotation and individual differences in spatial ability. *Psychological Review, 92,* 137–172.

Kaufman, A. S., & Kaufman, N. L. (1983). *Kaufman Assessment Battery for Children* (K–ABC). Circle Pines, MN: American Guidance Service.

Larkin, J. H., McDermott, J., Simon, D. P., & Simon, H. A. (1980). Expert and novice performance in solving physics problems. *Science, 208,* 1335–1342.

MacLeod, C. M., Hunt, E. B., & Mathews, N. N. (1978). Individual differences in the verification of sentence–picture relationships. *Journal of Verbal Learning and Verbal Behavior, 17,* 493–507.

Mulholland, T. M., Pellegrino, J. W., & Glaser, R. (1980). Components of geometric analogy solution. *Cognitive Psychology, 12,* 252–284.

Posner, M. I., & Mitchell, R. F. (1967). Chronometric analysis of classification. *Psychological Review, 74,* 392–409.

Scribner, S. (1984). Studying working intelligence. In B. Rogoff & J. Lave (Eds.), *Everyday cognition* (pp. 9–40). Cambridge, MA: Harvard University Press.

Shepard, R. N., & Metzler, J. (1971). Mental rotation of three-dimensional objects. *Science, 171,* 701–703.

Sternberg, R. J. (1977). *Intelligence, information processing, and analogical reasoning: The componential analysis of human abilities.* Hillsdale, NJ: Lawrence Erlbaum Associates.

Sternberg, R. J. (1979). The nature of mental abilities. *American Psychologist, 34,* 214–230.

Sternberg, R. J. (1984). Toward a triarchic theory of human intelligence. *Behavioral & Brain Sciences, 7,* 269–287.

Sternberg, R. J. (1985a). *Beyond IQ: A triarchic theory of human intelligence.* New York: Cambridge University Press.

Sternberg, R. J. (1985b). Human intelligence: The model is the message. *Science, 230,* 1111–1118.

Sternberg, R. J., & Davidson, J. E. (1982). The mind of the puzzler. *Psychology Today, 16,* June, 37–44.

Sternberg, R. J., & Gardner, M. K. (1982). A componential interpretation of the general factor in human intelligence. In H. J. Eysenck (Ed.), *A model for intelligence* (pp. 231–254). Berlin: Springer–Verlag.

Sternberg, R. J., & Gardner, M. K. (1983). Unities in inductive reasoning. *Journal of Experimental Psychology: General, 112,* 80–116.

Sternberg, R. J., & Weil, E. M. (1980). An aptitude-strategy interaction in linear syllogistic reasoning. *Journal of Educational Psychology, 72,* 226–234.

Thurstone, L. L. (1938). *Primary mental abilities.* Chicago: University of Chicago Press.

Chapter 6

Construct Validity of Computer-Based Tests

Bert F. Green
Johns Hopkins University

Testing by computer offers several advantages: better experimental control, greater efficiency through adaptive, or tailored testing, and a wider range of psychological attributes to measure. But a computer test is still a test—that is, a succession of separate items eliciting simple responses from which a score is fashioned. As such, examining validity is, in most respects, no different for computer and conventional tests. One profoundly different issue *has* arisen from computer-based personality and ability assessments, which often go beyond scores, to produce narrative assessments of the individual. Determining the validity of a verbal description is a serious problem that has received a lot of attention, most of which is not very satisfactory. However, this chapter will not consider narratives, it will stay in the more familiar realm of test scores.

I wish to address first the problems that arise when an existing conventional test is transferred to the computer, and second, the problems of validating new behavioral measures.

CONVENTIONAL AND COMPUTER TESTS

When a conventional test is transferred to the computer, it brings its validity with it. At least, we hope it does. To the extent that the computer merely provides better control, and more efficient use of testing time through adaptive item selection, the computer is affecting measurement error, not measurement validity. If computer presentation changes the score scale, by making the test more or less difficult, or altering the test score distribution, and if the effect goes undetected or is ignored, validity is jeopardized. But the effect is essentially a constant that can easily be removed by score calibration, hence permitting the valid interpretation of test scores. However, if computer presentation changes the task, so that the correlation between scores on the computer and conventional versions is low, then validity is threatened. A different construct is being measured.

A brief review of the known differences between computer and conventional presentation modes will help in evaluating the potential threat.

Passive Omitting

When an item appears on a computer screen, to be answered, the examinee must make a response. He or she cannot simply look at the next item, without leaving a record of his or her action. Even if the test permits "SKIP" or "NEXT ITEM" as a response option, that button must be pressed, and even that can alter the test. So far, serious problems have only been observed on questionnaires and personality inventories. The Minnesota Multiphasic Personality Inventory (MMPI) lists only two response alternatives: YES and NO to items such as "I like to sleep until noon." On the conventional test, the respondent is told that a few items may be left blank. In fact, if very many are left blank, the test is invalidated. Some computer versions offer two responses: YES and NO; others offer three: YES, NO, and CAN'T SAY. White, Clements, and Fowler (1985) reported that when offered CAN'T SAY, people use it too much. Apparently a forced choice between YES and NO is better, but it is slightly different, because the conventional MMPI permits a few omissions.

Allred (1986) found a similar effect on Gough's adjective check list. The respondent is offered a list of 300 adjectives, and is asked to check those that are self-descriptive. On the conventional form, the person may skip the adjective by *not* placing a check by it, but on the computer, a key must be pressed for each adjective. When the keys are labeled YES and NO, people select many more adjectives as self-descriptive than on the paper-and-pencil version. When the keys are labeled CHECK and NEXT ITEM, there is less selecting than with YES and NO, but there are still more selections than with the conventional form. Further, the extra adjectives tend to be more positively toned. Apparently, people will passively omit adjectives that are not especially salient in a description of themselves, but are not willing to specify, "No, the adjective does not apply to me." The effect is mainly a scale change, but is to some extent a construct change.

Passive omitting is impossible with keyboard responding. The use of a light pen, touch screen, or mouse as a response device would permit passive omitting on check lists, with several items per screen, but it might also create differences due to computer familiarity that are minimal when only a few keys are to be pressed.

Backtracking

The computer cannot conveniently permit students to review questions, or to change their answers, or to postpone trying to answer a question. A backtracking system could be devised, but it might be awkward and time consuming, and could create an advantage for students with computer experience. Furthermore, backtracking, either returning to an omitted item or changing an answer to an earlier item probably promotes dependence of item error components. One item may reveal the answer to another, or may remind the examinee of the method for solving an earlier problem. Consequently, it would be better psychometrically to prohibit review. Empirical research (Lee, Moreno, & Sympson, 1984; Sacher & Fletcher, 1978) has found that backtracking raises scores on a math test, slightly, but does not affect scores on a test of word knowledge. The effect is small.

Screen Capacity

A computer screen can hold only so much information. Most items are short enough to fit onto a screen with no trouble. Paragraph comprehension items are long. If the paragraph fits, only one question is likely to fit, not a whole series. The tendency is to use shorter paragraphs for the computer, with only one question per paragraph. Hence, there is a chance that the task will change somewhat. We will present some indications of that possibility.

Graphics

Computer graphics are limited, especially on the inexpensive instruments likely to be used for computer-based testing. Ordinary charts and graphs are within reach, but some line drawings that accompany tests of mechanical knowledge or spatial perception are difficult to translate to the computer screen. No systematic study has yet been made of the effect of computer graphics. Such a study might be futile; while the paper was away being reviewed by the journal, a new generation of display hardware could be announced.

Responding

Pressing a key is easier, faster, and probably surer than marking a bubble on an answer sheet. This is only a threat to the validity of highly speeded tests. Speeded tests, such as crossing out 0s, or counting 9s, or doing simple numerical sums, are best scored differently on the computer. The conventional score is the number correct in a fixed time period, which can be interpreted as a rate of speed—the number of correct responses per time period, because the denominator, time, is fixed. Greaud and Green (1986) showed that, on a computer, it is better to compute speed by keeping the number of items fixed, and using the computer to measure both number correct and time to finish. The inverse of speed is reaction time, which is the favorite measure of cognitive psychologists. For assessing individual differences, speed is the better measure (Greaud & Green, 1986; Wainer, 1977).

Greaud and Green also examined construct differences, using a modification of the multitrait, multimethod matrix. Four versions of a test of numerical operations were given; two by computer, two conventionally. The within-mode correlations provided reliability coefficients that were used to correct the cross-mode correlations for attenuation. This is probably the canonical use for such a correction, because we want to know exactly what it purports to give, the correlation between the "true" parts of the scores. If the disattenuated correlations are nearly one, the construct has not changed. Table 6.1a shows that in fact the construct has not changed much for the test, numerical operations, although Form 3 does not seem to be quite parallel with the other three forms. But Table 6.1b shows that the construct tested by Coding Speed was changed considerably. That, however was easily traced to a change in item format, as shown in Fig. 6.1. Putting only one item on the screen at once was expedient for the programmer, but disastrous for the test. This appears to be a good method for investigating the issue of construct change.

TABLE 6.1a
Correlations within and across Modes of
Presentation of Short Forms of a Test of Numerical
Operations. Correlations are corrected for
attenuation (from Greaud & Green, 1986)

Forms		1	2	3	4
Conventional	1	——	1.00	.81	.97
	2	1.00	——	.81	.98
Computer	3	.81	.81	——	1.00
	4	.97	.98	1.00	——

TABLE 6.1b
Correlations within and across Modes of
Presentation of Short Forms of a Test of
Coding Speed. Correlations are corrected
for attentuation

Forms		1	2	3	4
Conventional	1	——	1.00	.38	.54
	2	1.00	——	.74	.84
Computer	3	.38	.74	——	1.00
	4	.54	.84	1.00	——

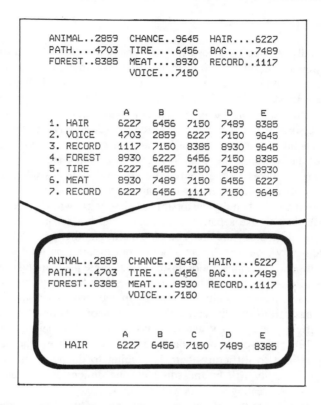

FIG. 6.1. Formats for the coding speed test of the ASVAB. (a) Conventional version; (b) Greaud and Green's computer version.

Time Limits

Because the computer administers each test individually, customary time limits can be abandoned. They are used only as a matter of convenience in conventional group administration. The bulk of the evidence on timed versus untimed cognitive tests indicates some change in mean, but very high correlation between timed and untimed administration. Unfortunately, most studies use an equivalent groups design, which can only address the question of scale change, not construct change.

Some early studies found that speed scores on cognitive tests tended to form a separate speed factor that was essentially uncorrelated with the "power" factors (French, 1951). Lately, some workers, including Jensen (1980), have argued that if the right speed is measured, it can be very informative about cognitive capacity. But a speed score on a cognitive item qualifies as new information, which is discussed later.

Dimensionality

A test is usually viewed as measuring one construct. But some tests may be multidimensional, measuring two or more different things. The single resulting score is then a combination of the different dimensions. This is likely to be the case in some achievement tests. For example, the advanced test in psychology on the Graduate Record Exam (GRE) measures at least three things: experimental, social (and personality), and statistics. Subscores are actually reported in experimental and social; there aren't enough statistics questions to yield a reliable subscore, but the overall score is an amalgam of all three areas.

When everyone takes all the items, multidimensionality is not very bothersome. The problem is more serious in adaptive testing, where each examinee takes a different test. When dimensionality is clearly known, the best procedure would probably be to use separate item pools, and get separate scores, adaptively, for each dimension, and then combine them. Another possibility would be to select alternately from the different pools, but to tailor on total score.

When multiple dimensions are only suspected, some prior analysis is needed. This is generally some form of factor analysis. Unfortunately, no matter how careful one is, so-called difficulty factors turn up regularly. These are factors that separate the easy from the difficult items. Some people believe there really is something different about easy and difficult items. Others suspect an artifact (McDonald, 1981; McDonald & Ahlawat, 1974). In any case, when the factors are strongly related to difficulty there is nothing to do but grin and bear it. Students of low ability will be measured on one dimension, students of high ability on the other; creating subtests won't help because the low-ability students won't be able to answer the difficult questions and the high-ability students will correctly answer all the easy questions. The same result will occur on an adaptive test.

Adaptive Testing

So far, no one has demonstrated an effect due solely to the adaptive nature of a test. But a computerized adaptive test (CAT) is subject to all the effects mentioned. First, passive omitting is not possible. Furthermore, in an adaptive framework, backtracking is not possible. The student may not postpone an item. The logic of CAT seems to require treating an omitted item like an error. Likewise, it is probably illegitimate to permit changing any answer. In CAT the sequence of items cannot be undone and should not be retraced.

CAT requires a computer, which means that problems of screen size, graphics, and response devices are inevitable. CAT does not need to insist on time limits, although it may be necessary to have some very generous limits, for administrative reasons. The dimensionality issue is especially critical for CAT because CATs tend to be short, and it is very difficult to ensure that all facets are covered in a short test.

EXAMINING CONSTRUCT VALIDITY

How robust is CAT likely to be to these potential threats to validity? The Navy Personnel Research and Development Center conducted a large-scale study of a computerized adaptive version of the Armed Services Vocational Aptitude Battery (ASVAB). The experimental CAT-ASVAB was given to a large number of service recruits, as part of a larger study of the predictive validity of CAT (Moreno, Wetzel, McBride, & Weiss, 1984; Vicino & Hardwicke, 1984). That study was reported at the American Educational Research Association meetings in 1984. One part of that study was a factor analysis of the scores obtained from both conventional and CAT versions of the battery. As part of a different study, NPRDC furnished the data to me. Rather than reiterating the Vicino and Hardwicke report, I shall report the result of a separate analysis, done by Allred and myself, based on only part of the data—some 1,500 Navy recruits.

There are 10 subtests on the conventional ASVAB and 11 on the CAT version. A factor analysis was made of the 21×21 correlation matrix. Table 6.2 shows the 4-factor solution, from an exploratory factor analysis, with factor rotation by direct oblimin, yielding correlated factors. Those familiar with the ASVAB will recognize the four factors, which always seem to emerge (Wilfong, 1980). The results are remarkable, and comforting. Plainly, with a few minor exceptions, the factor structure is the same for the two modes of administration of the test battery. I should note that the items were different across modes.

With 1,500 cases, fairly small differences in factor pattern coefficients probably deserve attention. First, factor analyses of the ASVAB generally show the four factors found here: verbal, quantitative, technical, and speed. Second, each test furnishes some specific variance—the reliability of most of the individual tests is usually at least .80–.85, which is often higher than the communality. Third, bear in mind that the CAT scores are estimated abilities, using item response theory (IRT). IRT ability scales show an ogival-shaped relation of ability scores to number-right scores. IRT spreads out ability at the top and bottom of the scale much more than conventional number-right scores do. This nonlinearity affects only the top and bottom 10% of the cases.

General science (GS) and word knowledge (WK) show no surprises. Paragraph comprehension (PC) weighs higher on the verbal factor in the CAT mode, and has a higher communality. Partly this is because it is a bit more reliable; partly it reflects the change to only one question per paragraph and shorter paragraphs. Paragraph comprehension is a little more like word knowledge on the computer. This may represent a loss of useful information. It should be noted that in practice, paragraph comprehension and word knowledge are always combined to form a verbal score for use in predicting performance.

The two speed tests, numerical operations (NO) and coding speed (CS), are by themselves. The two quantitative tests, arithmetic reasoning (AR) and math knowledge (MK) are together. AR has a somewhat higher weight on CAT, which may indicate better measurement in CAT, possibly because of no time limit.

TABLE 6.2
Factor Pattern of Armed Services Vocational Aptitude Battery
(ASVAB) in Both Paper-and-pencil (PP) and Computerized
Adaptive Test (CAT) Modes

Tests	Mode	Factors				Common variance
		Verbal	Quant.	Tech.	Speed	
General science	PP	.65	.16	.13	.08	.67
	CAT	.70	.18	.09	−.05	.74
Word knowledge	PP	.97	−.10	−.07	−.02	.77
	CAT	.94	−.06	−.01	.00	.80
Paragraph comprehens.	PP	.55	.05	.00	.11	.37
	CAT	.65	.13	.01	.04	.57
Numerical operations	PP	−.13	.10	.00	.65	.45
	CAT	.02	.20	−.07	.58	.47
Coding speed	PP	.03	−.06	.08	.67	.43
	CAT	.09	.04	−.04	.73	.54
Arithmetic reasoning	PP	.05	.71	.11	.11	.69
	CAT	.03	.82	.07	.04	.77
Math knowledge	PP	.06	.86	−.09	.05	.80
	CAT	.07	.80	−.12	.08	.72
Mechanical comprehens.	PP	.16	.38	.43	−.04	.58
	CAT	.06	.30	.42	−.08	.39
Electronic information	PP	.37	.12	.40	.03	.53
	CAT	.28	.19	.45	−.02	.55
Auto/Shop	PP	.15	−.02	.76	.10	.70
Auto Info.	CAT	−.10	−.11	.91	.02	.72
Shop Info.	CAT	−.03	−.02	.72	−.05	.50

Factor Intercorrelations

Factors	V	Q	T	S
Verbal	1.00	.65	.43	.16
Quantitative	.65	1.00	.32	.39
Technical	.43	.32	1.00	−.06
Speed	.16	.39	−.06	1.00

Mechanical comprehension (MC) has a lower weight on quantitative and a low communality. The may be due to the large amount of graphics on this test, and the relatively poor quality of graphics on the experimental system.

Electronic information (EI) has less verbal weight in CAT, which probably reflects something different about the items in the CAT pool. The final test, auto shop (AS) is one conventional test and two CAT tests. When auto information (AI) is separated from shop information (SI), AI turns out to provide the best definition of the technical factor. On the ASVAB, technical seems to be blue-collar, applied technical, more than mechanical theory. On the whole, then, the construct validity of CAT-ASVAB would seem to be supported.

NEW TESTS AND NEW CRITERIA

One of the advantages of putting tried and true tests on the computer is that the validity can be imported. If the conventional and computer tests are equivalent then the validity of one is the validity of the other. On the chance that equivalence might not be realized, the NPRDC group actually did some predictive validity studies, and found equivalent validities (Vicino & Hardwicke, 1984).

When new tests are made, new validity studies will be needed. Many of the tests now being tried on the computer are perceptual tests, simple memory tests, tests of choice reaction time, eye–hand coordination, and other tasks that are less complex than verbal, quantitative, or technical measures. Whether these tests will be operationally useful in military selection remains to be seen, but it seems clear that if they are to be useful, then training grades, the usual criterion, or even job knowledge tests, will have to be supplemented. There is a very good chance that perceptual-motor tests will not be highly related to the current verbally oriented ASVAB. If such tests are to make good predictions, they will have to predict nonverbal performance.

There is a large, ongoing, joint-service project to develop on-the-job performance measures for military jobs. Many types of performance measures are being tried. Hands-on job tests are job samples, requiring an enlisted person to do several parts of his job. For example, a motor mechanic might be asked to install a new oil pump, or adjust the clutch. Scoring the tests involves careful rating of each step of the task by a trained observer. Walk-through tests are similar to hands-on tests, but the examinee merely shows an interviewer what he or she would do, rather than actually doing it. Job knowledge tests are more familiar conventional tests of procedural knowledge. Elaborate simulations will be used for some jobs. The researchers may even try to get the usual supervisor's ratings, despite the usual difficulties.

The details of this elaborate project can be found elsewhere. (For an overview and further detail, see Wigdor & Green, 1986; Office of the Assistant Secretary of Defense, 1985.) I merely wish to emphasize the great importance of developing such criteria, because only with such criteria will the true value of many new types of tests be revealed. Fredericksen (1984) has repeatedly made the point that understanding test validity requires valid criteria. He is right. If we keep using measures of training success as criteria, we run the risk of finding little additional value in the new predictors.

I do not mean to suggest that real job performance is largely nonverbal. In fact, on some of the hands-on performance tests, if the examinee doesn't know how to perform a specific task, a few points are deducted, and then use of the job manual is permitted. Of course, working with a manual is not a "shoo-in." I once observed a fellow who seemed to be having difficulty doing the task, even with the manual right in front of him. When I quietly asked the test administrator about it, he told me that the fellow had the manual opened to the wrong page. Having just had trouble installing a new board in my personal computer, I knew how he felt. Even when you find the right page, the picture doesn't look much like your machine, and there's nothing in the manual about how to fish out that screw you dropped. In that situation, high verbal and quantitative scores don't help much.

In short, new computer tests offer the opportunity for a great expansion of the space of predictor variables. Concurrently, but in order for the new predictors to have criterion-related validity there must be an accompanying expansion of the space of criterion variables.

REFERENCES

Allred, L. J. (1986). *Sources of non-equivalence between computerized and conventional psychological tests*. Unpublished doctoral dissertation, Johns Hopkins University, Baltimore.

Fredericksen, N. (1984). The real test bias: Influences of testing on teaching and learning. *American Psychologist, 39*, 193–202.

French, J. W. (1951). The description of aptitude and achievement tests in terms of notated factors. *Psychometric Society: Psychometric Monographs*, No. 5.

Greaud, V., & Green, B. F. (1986). Equivalence of conventional and computer presentation of speed tests. *Applied Psychological Measurement, 10*, 23–34.

Jensen, A. (1980). *Bias in mental tests*. New York City: Free Press.

Lee, J. A., Moreno, K. E., & Sympson, J. B. (1984, April). *The effects of mode of test administration on test performance*. Paper presented at the annual meeting of the Eastern Psychological Association, Baltimore.

McDonald, R. P. (1981). The dimensionality of tests and items. *British Journal of Mathematical and Statistical Psychology, 34*, 100–117.

McDonald, R. P. & Ahlawat, K. S. (1974). Difficulty factors in binary data. *British Journal of Mathematical and Statistical Psychology, 27*, 82–99.

Moreno, K. E., Wetzel, C. D., McBride, J. R., & Weiss, D. J. (1984). Relationship between corresponding Armed Services Vocational Aptitude Battery and computerized adaptive testing subtests. *Applied Psychological Measurement, 8*, 155–163.

Office of the Assistant Secretary of Defence, Force Management and Personnel. (1985). *Joint-Service Efforts to Link Enlistment Standards to Job Performance*. Fourth Annual Report to the House Committee on Appropriations. Washington, DC: U.S. Department of Defense, December.

Sacher, J., & Fletcher, J. D. (1978). Administering paper-and-pencil tests by computer, or the medium is not always the message. In D. J. Weiss, *Proceedings of the 1977 Computerized Adaptive Testing Conference*. Department of Psychology, University of Minnesota, Minneapolis, July.

Vicino, F. L., & Hardwicke, S. B. (1984). *An evaluation of the utility of large scale computerized adaptive testing*. Paper presented at the AERA convention, March.

Wainer, H. (1977). Speed vs. reaction time as a measure of cognitive performance. *Memory & Cognition, 5*, 278–280.

White, D. M., Clements, C. B., & Fowler, R. (1985). A comparison of computer administration with standard administration of the MMPI. *Computers in Human Behavior, 1*, 153–162.

Wigdor, A. & Green, B. F. (Eds.). (1986). *Assessing the performance of enlisted personnel: Evaluation of a joint-service research project*. Washington, DC: National Research Council.

Wilfong, H. D. (1980). *ASVAB technical supplement to the high school counselor's guide*. Directorate of Testing, U.S. Military Enlistment Processing Command, Fort Sheridan, Chicago.

Section **III**

TESTING VALIDITY
IN SPECIFIC SUBPOPULATIONS

The "validity of a test" is a misnomer. As Cronbach (1971) has pointed out, it is the inferences that one draws from the test scores that need to be validated. This is oftentimes a difficult and expensive process and becomes more so when it is done for specific subgroups of the examinee population. In this section we explore some of these difficulties.

The first chapter, by Warren Willingham, discusses the challenges involved in testing handicapped people. The second, by Richard Durán, investigates issues involved in testing students who have non-English backgrounds. Although the roots of these problems relate strongly to those of the handicapped, there are a number of differences which are worthy of serious consideration. While we agree with Willingham that many of these issues will not be resolved by mathematical specialists, we more strongly agree that "better facts will surely encourage wiser policy and fairer practice." It is toward this end that the following chapters are aimed.

A principal question when concerned with test validity among specific subgroups must be "does this test perform the same in this focal group as it does in the more general reference group?" If it does than we can be well assured that, for better or for worse, the test is equally fair. Two chapters in this section are concerned with the statistical methodology involved in the accurate measurement of any differential performance of test items (DIF). The two methods proposed are, each in its own way, the best that can be done. The chapter by Paul Holland and Dorothy Thayer does not utilize item response theory to study DIF; instead, they condition on raw score and summarize the differential effect with the Mantel–Haenszel (1959) statistic.

The chapter by David Thissen, Lynne Steinberg, and Howard Wainer, uses a model-based approach. This should be more flexible and powerful than the Mantel–Haenszel *when the model fits* although its robustness to deviations from the model was not examined. Each method represents a significant advance over its predecessors.

Rubin's discussion (p. 241–256) provides some additional insights into these methods. He also proposes adapting the methodology of low-dose extrapolation, common in drug testing, toward ameliorating some other problems involved in testing the handicapped.

REFERENCES

Cronbach, L. J. (1971). Test Validation. In R. L. Thorndike (Ed.), *Educational measurement* (2nd ed., pp. 443–509) Washington, DC: American Council on Education, pp. 443–507.

Mantel, N., & Haenszel, W. (1959). Statistical aspects of the analysis of data from retrospective studies of disease. *Journal of the National Cancer Institute, 22,* 719–748.

Chapter 7

Testing Handicapped People—
The Validity Issue

Warren W. Willingham
Educational Testing Service

Admissions testing programs provide modified tests and test procedures for handicapped individuals in order to reduce the likelihood that a sensory or physical disability may spuriously lower test scores. Regulations under Section 504 of the Rehabilitation Act require that the validity of such tests be demonstrated. The meaning of validity in this instance is examined in consideration of federal legislation, current test theory and practice, and unusual circumstances encountered in the testing of handicapped people. It is concluded that test validity for handicapped subgroups means primarily test fairness and the measure of test fairness is comparability. Five measures of comparability between test scores for handicapped and nonhandicapped examinees are distinguished. For considerations of equity as well as the inherent difficulty in establishing score comparability, it is important to give careful attention also to the comparability of the task presented by the assessment procedure.

INTRODUCTION

Attention to admissions testing procedures for handicapped people greatly increased as a result of Section 504 of the Rehabilitation Act of 1973. Among other stipulations the implementing regulations for Section 504 prevent the use of a test showing disproportionate adverse effect on handicapped people unless the test has been validated. This is significant because it is the only instance of a federal mandate concerning higher institutions' use of tests in admissions. In keeping with this legislation the recently revised Standards for Educational and Psychological Testing (APA, AERA, NCME, 1985) now exhibit far greater concern with testing of handicapped persons than did earlier editions. The *Standards* state, for example, "In addition to modifying tests and test administration procedures for people who have handicapping conditions, validating these tests is urgently needed." (p. 80)

What is implied by "validating these tests?" My purpose is to consider that question from several points of view: The impact of federal regulations, the special circumstances involved in the testing of handicapped people, and current theory and practice concerning validity. In the end I conclude that in validating tests for handicapped people, the essential issue is fairness and the important questions concern the comparability of tests for handicapped and nonhandicapped people.

I will draw upon recent experience that a group of us have had in undertaking a series of studies on this topic. That work has not reached the point of summative conclusions, but some findings, already apparent, are particularly relevant to this discussion. First, it is necessary to provide some background on testing of handicapped people and implications of the legislation.

ADMISSIONS TESTING AND THE 504 REGULATION

Testing Handicapped Applicants

There are a wide variety of sensory, motor, and cognitive disabilities normally referred to, somewhat inaccurately, as handicaps (see Susser, 1973, p. 5). They are often categorized into one of four types: hearing impairment, learning disability, physical handicap, and visual impairment. Within these four types, individual functioning may range from essentially normal to severely disabled. Equally important, these four types of handicap are quite different with respect to cognitive functioning and implications for testing—so different in fact that it is a serious error to think of handicapped people as one subgroup of examinees.

All of the major testing programs administered by ETS (e.g., Scholastic Aptitude Test and Graduate Record Examinations), provide formal procedures whereby handicapped examinees may take tests in a manner that attempts to accommodate their particular disability (Kirsh, in preparation). The purpose is to provide a test that is equivalent to that taken by nonhandicapped individuals in the sense that sources of difficulty irrelevant to the constructs measured are eliminated, insofar as possible.

For example, special administrations of the SAT are offered in four test formats: regular, large type, Braille, and audio cassette. A reader or amanuensis may be used as necessary. Special administrations are individually arranged and supervised on flexible dates in the student's own school. They normally involve extended time, frequently unlimited time (College Entrance Examination Board, 1985).

Special testing arrangements have been offered since 1939, though until recently they were few in number. In 1975 there were some 1,500 such special accommodations. That number doubled in approximately 5 years; and more than doubled again in the next 5. Most of the increase was due to larger numbers of students identified as learning disabled. From 1975 to 1985 this category increased from about 50% to 80% of the total. SAT scores for the handicapped groups vary somewhat from year to year but run approximately as follows: The SAT mean for both the physically handicapped and visually impaired is about one-quarter of a standard deviation below the national average for all examinees. The SAT mean for the learning disabled group is about two-thirds of a standard deviation below average. For the hearing impaired, scores average about 1 standard deviation below the national mean.[1]

The 504 Regulations

As part of the Rehabilitation Act of 1973 (Public Law 93–112), Congress enacted Section 504, which states in its entirety:

> No otherwise qualified handicapped individual in the United States as defined in Section 7(6), shall, solely by reason of his handicap, be excluded from the participation in, be denied the benefits of, or be subjected to discrimination under any program or activity receiving federal financial assistance.

The regulations implementing Section 504 contain three key mandates affecting college admissions tests (Department of Health, Education, and Welfare, 1977a, 22683, Sec. 84.42). An institution receiving federal funds:

> (b)(2) May not make use of any test or criterion for admission that has a disproportionate, adverse effect on handicapped persons or any class of handicapped persons unless the test or criterion, as used by the recipient, has been validated as a predictor of success in the education program or activity in question. . . .

> (b)(3) Shall assure itself that admissions tests are selected and administered so as best to insure that, when a test is administered to an applicant who has a handicap that impairs sensory, manual, or speaking skills, the test results accurately reflect the applicant's aptitude or achievement level or whatever other factor the test purports to measure, rather than reflecting the applicant's impaired sensory, manual, or speaking skills (except where those skills are the factors that the test purports to measure) . . . .

---

[1]These data refer to special test administrations, not to any tests taken by handicapped individuals in regular national administrations. The same is true for all other data or references to testing of handicapped examinees throughout this chapter, unless otherwise specified (Ragosta, in press).

(b)(4) . . . may not make preadmission inquiry as to whether an applicant for admission is a handicapped person.

A curious inconsistency may be noted from the fact that in the original legislation, Section 504 specified that "no *otherwise* qualified handicapped individual" shall be denied admission because of a disabling condition. The 504 regulations then define handicapped persons as anyone who has a physical or mental impairment including a wide range of physiological or neurological disabilities including "any mental or psychological disorder such as mental retardation, organic brain syndrome, emotional or mental illness and specific learning disabilities." Superficially it appears that a mentally ill or retarded person may not be rejected by a college if he or she meets other standards of admission. Clearly, no such mandate was intended, but the original language of the bill did not allow for the fact that particular handicaps differ as to their relevance to various educational programs or occupational activities, and that disabilities may be directly reflected in admissions tests because the skills have been shown to be valid admissions criteria. Accordingly, the word "otherwise" was deleted from corresponding language in the 504 regulations, and (b)(3) provides exception to the rule that an admissions test not reflect disabilities. I will return to this point.

Testimony concerning the draft regulations soon revealed a less tractable inconsistency. Test publishers offer modified tests in the spirit of (b)(3), but being unable to guarantee comparability of the modified test, they commonly flag (i.e., identify) the scores in order to caution users and to protect the integrity of standardized test procedures generally. But this step constitutes a violation of (b)(4) because flagging the score reveals that the student is handicapped. Faced with this dilemma, the Office of Civil Rights took two steps. One was to endorse on a temporary basis, interim guidelines permitting flagging and the use of scores not yet validated (Redden, Levering, & DiQuinzio, 1978).

The second step was to impanel a committee under auspices of the National Academy of Sciences (NAS) to reconcile the testing requirements of the 504 regulations with available testing technology and practice. In its report, (Sherman & Robinson, 1982) the panel recommended a 4-year period of research directed particularly to validating tests that are modified for handicapped examinees and making those tests as comparable as possible with standardized tests. One suggestion was the possibility of rescaling test scores through the grade average criterion so that predictions would be comparable, and there would be no need flag the test scores of handicapped examinees. A series of studies at ETS were initiated jointly by College Board, Graduate Record Examinations Board, and ETS in response to the panel report. Some of the work has been reported in technical reports; accounts of additional studies and the final project report are in preparation.[2]

---

[2]Willingham, W., Ragosta, M., Bennett, R., Braun, H., Rock, D., Powers, D. *Testing handicapped people* (in preparation).

SPECIAL CIRCUMSTANCES

Questions raised by the 504 regulations must be considered for each of the several types of handicaps because the disabilities differ so substantially, one from the other. Contributing also to a profusion of validity issues are several unusual characteristics which make this validity problem instructive. There are seven such special circumstances, each of which raises additional complications in assessing the validity of tests for handicapped students. For the purposes of this discussion, we refer here only to tests administered to handicapped students under modified conditions.

1. First, handicapped examinees provide the only instance of evaluating test validity for a particular subgroup in which the test is not actually the same test as that administered to the majority group. With admissions tests the content does not typically vary (Solomon, 1982). The main test variations that raise additional validity questions are physical format (large type, cassette, Braille) and extended time in administration. Visually impaired examinees are most likely to use modified test formats though some other handicapped students do as well. Extended timing is common in all groups and poses an especially vexing issue as to comparability.

2. With many special tests administered to handicapped people, it is not only the test that looks different; the score does as well. It comes with a notation: "NON STA." That flag on the score tightens the connection between validity and test use in a unique way. The problem is that the very appearance of the flag, put there by the test developer or sponsor, may prompt invalid inferences or prejudicial admissions decisions on the part of users. That is the concern of many handicapped people, and a main reason why they object to the flag. The NAS panel was concerned over both positive and negative stereotyping that test score flags may foster.

3. Comparability of criterion data is always an uncertainty in predictive validity studies, but in most cases one assumes that its main effects are to add noise and lower validity coefficients (Goldman & Slaughter, 1976). Noncomparable criteria are more likely when subgroups have different educational experiences. Many handicapped students, particularly those with hearing impairment, are enrolled in special college programs that are designed to meet their particular educational needs and provide support services as necessary. It would not be surprising if both grading standards and admissions standards were more lenient in such programs. Our preliminary data suggest that both assumptions are correct. The effect is to give an impression of noncomparable test scores when noncomparable criteria are an equally likely explanation.

4. Availability of data is certainly not a problem unique to handicapped examinees, though it has always been recognized as a paramount issue. If anything, the problem appears to be worse than imagined a few years ago. Obtaining adequate data is especially difficult for visually impaired, hearing impaired, and physically handicapped examinees. Each of these groups number only a few

hundred nationally each year for a major test like the SAT; the students then fan out into hundreds of institutions. Without Bayesian methods developed quite recently (Braun & Jones, 1985; Braun, Jones, Rubin, Thayer, 1983; Rubin, 1980) most of the prediction work in which my colleagues are now engaged would be quite impossible. Nonetheless, many questions concerning modified versions of the SAT and GRE are never likely to be addressed simply for lack of adequate data. Most admissions tests covered by the 504 regulations have far less data on handicapped examinees. It is unreasonable to assume that empirical studies can go very far in validating such tests for specific types of handicapped people.

    5.   There are several special circumstances concerning learning disabilities that are particularly important because, among those who take special test administrations, this category is very large and continues to grow. An uncertainty arises when the characteristic defining the handicapped group appears to overlap the construct measured by the test being evaluated. For example, federal regulations (Department of Health, Education, and Welfare, 1977b, p. 65083) define specific learning disability as:

> A disorder on one or more of the basic psychological processes involved in understanding or in using language, spoken or written, which may manifest itself in an imperfect ability to listen, think, speak, read, write, spell, or to do mathematical calculations. The term includes such conditions as perceptual handicaps, brain injury, minimal brain dysfunction, dyslexia, and developmental aphasia. The term does not include children who have learning problems which are primarily a result of visual, hearing, or motor handicaps, of mental retardation, of emotional disturbance, or of environmental, cultural, or economic disadvantage.

Learning disabled (LD) students are eligible for special administrations of admissions tests so that such imperfect abilities do not (in the language of the NAS panel) distort the resulting scores. If an LD student's problem is reading, then the extended time available in a special administration of the SAT, for example, might result in a score more representative of the student's reasoning ability, but the SAT is also a measure of reading. In fact, it includes reading comprehension items and provides a subscore for reading. The rationale for providing extended time to students who have difficulty reading rests on a distinction between decoding and understanding. Like someone who is blind, the LD examinee has a specific visual deficit, but with more time to get the words off the page, can demonstrate normal verbal reasoning ability. The validity of this analysis is debated in research literature. Stanovich (1986) argued that a large body of evidence does not support an assumption of such specificity, and that reading disabled individuals are characterized by pervasive language problems. In this case the rationale and basis for establishing a comparable test for learning disabled examinees is not clear (especially what would constitute an appropriate amount of extended time).

    As noted earlier, the regulations acknowledge the possibility of exceptions to the rule that tests must not reflect those imperfect abilities or impaired skills by adding the qualification "except when those skills are the factor that the test purports to measure" (DHEW, 1977a, p. 22683). When this exception applies is unclear, especially because of ambiguity in the way that the LD category is defined. Whether the exception applies is consequential because it carries with it federal regulations as to validity standards.

6. The LD category poses special problems because there is substantial confounding between the method by which the group is defined and the method for determining whether test scores for that group are valid. In a report of a special work group appointed by the Department of Education (Reynolds, 1985) the development of the LD definition is described along following lines.

> For many years but particularly since the passage of public law 94–142 the diagnosis and evaluation of learning disabilities has presented major problems. . . . When the rules and regulations for PL 94–142 were being developed, many experts testified in Office of Education hearings, wrote numerous papers, and were convened for discussion and debate. . . . The only consensus regarding the characteristics of this "thing" called learning disability was that it resulted in a major discrepancy between what you would expect academically of learning disabled children and the level at which they were actually achieving.

Thus federal regulations stipulate that the operational criteria for determining the existence of a specific learning disability should be based on "(1) whether a child does not achieve commensurate with his or her age and ability when provided with appropriate educational experiences and (2) whether the child has a severe discrepancy between achievement and intellectual ability in one or more of seven areas related to communication skills and mathematical abilities" (Department of Health, Education, and Welfare, 1977b, p. 65083).

A recent 50-state survey confirms that definitions of learning disability currently in use in the public schools emphasize the aptitude-achievement discrepancy (Chalfant, 1984). One might expect such an aptitude-achievement discrepancy to be common among LD students who take an extended time version of the SAT since it is the school documentation of the LD condition that establishes who is eligible for the special administration of the SAT. The data of Braun, Ragosta, and Kaplan (in press) do show that pattern for LD students. Among the four handicapped groups, LD students had by far the lowest high school grades and were the only group to rank substantially lower on high school average than on SAT scores relative to nonhandicapped students.

When college grades of LD students were predicted on the basis of their scores on an SAT administered with extended time, performance was overpredicted by .39 standard deviations—the only handicapped group who showed nearly such a strong pattern of underachievement (or overprediction). Does this mean that the extended time version of the SAT is seriously biased *in favor* of LD students or simply that the group had been identified as underachievers earlier and continued that pattern in college? In the face of this apparent confounding effect, how much confidence can one have in over- or underprediction as a basis for determining the comparability of scores for LD students? Or as a basis for lowering scores reported for LD students in order to make them "more comparable" to those of nonhandicapped students?

7. A final issue is accuracy of classification—an essential assumption in any analysis of comparability of tests across groups. Reliable identification, particularly as to severity of disability, is a significant issue within each of the four main types of handicap. But learning disability poses by far the most serious problem as the previous discussion might suggest. In Chalfant's view (1984), the problem starts with the fact that, in defining operational criteria for determining learning disability, federal regulations omit any reference to psychological process (e.g., visual deficit) and the result is that academic failure becomes defined as learning disability (Department of Health, Education, and Welfare, 1977b, Sec. 121a.541). Given an inherently unreliable diagnostic procedure that lags behind the state-of-the-art (Reynolds, 1985) and a low incidence of learning disabilities, Shepard (in press) points out that a substantial proportion of misidentifications are statistically inevitable. An extensive study in Colorado (Shepard, Smith, & Vojir, 1983) indicated that some 3 in 5 students labeled "LD" failed to meet even a weak criterion for LD classification. The misclassified proved to have a variety of other problems: language difficulties, emotional problems, absenteeism, or were slow learners, or average learners in high SES districts. Elsewhere, Shepard (1983) described two motives at work: first, the strong interest of many parents to have their low achieving children labeled learning disabled in the belief that it is more socially acceptable than other alternatives and second, the professional interest of teachers and program administrators to move pupils into this category. As Chalfant (1984) noted, "prevalence data reported by state and federal agencies indicate that many students are being inappropriately classified as learning disabled."

One manifestation of these dynamics is that LD classifications have risen dramatically, increasing every year since the federal government first required states to count students in special education programs funded under public law 94–142. In 1976–77 there were 797,000 LD students; in 1982–83 the number was 1,741,000. During this period the number of students classified in several other categories, including mentally retarded, actually declined (*Education of the Handicapped,* June 29, 1983, January 8, 1986). From a scientific standpoint, LD classification seems to be partly a moving target and partly a diverse collection of students with quite different educational problems—all of which poses exceptional difficulty for establishing the comparability of test scores for this group.

DEFINING THE VALIDITY PROBLEM

Due to the generally acknowledged discrepancy between the intent of the 504 regulations and present technical capabilities, there has been considerable uncertainty as to exactly what would constitute acceptable validation of admissions tests for handicapped people. The regulations stipulate that a test should not be used unless it has been validated "as a predictor of success in the education program or activity in question," [(b)(2)], referring apparently to a conventional validity study based on the total class since one based only upon specific types of handicapped students would be quite impossible in all save a few institutions. But the regulations also mandate [(b)(3)] that "test results accurately reflect the applicant's aptitude or achievement level or whatever other factors the test purports to measure rather than reflecting the applicant's [impairment]"

In the latter case the implication is that the testing procedure should appropriately take account of the disability so that the scores have comparable meaning. When the NAS panel speaks of validating tests for handicapped people it is clearly within this larger compass. The panel suggests a variety of activities in the spirit of establishing such comparability. The language of the regulations, it should be noted, gives a much stronger mandate to the narrow as opposed to the broad interpretation of validate. To wit; the institution *may not make use of* a test unless it has been validated in the narrow sense of (b)(2); in the broader sense of (b)(3) it only need assure itself that tests are selected and administered so as *best to ensure* that modified tests accurately reflect the applicant's aptitude.

Standards for Educational and Psychological Testing (APA, AERA, NCME, 1985) follow in that spirit. Standard 14.6 stipulates that, *when feasible,* the validity and reliability of tests administered to handicapped people should be investigated as well as the effects of test modifications. The standard is silent on what constitutes adequate validation, leaving that question to professional judgment based on current theory and practice with respect to other subgroups of examinees.

In selective admissions, we are used to thinking of test validity for a subgroup where that subgroup represents applicants to an educational program or a job. In that case validity is much associated with utility: Does an admissions test, for example, make a useful contribution, not only to enrolling more able students in a particular institution, but to an effective admissions process within the educational system at large? On the other hand, in considering the validity of that test for a subgroup of examinees such as handicapped people, minority students, or women, accuracy of inferences has more to do with fairness to individuals and groups than with utility to programs and institutions. In broad perspective, both utility and fairness are cornerstones of a valid selection test. It is important to note the connection of this problem with the more fundamental issue of construct validity. As Cronbach (1971) made clear, "one validates, not a test, but an interpretation of data arising from a specified procedure." In other words, does the score mean what we take it to mean? The meaning of a construct can be distorted in any number of ways: inclusion of inappropriate items, undue speededness, misscoring, etc. An important mark of accurate and consistent meaning in a construct is, as Messick (1975) noted, "the extent to which a measure displays the same properties and patterns of relationships *in different population groups* and under different circumstances. . . ."

Such population validity links test bias directly to construct validity (Willingham, 1976). Test bias represents various possible discrepancies across subgroups that constitute spurious sources of variance having no intrinsic connection with the construct, i.e., the knowledge and skill being measured. Thus test bias or population invalidity reduces construct validity by introducing systematic error, much as would including inappropriate items or giving unfair advantage or disadvantage to some examinees.

An important additional attribute of test bias as a threat to construct validity is the fact that the discrepancies center upon a particular group and consequently may result in inappropriate decisions or unfair treatment of that group. These various considerations point in the same direction: For a particular subgroup of examinees, such as handicapped people, test validity means primarily test fairness and the measure of test fairness is comparability.

Comparable in what sense? Over the past two decades there has developed a very considerable body of literature concerning the test performance of subgroups. Some very useful reviews and analyses have focused on particular ethnic groups (Durán, 1983), sex differences (Clark & Grandy, 1984), intelligence tests (Jensen, 1980), admissions tests (Breland, 1979), statistical methodology (Berk, 1982), and so on.

Cole (1981) provided a particularly useful discussion of longstanding frustrations in dealing effectively with the policy aspects of test bias and the difficulty of rectifying disparate scientific and the social views of the topic. Part of the problem is the difference in value orientations implied by Messick's (1975) well-known distinction between the evidential and the consequential basis for evaluating tests and their use. Part of the problem is also the complexity of the issues and the inherent limitations in understanding comparability and fairness in scientific terms.

Perhaps in recognition of this difficulty, the NAS panel did not restrict itself to research recommendations concerning ways to achieve scientific or psychometric comparability of modified tests. The panel also discussed in some detail the problem of establishing comparable test content, conditions of administration, and so on (Sherman & Robinson, 1982, chapter 5; see also Schmeiser, Kane, & Brennan, 1983 for a useful discussion). These two orientations to the topic can be distinguished as *score* comparability and *task* comparability.

Score comparability implies comparable meaning and interpretation; that is, all aspects of construct generalizability or test fairness that have come to be associated with research on subgroups of examinees. It is a psychometric construction that is examined and established empirically on the basis of the outcome of the testing procedure. On the other hand, establishing comparability of the task—especially comparable content and conditions of administration—is something one does, a priori, on the basis of experience, expert judgment, and relevant data.

Task comparability comes especially into play with respect to modified tests for handicapped examinees for the obvious reason that the task is different to some degree. Ensuring task comparability, in the face of a disability irrelevant to the construct measured, is fully in the spirit of standardizing a test in order to provide a fair assessment for all examinees (Angoff & Anderson, 1963). Thus, efforts to improve score comparability and task comparability can be seen as complementary ways of providing fair (i.e., valid) tests for handicapped people. The one supports the other; in particular, empirical evidence of score comparability is often helpful in making sound judgments about task comparability. The ongoing research to which I have referred provides data relevant to several aspects of task comparability (especially speededness, testing conditions, and test content), but these studies focus primarily on five important types of score comparability.

1. *Factor structure.* If sensory or cognitive dysfunction occasion a handicapped student taking a modified test, it is certainly plausible in that instance that the test may not measure the same construct; that is, the score may not have quite the same meaning for those examinees. That possibility is enhanced when the comparability of the task is uncertain. Such resulting differences in the construct could cause misinterpretation in educational advising or instructional placement even if the score is comparable for admissions purposes. Studies involving confirmatory factor analysis with both the SAT and GRE have recently been completed (Rock, Bennett, Jirele, 1986; Rock, Bennett, & Kaplan, 1985). Results indicate some differences but that generally the factor structure of these tests is quite similar for various groups of handicapped and nonhandicapped examinees.

2. *Item functioning.* Even if modified tests measure quite similar constructs, it is certainly possible that particular types of items may be unfair because they are differentially difficult for reasons connected with particular disabilities. Furthermore, the selection of items, their wording, or the way they are presented may have been modified for the specific purpose of avoiding unfair difficulty. Studies of item functioning for different groups of handicapped examinees are a useful empirical check on that process. Such studies have recently been completed for two forms of the SAT and one of the GRE (Bennett, Rock, & Jirele, 1986; Bennett, Rock, & Kaplan, 1985). To a surprising degree, particular types of items appear to have comparable difficulty for different groups of handicapped and nonhandicapped examinees, once total score is taken into account. The items that proved to be more difficult for handicapped examinees were certain mathematics problems on a Braille test version that involved graphics or unfamiliar symbols.

3. *Reliability.* Ordinarily reliability is not seen as an aspect of validity, but it is relevant as an indicator of the comparability of the measure across subgroups. Namely, are test results as consistent for handicapped as for nonhandicapped examinees, or is the score likely to fluctuate more in the case of modified tests?

Given the findings just cited, it is perhaps no surprise that reliability—that is, internal consistency—appears to hold up quite well (Bennett et al., 1985, 1986).

4. *Predicted performance.* More than any other type of evidence, the validity of an admissions test for a subgroup is likely to be judged on the basis of how accurately it predicts the performance of the group. Accuracy of prediction engages two critical questions: whether the test performs its main function— discriminating between successful and unsuccessful students—as well for this subgroup as for applicants generally, and whether the test promotes fair admissions decisions by not systematically over- or underestimating the academic performance of the group. The importance of this form of comparability led the NAS panel to propose rescaling test scores for handicapped examinees in the hope of avoiding any systematic prediction errors. Our studies of predictive accuracy are not completed, though some outcomes are reasonably clear. While predictive validity seems generally acceptable overall there are important instances of over- as well as underprediction for particular groups of handicapped students. There are serious problems in interpreting those differences for reasons already cited: confounding effects, noncomparable criteria, and limited data for many key comparisons.

5. *Admissions decisions.* Additional grounds for questioning comparability of tests modified to accommodate handicaps arise from the fact that the scores carry a flag. Does the flag, signifying something unusual about the score, actually inspire invalid inferences? There is possibly no very satisfactory way of determining whether and how often the flag actually leads to incorrect inferences, though evidence of comparable admission decisions does bear on the question. If disabled applicants are less likely to be admitted than nondisabled applicants with comparable credentials, it can be argued that the flag is detrimental; that is, harmful in that it may facilitate a prejudicial practice by making it easier to identify handicapped individuals. If that were the case, the score would, through its appearance alone, tend to invalidate itself by inviting different inferences than those that might otherwise be drawn by users. A study of admissions decisions is in progress.

I conclude with a few general observations. Some of these validity issues are unusual compared with those that are typical for other subgroups of examinees that have received much attention in recent years. To some degree, however, these issues may be a harbinger of things to come, or perhaps they are part of the tide: more federal involvement in testing, increasingly subtle validity issues. Two examples of the latter suffice. Computer adaptive testing is gaining momentum. Like modified tests for handicapped students, the CAT version is seldom exactly the same test. Durán's paper at this conference bears witness to the increasing concern with the effects of language on test validity. As with testing handicapped people, the construct that operationally defines the group (e.g., facility in English) often overlaps with the construct being measured.

The NAS panel acknowledged that it is unlikely that conditions of handicap can be disentangled from the skills required by admissions tests—or college coursework, I would add. Some might contend that there is an element of wrongheadedness here—that in the case of handicapped people tests are being expected to serve functions they can not do well, and perhaps we should not make the effort to provide comparable tests. That view may be expedient but seems much outweighed by other considerations. Certainly there are substantial numbers of students whose test performance can be hampered by disabilities unrelated to the cognitive skills those tests measure. In the spirit of the law as well as social responsibility, every reasonable effort must be made to provide handicapped students with the most valid tests possible. How best to do that is the point at issue.

It is accomplished partly by recognizing that test validity for handicapped people is not exclusively an empirical question. Relevant data are important in demonstrating fairness, but given the problems outlined above and research experience we have accumulated over the past several years, the evidential basis seems likely to be shaky. It would be ill-advised to rely solely on score comparability because demonstrating such comparability may not be feasible in many cases. Also important is the perception of fairness and the credibility of the assessment process for handicapped persons as well as the equity of admissions testing for all. That is why careful attention to task comparability is an important element in ensuring valid tests for examinees with disabilities.

Finally, fairness is a social not a psychometric concept. Whether inferences regarding the test scores of handicapped examinees are correct or incorrect is not always a straightforward question. Facts are easily disputed; test use in selective admissions will always be influenced by value considerations. In some instances there are strong arguments for preferential enrollment of handicapped students, but as with all social policy, not everyone agrees. As Cronbach (1976) noted in a similar context, "These issues will not be settled by mathematical specialists." No doubt and rightly so, but better facts will surely encourage wise policy and fair practice.

REFERENCES

American Educational Research Association, American Psychological Association, and National Council on Measurement in Education. (1985). *Standards for educational and psychological testing*. Washington, DC: American Psychological Association.

Angoff, W., & Anderson, S. (1963). The standardization of educational and psychological tests. *Illinois Journal of Education*, 19–23.

Bennett, R., Rock, D., & Jirele, T. (1986). *The psychometric characteristics of the GRE for nine handicapped groups*. (ETS RR–86–6). Princeton, NJ: Educational Testing Service.

Bennett, R., Rock, D., & Kaplan, B. (1985). *The psychometric characteristics of the SAT for nine handicapped groups* (ETS RR–85–49). Princeton, NJ: Educational Testing Service.

Berk, R. (1982). *Handbook of methods for detecting test bias.* Baltimore: Johns Hopkins University Press.

Braun, H., & Jones, D. (1985). *Use of empirical Bayes methods in the study of the validity of academic predictors of graduate school performance* (GREB Report No. 79–13). Princeton, NJ: Educational Testing Service.

Braun, H., Jones, D., Rubin, D., & Thayer, D. (1983). Empirical Bayes estimation of coefficients in the general linear model from data of deficient rank. *Psychometrika, 48,* 71–181.

Braun, H., Ragosta, M., & Kaplan, B. (in preparation). *The predictive validity of the Scholastic Aptitude Test for disabled students.* Princeton, NJ: Educational Testing Service.

Breland, H. (1979). *Population validity.* (Research Monograph No. 8). New York: College Entrance Examination Board.

Chalfant, J. (1984). *Identifying learning disabled students: Guidelines for decision making.* Burlington, VT: Northeast Regional Resource Center.

Clark, M., & Grandy, J. (1984). *Sex differences in the academic performance of Scholastic Aptitude Test takers.* (College Board Report no. 84–8). New York: College Entrance Examination Board.

Cole, N. (1981). Bias in testing. *American Psychologist, 36*(10), 1067–1077.

College Entrance Examination Board. (1985). *ATP services for handicapped students: 1985–86 information for counselors and admissions officers.* New York: Author.

Cronbach, L. (1976). Equity in selection—Where psychometrics and political philosophy meet. *Journal of Educational Measurement. 13*(1), 31–41.

Cronbach, L. (1971). Test validation. In R. L. Thorndike (Ed.), *Educational measurement* (2d ed., p. 76). Washington, DC: American Council on Education.

Department of Health, Education, & Welfare. (1977a). Nondiscrimination on basis of handicap. *Federal Register, 42*(86), p. 22683, Sec. 84.42.

Department of Health, Education, & Welfare. (1977b). Assistance to states for education of handicapped children: Procedures for evaluating specific learning disabilities. *Federal Register, 42,* 65082–65085.

Durán, R. (1983). *Hispanics' education and background: Predictors of college achievement.* New York: College Entrance Examination Board.

Education of the Handicapped, (1986, January 8) p. 7.

Education of the Handicapped, (1983, June 29). Alexandria, VA: Capitol Publications, pp. 1–3.

Goldman, R. D., & Slaughter, R. E. (1976). Why college grade point average is difficult to predict. *Journal of Educational Psychology, 68*(1), 9–14.

Jensen, A. R. (1980). *Bias in mental testing.* New York: Free Press.

Kirsh, B. (in preparation). *Availability of services for handicapped examinees: 1985 survey results.* Princeton, NJ: Educational Testing Service.

Messick, S. (1975). The standard problem: Meaning and values in measurement and evaluation. *American Psychologist, 30*(10), 955–966.

Ragosta, M. (in preparation). *Handicapped students described.* Princeton, NJ: Educational Testing Service.

Redden, M., Levering, C., & DiQuinzio, D., (and the Task Force on a Model Admissions Policy). (1978). *Recruitment, admissions, and handicapped students: A guide for compliance with Section 504 of the Rehabilitation Act of 1973.* Washington, DC: American Association of Collegiate Registrars and Admissions Officers and the American Council on Education.

Rehabilitation Act of 1973. (September 26, 1973) PL 93–112; 87 Stat. 355.

Reynolds, C. (1985). Critical measurement issues in learning disabilities. *Journal of Special Education, 18*(4).

Rock, D., Bennett, R., & Jirele, T. (1986). *The internal construct validity of the GRE General Test across handicapped and nonhandicapped populations.* (ETS Research Report 86–7). Princeton, NJ: Educational Testing Service.

Rock, D., Bennett, R., & Kaplan, B. (1985). *The internal construct validity of the SAT across handicapped and nonhandicapped populations.* Princeton, NJ: Educational Testing Service.

Rubin, D. B. (1980). Using empirical Bayes techniques in the law school validity studies. *Journal of the American Statistical Association, 75,* 801–816.

Schmeiser, C., Kane, M., & Brennan, R. (1983). Testing the handicapped: An issue of comparability. *Bar Examiner, 52*(2) 16–23.

Shepard, L. (in press). Identification of mild handicaps. In R. Linn (Ed.), *Educational measurement* (3d ed.). New York: Macmillan.

Shepard, L. (1983). The role of measurement in educational policy: Lessons from the identification of learning disabilities. *Educational Measurement Issues and Practices, 2*(3), 4–8.

Shepard, L., Smith, M., & Vojir, C. (1983). Characteristics of pupils identified as learning disabled. *American Educational Research Journal, 20*(3), 309–331.

Sherman, S., & Robinson, N. (1982). *Ability testing of handicapped people: Dilemma for government, science, and the public.* Washington, DC: National Academy Press.

Solomon, C. (1982). *A manual for preparing special test editions for the handicapped.* Princeton, NJ: Educational Testing Service.

Stanovich, K. E. (1986). Cognitive processes and the reading problems of learning disabled children: Evaluating the assumption of specificity. In J. K. Torgesen & B. Y. L. Wong (Eds.). *Psychological and educational perspectives on learning disabilities.* Orlando, FL: Academic Press.

Susser, M. (1973). *Causal thinking in the health sciences concepts and strategies of epidemiology.* New York: Oxford University Press.

Willingham, W. (1976). *Validity and the Graduate Record Examinations program.* Princeton, NJ: Educational Testing Service.

Willingham, W., Ragosta, M., Bennett, R., Braun, H., Rock, D., & Powers, D. (in preparation). *Testing handicapped people.* Princeton, NJ: Educational Testing Service.

Chapter 8

Validity and Language Skills Assessment: Non-English Background Students

Richard P. Durán
Graduate School of Education,
University of California at Santa Barbara

INTRODUCTION

English language proficiency testing is widely used in American schools at two levels of schooling. At the elementary school level—and to a lesser extent at the secondary school level—it is used in assessing language minority students' ability to benefit from instruction in English and as an indicator of students' need for language services such as bilingual education or instruction in English as a second language. At the college level, proficiency testing is widely used in evaluating non-English background students' ability to undertake advanced academic work through the medium of English. While existing proficiency tests have proven useful in these domains of application, there is nonetheless a recurrent call for the development of new types of language proficiency tests which could provide richer qualitative information about students' mastery or lack of mastery of critical English language skills for academic study (Durán, in press a, b; Rivera, 1984).

The challenge of creating better language proficiency tests is intrinsically tied to basic questions regarding validity in testing. First, examinees taking English proficiency tests can come from very diverse social, ethnic, and educational backgrounds. This requires that these tests along with other tests for use with non-English background examinees demonstrate appropriate population validity for use with target groups of examinees. These concerns are articulated well in a section on the testing of linguistic minorities provided in the *Standards for educational and psychological testing* (American Psychological Association, 1985). Concern for the predictive validity of language proficiency tests represents yet another fundamental issue. Language proficiency tests are intended to predict the ability to use a language in criterion settings, and are not intended to predict performance on criterion variables reflecting academic achievement or cognitive abilities divorced from language functioning. Language proficiency test scores, however, can be used as moderator variables to predict achievement and cognitive criterion measures from appropriate predictors of these criterion variables (Alderman, 1982). In this case language proficiency scores provide information about the importance of considering language proficiency as a factor influencing display of skills and aptitudes in a nonnative language.

This chapter concentrates on yet another important aspect of validity surrounding development and use of language proficiency tests. It explores the possibility of developing improved language proficiency tests by altering and refining prevalent notions of the construct and content validity of proficiency tests based on advancements in theory and research. Existing research studies suggest obvious relationships between language proficiency test scores and measures of cognitive aptitudes in a language (Durán, in press, b). However, what is missing are insights into new procedures which might lead to substantial improvements in the quality of information which might be obtained from proficiency tests—especially insights that in the long run might contribute to educational interventions accelerating acquisition of English as a second language.

In pursuing a discussion of possible directions for new assessment techniques this chapter develops a perspective consistent with the advice of Glaser (1985), Pellegrino (this volume), and Bejar (1984) pertinent to improvements which might be made in the design and validation of tests of cognitive skills. These investigators argue there is a need for tests providing diagnostic information about students' cognitive skill development which can be linked to instruction enhancing the development of target skills. They indicate that the design of new cognitive aptitude and achievement tests should draw upon cognitive theory and research findings concerning the target skills to be assessed and that the development of tests items themselves should reflect systematically what is known about the skills in question. Each of the forgoing points is intimately related to the question of the construct and content validity of tests and with empirical sources of information which can be investigated to establish validity.

Going beyond concern for assessment of cognitive skills, these views are pertinent to the design of improved language proficiency tests and in particular to the design of new tests measuring important language-processing skills which are not assessed currently. Theoretical accounts of language processing, based on the notion of ''communicative competence,'' are emerging, and these permit a more refined and extended description of language-processing skills involved in problem solving, reading, and writing, and face-to-face interaction, than has been possible in the past. Drawing on cognitive psychology and discourse analysis research, it is becoming possible to analyze the language-processing requirements of problem-solving tasks arising in academic settings and to plan the design of assessment techniques evaluating examinees' mastery of the language skills in question. The new approaches have the potential of providing a richer basis for the design of language instruction than has been possible in the past. This is so because they can provide a diagnosis of students' ability to perform specific kinds of tasks with language (e.g., ability to answer questions based on a text and to summarize points made in passage, etc.) which are amenable to language instruction given information about students' familiarity with the content knowledge at hand. An important cornerstone of the new approaches to designing these new procedures for assessing second language skills rests with enlarging and refining the construct of "language proficiency."

The next section discusses the emergence of "communicative competence" as a construct replacing "language proficiency" among a number of language testing researchers. This discussion is followed by an examination of cognitive studies suggesting ways to devise assessment of communicative competence skills relevant to academic functioning of students. A subsequent section of the chapter briefly mentions progress in the field of discourse linguistics, which provides yet another basis for improving assessment of students' communicative competence in English for academic purposes. The chapter concludes with a discussion of the contributions which the foregoing approaches make to the general question of establishing the validity of a test.

LANGUAGE ASSESSMENT RESEARCH

Over the past several years increasing attention has been given to the construction of theoretical models of second language skills which might better inform development of proficiency tests. Bernard Spolsky (1979, 1981) has commented on historical trends in the definition of "language proficiency" as it has been operationalized in tests. He noted that over the past 20 years many of the most widely used language proficiency tests have emphasized assessment of examinees' mastery of discrete points of grammar, vocabulary, word knowledge, and sentence or paragraph meaning in either the spoken or written modalities of language.[1] This philosophy of test development has stressed the construction of tests made up of a small number of sections, each section targeted at a different skill area. Each section is made up of numerous independent items, each item testing a specific skill using multiple-choice response procedures. A test such as the Test of English as a Foreign Language (TOEFL) epitomizes this sort of discrete point instrument. The items in each of the three TOEFL sections (Listening Comprehension, Structure and Written Expression, and Reading Comprehension) are intended to examine knowledge of specific skills drawn from a set of test specifications guiding the development of items.

---

[1]The term "discrete point" is used in the language testing field to refer to a specific feature of language knowledge assessed by a given test item.

As Spolsky noted, in contrast, other approaches to language proficiency testing have acquired momentum. This momentum has been captured by two developments. First, new tests of language proficiency have been developed and implemented, which require examinees to process language in a more complex fashion than is possible utilizing multiple-choice test items relying on abbreviated language stimuli. Oller (1979), for example, described the construction and construct validation of "pragmatic" tests of language proficiency that require examinees to combine many language skills together for the purpose of performing meaningful problem-solving tasks. As another example, Lowe (1981), Clark (1978), TOEFL Program (1984), and the Interagency Language Roundtable (1983) described direct tests of language proficiency which provide ordinal ratings of examinees' overall level of skill development in areas including speaking, writing, reading, oral understanding, culturally appropriate language usage, and subareas of some of these domains. These new forms of assessment differ from more widely used proficiency-testing procedures in that they provide capsule summaries of examinees' language skills indicating expected strengths and weaknesses in examinees' capabilities in the various areas under assessment.

The second major development characterizing trends in language-testing research has focused on creating improved theoretical accounts of the nature of language and language-processing skills which should be amenable to assessment. These new accounts have drawn systematically on theories and research findings from a diverse number of fields, including applied linguistics and discourse analysis, sociolinguistics and ethnography of communication, and cognitive psychology studies of problem solving and language processing. These approaches ask: How do people actually use language in everyday contexts and what forms of knowledge underly these capabilities? As discussed subsequently, investigators have been able to identify numerous, important, language-processing skills which are not assessed systematically at present by existing proficiency tests, but which might be assessed by altering our models for the development of language proficiency tests.[2]

One of the most widely cited of these new theoretical perspectives was proposed by Canale and Swain (1980) and Canale (1983). In place of the notion of "language proficiency" they substitute the notion of "communicative competence." The construct of communicative competence is broader than the notion of language proficiency as the latter is operationalized in the development of items for most existing language proficiency tests. Like existing notions of language proficiency, communicative competence is intended to encompass knowledge of sentence-level grammar, punctuation, word formation, usage and

---

[2]From a test validity perspective, these calls for new language assessment procedures resemble previous movements in the test development field as a whole which have called for simulated task and performance-based tests of abilities as a complement to pencil-and-paper, multiple-choice tests of abilities (see e.g., Frederiksen, Jensen, & Beaton, 1972; Frederiksen & Ward, 1978).

diction, vocabulary, and recognition of sentence-level meaning. In addition, however, the construct of communicative competence encompasses knowledge of the social appropriateness of language form and register, knowledge of how discourse and speech acts are structured to meet communicative goals, and knowledge of strategies to monitor and adjust language processing on-line to meet communicative goals. Canale (1983) described four dimensions of communicative competence which can be summarized as follows:

Grammatical competence: Mastery of the language code (e.g., vocabulary and rules of word formation, sentence formation, pronunciation, and spelling).

Sociolinguistic competence: Mastery of appropriate use (in comprehension and production) of language in different sociolinguistic contexts, with an emphasis on appropriateness of (a) meanings (e.g., topics, attitudes, and functions) and (b) forms (e.g., register, formulaic expressions).

Discourse competence: Mastery of how to combine meanings and forms to achieve unified text in different genres—such as casual conversation, an argumentative essay, or a business letter—by using both (a) cohesion devices to relate forms (e.g., use of pronouns, transition expressions, parallel structures) and (b) coherence principles to organize meanings (e.g., concerning the development, consistency, and balance of ideas).

Strategic competence: Mastery of verbal and nonverbal strategies both (a) to compensate for breakdowns in communication due to insufficient competence or to performance limitations (e.g., use of prarphrase, dictionaries) and (b) to enhance the rhetorical effect of language (e.g., use of slow and soft speech, use of literary devices).

Each of these dimensions of communicative competence is relevant to the four modalities of language use: speaking, writing, oral comprehension, and reading. For each dimension and modality, it is possible to go beyond the skills outlined to a much more detailed listing of skills, each of which, in principle, might be made amenable to assessment. Appendix A displays an expanded outline of this sort; it was used as the starting point for an even more detailed outline by Durán, Canale, Penfield, Stansfield, and Liskin–Gasparro (1985) in their evaluation of the content validity of items found on the Test of English as a Foreign Language.

Discussion of this content validity study of the TOEFL is useful at this point because it highlights ways in which redefinition of a construct may fundamentally affect the evaluation of the content validity of a test. The three sections of the TOEFL are intended to assess students' proficiency in understanding oral language, recognizing grammatical structures and word usage appropriate to writing, and ability to comprehend vocabulary and brief, written text passages.

One notes immediately that TOEFL does not require the actual production of language by examinees, though the Structure and Written Expression section is designed to be an indirect test of writing ability.

The communicative competence skills directly assessed by the TOEFL, however, do not involve skills which can only be demonstrated through the actual production of language. This is especially evident in areas of sociolinguistic, discourse, and strategic competence. Communicative competence in these areas of language production requires that individuals apply knowledge of topic, situation, purpose of communication, and audience in order to regulate spoken and written language production. These skills are very difficult to assess indirectly because in the real world they are composed and arise on the basis of marshaling skills tailored to meet authentic needs for communication of personal value to individuals. It is difficult to create such circumstances in a testing context—even if language production is required.

Issues of communicative competence in language production aside, one can inquire about the communicative competence properties of items requiring only language reception. Relevant to this point, one of the main conclusions of the TOEFL study in question was that item types requiring comprehension of the most complex discourse assessed a greater range of communicative competence skills. That is, items involving comprehension of audiotaped segments of simulated lectures, conversation segments involving several turns of discourse, and the reading and understanding of multiple-sentence paragraphs on an academic topic tapped a broader range of receptive communicative competence skills than other items. The item types mentioned involved more complicated language structures and they also placed more emphasis on the development of semantic meaning. These items required that examinees infer the meaning of language across sentence boundaries and they required examinees to sense dependencies and qualifications among the ideas expressed by the language of item stems. In contrast, item types involving comprehension of brief, one- or two-sentence statements presented via audiotape or print, with little description of a context for communication, were found to be limited in their coverage of communicative competence skills. In these cases, items did a good job of covering basic skills related to recognizing phonological, graphemic, lexical, and grammatical information. However, the items did not appear to be effective in requiring examinees to integrate and evaluate the intention of speakers or authors, nor to detect and evaluate connections among multiple ideas.

Findings of this sort are not likely to be specific to the TOEFL. Indeed, one of the thorniest issues stimulated by communicative competence descriptions of language proficiency has been the extent to which language proficiency assessment items should reflect the characteristics of authentic communication. Spolsky (1985) commented that all language-proficiency testing contexts must differ from everyday language use. They are perceived by examinees as formalized language assessment situations rather than as situations driven by the demands of everyday communicative activity. In devising enhanced tests of language proficiency, based on a communicative competence approach, it is essential to recognize the deep and immediate connection which exists between the particular language constructs under assessment and the methods used in an assessment.

Bachman and Palmer (in press) have given extended attention to ways in which language testing situations might distort the performance of examinees on language proficiency tests. They note, for example, as does Spolsky, that language-testing situations are likely to focus the primary attention of the examinee on language form and less on the purposes of language use. In addition, Bachman and Palmer noted that in assessment circumstances examinees may not be able to request or receive reactions, or feedback regarding their language production or interpretation of language. In true oral interaction, for example, interlocutors are able to interrupt each other and to carry out forms of verbal and nonverbal communication that help them to monitor and adjust their language, given their communicative ends. Such circumstances are less likely to arise in a spontaneous fashion in tests of speaking proficiency. In a similar vein, in tests assessing examinees' reading comprehension, examinees can rely solely on their immediate interpretation of the meaning that might be inferred from item stems and questions. This restriction, of course, makes sense if the goal of assessment is restricted to those reading skills immediately available to individuals. The point here, however, is that examinees may exhibit additional skills affecting a broader assessment of their academic reading ability.

Our current design of reading assessments does not yet allow us to assess how examinees might adjust their interpretations of text and reading strategies, given self-generated or external feedback on their comprehension of a text. Thus, reading-comprehension test items that we typically encounter today are likely to tap an important but narrow range of reading skills. Research by Cohen (1984) suggests that even within the confines of existing reading comprehension tests, we have yet to understand the reading strategies exercised by examinees on language proficiency tests.

In contrast to the objectives of assessment of current reading proficiency items, it is interesting to note accounts of reading associated with Hermeneutic perspectives on reading and with sociolinguistic accounts of reading (Bloom & Green, 1984). From these perspectives, understanding of a text can be viewed as a dialectical process, occurring over time and repeated rereadings, guided by developing knowledge and the varying nature of tasks requiring reading. Translated into the contexts of everyday schooling, one can sense how a broadened account of reading skills and reading behavior might be required. Use of notes to summarize points in a text, underlining of terms and important statements in a text, use of dictionaries to uncover word meanings, etc., suggest a broad range of higher-order reading skills facilitating comprehension processes. These forms of extended reading skills would seem of special importance to assess among non-

English background students expected to cope with the reading demands of academic study in English.

In the next section, a more extended discussion is given to ways in which it might prove possible to improve assessment of communicative competence in reading. Reading comprehension is selected for discussion because of the extended body of research in cognitive psychology and discourse analysis which can inform development of innovative assessments in this domain. The discussion again suggests how improving the construct validity of language proficiency tests benefits by linking the content of research theory and research findings to the design of test items and tests. Attention is also given to ways in which theory and research can help identify performance measures for reading comprehension skills not assessed by current tests of reading proficiency in a second language.

INSIGHTS FROM COMPREHENSION RESEARCH

There is a large body of cognitive research on reading which is of potential value for designing improved assessment of reading skills among non-English and native English students. It is fair to state, however, that the application of research findings to the improvement of reading assessment has been slow to develop despite the fact that there are many possible starting points. For example, it is well known that readers who are faster and most accurate in their text comprehension are also readers who concentrate on extracting the meaning of texts. These readers are also more likely to be more accurate and efficient in the decoding of individual words in a text than poor readers. Poor readers spend more attention than good readers in trying to recognize and understand individual words and syntactical structures underlying sentences.

Thus, one possible avenue for new reading comprehension assessment research, might be to design assessments of the word-decoding and sentence recognition efficiency of readers from a non-English background. While tests of second-language vocabulary and sentence understanding exist, they are not designed to assess the degree to which examinees have automated the skills in question. A theoretical basis for the pursuit of this latter work could be adapted from psycholinguistic research on monolinguals such as that by Frederiksen, Warren, and Rosebery (1985a, b), which combines assessment of word-decoding and sentence recognition skills with the training of these same skills. Similar research without the training component, but with bilingual subjects has been pursued by Chang (1984) and Durán (1985). All of these investigators rely on information-processing models of word-decoding and sentence recognition processes and they examine variation in speed and accuracy of performance as a function of explicit manipulations in the tasks presented subjects. The findings of the bilingual research indicate that subjects process information less quickly, but with similar levels of accuracy in the less familiar language versus the more familiar language. For simple language-processing tasks, there are no differences in the underlying strategies which subjects use in performing tasks in one language versus another; the primary effect is that performance is slower in the less proficient language. As we have mentioned, however, formal tests of English language proficiency for everyday use have not been developed based on this or similar research. This remains a possibility for the future.

Another possibility close to implementation is the use of individualized computer administered reading training exercises designed to improve word decoding skills. Frederiksen (1987) has demonstrated that it is possible to enhance automation and accuracy of word decoding skills in bilinguals' second language using such procedures. This work is of fundamental importance because it suggests that word decoding skills share some common and some uncommon cognitive components across two language systems, and, hence, that reading skills assessments and training exercises should take these similarities and differences into account.

As an alternative to a focus on word decoding and sentence recognition skills, however, it is also possible to consider research on innovative assessment of reading skills at higher levels of reasoning and semantic processing which are related to the discourse and strategic competence skills of students in English. Cognitive research on the topic of comprehension monitoring helps illustrate this possibility. Research in this area is concerned with understanding readers' self-awareness of reading as an activity, and further, with understanding how readers regulate their reading behavior as they go about interpreting a text. Comprehension monitoring is a form of metacognition; it involves awareness and strategic thinking about the reading process itself. At present we have just begun to devise ways to assess the occurrence of comprehension-monitoring skills among students functioning in a second language. This line of investigation would seem especially productive given current theories of second-language skills acquisition and metacognitive functioning (Bialystok & Ryan, 1985; McLaughlin, Rossman, & McLeod, 1983).

Brown, Armbruster, and Baker (1986) presented a comprehensive review of research in the area as it pertains to students' reading for the purpose of studying. The concerns they raise are relevant to characterizing students' reading of academic materials in a second language though they themselves only addressed research on monolinguals. They noted four major classes of variables affecting the conduct of reading:

- *Text*. The features of reading materials that influence comprehension and memory (e.g., difficulty, clarity, structure).
- *Task*. The requirements of various tasks and purposes of reading that learners commonly encounter in schools.
- *Strategies*. The activities learners engage in to understand and remember information from the text.

- *Learner characteristics.* Characteristics such as ability, familiarity with the material, motivation, and other personal attributes and states that influence learning. (p.51)

Experimental research in the area investigates how variations in some small subset of factors is related to performance measures of reading and studying while holding constant or controlling for the influence of some of the other remaining variables. Such a constraint would also seem to be required if we were to attempt assessing the comprehension monitoring skills of non-English background students reading and studying in English. Further discussion of the dichotomy between text and task, on the one hand, and strategies and learner characteristics, on the other hand, is helpful in identifying ways in which useful comprehension constructs might be developed for assessment purposes.

As Brown and collaborators note, the variables we have outlined are interactive. Given a text and task, readers elect certain reading strategies and not others, and in turn, preference and enactment of strategies is affected by the characteristics of the learner. *Text* and *task* are in some sense independent of the individual student; they arise as embodiments of the instructional process which students encounter. In most instructional assignment requiring use of a text, the critical issue is whether students can arrive at a suitable cognitive representation of *text* and *task* for the purpose of completing assignments. Students' attempts to construct the appropriate representations of *text* and *task* are a function of a second set of variables—their *learner characteristics* and available *strategies* for the conduct of reading. Students' discourse competence and strategic competence in reading are critical to comprehension monitoring as it arises in carrying out assignments. As they go about an assignment, students must utilize their knowledge of discourse conventions, coupled with flexible reading strategies, in order to work back and forth between the stated information in a text, their perceptions of the requirements of the assignment, and their evaluation of progress in completing the assignment in question.

One new direction for language assessment suggested by these concerns is to measure how well students can understand various layers of meaning conveyed by English-language text, going from the individual word level up through the meaning of a passage as whole. Fillmore (1983), Kay (1987), and Langer (1987) have conducted relevant research on monolingual children's ability to understand the text of reading-comprehension test items, given the need to answer questions based on items. Their approach can be extended to assess second language learners' ability to understand text passages.

Fillmore and Kay postulated that comprehension of texts occurs at different "envisionment levels" representing an "ideal reader's" ability to derive different levels of understanding of a text passage. These envisionment levels are based on the "ideal reader's" analysis of the lexical, syntactical, and discourse features of a text and use of different reasoning strategies applied to this information. In projects under way at UCSB, Susan Goldman and I have adopted and slightly expanded this notion of envisionment levels so that it is useful for research on the academic reading skills of non-English background college students. The envisionment levels used in this work to characterize students' depth of comprehension are:

Envisionment Level	Comprehension and Reasoning
Level A	Understands isolated words signaling concepts and is capable of drawing on this knowledge in performing reasoning exercises.
Level B	Understands the meaning expressed by individual, isolated sentences and is capable of using this knowledge in performing reasoning exercises.
Level C	Can understand explicitly signaled or invited interrelationships between meanings expressed in different sentences. Can perform on reasoning exercises on this basis.
Level D	Can derive an envisionment of a specific situation or set of facts referred to by a text. In performing reasoning exercises can draw on knowledge derived from this envisionment as well as from information conveyed by interrelated or isolated sentences.
Level E	Can reason hypothetically on the basis of information derived at other levels of comprehension. Capable of understanding principles alluded to by a text and capable of reasoning about how principles might apply to situations beyond the situation described by the source text.

Goldman and I are investigating students' ability to answer questions about academic text passages designed to require different levels of envisionment on the part of students. Early findings from this work suggest that second language students' ability to answer questions are indeed sensitive to their depth of comprehension of a text. These early results suggest that envisionment-level analyses of text passages might prove useful in designing new kinds of reading assessment items tapping non-English background students' comprehension skills.

Appropriately designed items and questions could provide diagnostic information on students' reading comprehension ability. The envisionment-levels account is appealing because it is suggestive of an ordinal scaling of individuals' abilities to derive meaning in working questions based on a text. Students' ability to comprehend information appropriately at higher envisionment levels requires adequate comprehension of information at lower envisionment levels. Thus, it should be possible to design reading test items so that each item assesses examinees' ability to attain a target envisionment level. Over a collection of items it might be possible to derive measures representing examinees' propensity to read at each envisionment level, and to come up with a measure of examinees' maximal level of envisionment in given academic reading domain.

It is worthwhile to note that a test of reading comprehension exists which assesses constructs related to comprehension as conceived of in the envisionment-level approach. The Degrees of Reading Power Test (College Entrance Examination Board, 1981) utilizes a cloze-reading technique and it assesses students' ability to read texts at different levels of difficulty based on readability analysis of text characteristics. The cloze assessment technique requires examinees to fill in missing words in a target text based on multiple-choice options. The test can be administered for diagnostic purposes. Passages of varying levels can be administered examinees, and the scores on passages are scaled so that they can be interpreted to indicate the extent to which examinees can work assignments independently or with aid, given the difficulty level of texts. The Degrees of Reading Power Test can be used with examinees whose proficiency in English is limited, though validity research on this population would be essential as a complement to existing construct and predictive validity research on monolingual students.

The envisionment level characterization of reading just described differs from that of the Degrees of Reading Power approach in that the former, if implemented as an assessment, would require a more detailed and qualitative semantic and syntactical analysis of the texts used for assessment purposes. Freeman (1987) provides a detailed linguistic analysis of limitations inherent in use of readability formulas to characterize the comprehension requirements of texts used in the Degrees of Reading Power Test. Her criticisms do not weaken the grounds for use of the test, but they do point to the value of more detailed analysis of reading skills in developing assessments of students' reading comprehension skills. As an alternative, the envisionment-level approach to an assessment would have the potential of providing highly detailed diagnostic information on the particular kinds of vocabulary, syntactical structures, and discourse structures which prove problematic to students functioning at various levels of envisionment. Detailed information of this sort could be of considerable value in devising instructional interventions aimed at developing students' English language skills.

The envisionment-level account of comprehension merges nicely with another theoretical account of comprehension monitoring set forth by Collins and Smith (1982) who suggested additional reading comprehension behaviors which might be assessed but which are not currently assessed by reading comprehension tests.

Collins and Smith described different kinds of comprehension failure which readers encounter and the ensuing strategies that readers may undertake in order to compensate for the comprehension failure they encounter. Four kinds of comprehension failure were distinguished:

- Failure to understand a word in context.
- Failure to understand a sentence with adequate precision.
- Failure to understand how one sentence relates to another.
- Failure to understand how the whole text fits together. (pp. 175–176)

It is interesting to note that there is some correspondence between these points of comprehension failure and the levels of comprehension envisionment described previously. In essence each type of comprehension failure would make it difficult for readers to attain a corresponding level of envisionment. In the face of comprehension failure Collins and Smith suggested that readers might:

- Ignore an uncomprehended word, sentence, or relationship and read on;
- Suspend judgment about what a word or sentence or a relationship means;
- Form a tentative hypothesis about the meaning of a word, sentence, or relationship;
- Reread the current sentence or sentences;
- Reread the previous context leading to the current material;
- Go to an expert source to resolve an uncomprehended element.

Collins and Smith reported that research on the study skills of college students by others such as Baker (1979) indicated that students actually engage in the strategies listed. Further they suggested that the order in which the strategies are listed corresponds roughly to the degree to which they might disrupt reading behavior. The strategies listed earlier are thought to be less disruptive to maintaining the immediate flow of meaning derived from a text.

The overview of comprehension monitoring provided by Collins and Smith suggests several possibilities for the design of new reading assessments concerned with examinees' communicative competence in reading. First, one may ask: Can we devise assessments to detect the linguistic and discourse features underlying students' comprehension failures? A second and related question is: Can we devise assessments of different strategies which students undertake when they encounter comprehension failure? The answers to both of these questions is a qualified "yes." The next section on linguistic descriptions of discourse structure suggests some of the complexities of this undertaking and it helps make clear how the design of innovative reading test items can benefit from linguistic analyses of the structure of academic reading texts.

INSIGHTS FROM DISCOURSE ANALYSIS

Recent theoretical models of discourse structure by Quirk, Greenbaum, Leech, and Svartvik (1985), Celce–Murcia and Larsen–Freeman (1983), and Brown and Yule (1983) help identify numerous language structures beyond the word and single sentence level which learners of English must acquire in order to become proficient users of the language. The communicative competence skills outlined in Appendix A are relevant to such accounts, but the appendix materials do not highlight the importance of some analytical skills over others. A good deal of further research is needed in order to discern how the features of a text invite or signal particular meanings for a reader.

Most academic text passages (and passages in reading-test item stems) can be interpreted as performing a basic referential function. That is, their purpose is to convey information on some topic under the assumption that readers don't already know all of the information in question. Accordingly, texts of this sort follow grammatical and stylistic conventions in English that help readers detect the introduction of background information, introduction of new topics, development of topics, and interconnections among topics. Authors also insert additional information regarding the epistemic status of the information being reported, for example, whether a stated claim is a fact versus a conjecture, or whether other qualifications are in order in interpreting claims. In addition, authors might allude to examples of everyday experiences, or to information in tables and figures to help make discussion concrete. These and other kinds of information in texts must be detected by readers and their occurrence must be properly understood in light of the main flow of topics under development in the text.

The linguistic signals guiding interpretation of text at these higher levels is not always obvious; detection of the signals can require intensive familiarity with English and with ways in which the syntax and semantics of sentences can invite comprehension of nuances and shades of meaning. Consider, for example, the interpretation of the following two juxtaposed sentences taken from the research of Mann and Thompson (1986) on relational propositions in discourse:

This book claims to be a guide to all the trees of Indiana. It's so incomplete that it doesn't even have oak trees in it.

Good readers encountering these sentences in a book review would be able to sense how the word "claims" in the first sentence followed by the use of negative terms "so incomplete" and "doesn't even have" in the second sentence convey the author's message that the book in question is suspect as a reference about trees.

Obviously, designing innovative tests of readers' comprehension difficulties while reading texts on-line is a complex matter. In order to create such assessments it would seem necessary to query readers directly about the occurrence of such difficulties, to analyze the linguistic knowledge which is required to resolve such difficulties, and to interpret the significance of comprehension failures in light of examinees' ability to resolve meaning at various envisionment levels. While we have a long way to go toward this goal it is possible to suggest preliminary assessment research. One tactic might be to devise reading assessment methods which would ask examinees questions about their difficulties in answering reading comprehension items and about the strategies they undertook to answer reading test items in light of the difficulties they encountered.

SUMMARY

While this chapter has focused on improving language proficiency assessment the general line of argument pursued has implications for research on test validity at large. First and foremost, it suggests that improvements in the construct validity of tests (and hence on what it is they measure) should take serious advantage of theory and research in the performance domains in question. Theory and research findings can help extend and clarify constructs which are desirable to assess, but which may not be well developed within existing assessment approaches. In the context of this chapter, for example, the notion of communicative competence was examined as a way to expand and improve the account of important language skills which second language learners must acquire and which merit assessment. A related question concerns the extent to which current methods of assessment may constrain attainment of new constructs which would be valuable to measure.

This chapter also called attention to ways in which research from different disciplines might be integrated in the pursuit of new constructs and measures. Specifically, we have integrated viewpoints from language-testing research, cognitive psychology research, and linguistics research, offering insights on improvements which might be made in the design of language proficiency tests. It is possible to overcome differences in the conceptual perspectives of different disciplines to arrive at fresh insights regarding new assessments, though this effort requires a reasonable level of consistency across disciplinary perspectives on the fundamental constructs meriting analysis and research. This congruence was achieved, in large part, by replacing the notion of language proficiency by the notion of communicative competence as the focus of assessment.

As a final note, it is obvious that attempts to reconceptualize radically assessment such as we have suggested are inherently long-term programs of work susceptible to failure as well as to success. The optimistic side of this common-sense conclusion is that there is a cumulative history to testing research which records the evolution of attempts to improve and expand the validity of tests. Spolsky (1979, 1981), among others, has documented this evolution and there is little question but that it suggests a movement toward integrating research on language use in everyday contexts with the design of new language assessment procedures capturing more complex language and communication skills. What is most fascinating and new is a trend for cognitive psychology research to become merged with research on complex language usage. It is this merger which portends some of the most interesting and innovative suggestions for new forms of language skills assessment.

REFERENCES

Alderman, D. (1982). Language proficiency as a moderator variable in testing academic aptitude. *Journal of Educational Psychology, 74*(4), 580–587.

American Psychological Association. (1985). *Standards for educational and psychological testing.* Washington, DC.

Bachman, L., & Palmer, A. (in press). Fundamental considerations in the measurement of language abilities. Reading, MA: Addison–Wesley.

Baker, L. (1979). *Comprehension monitoring: Identifying and coping with text confusions* (Tech. Rep. No. 145). Urbana, IL: University of Illinois, Center for the Study of Reading.

Bejar, I. (1984). Educational diagnostic assessment. *Journal of Educational Measurement, 21*(2), 175–189.

Bialystok, E., & Ryan, E. B. (1985). A metacognitive framework for the development of first and second language skills. In D. L. Forrest-Pressley, G. E. MacKinnon, & T. Gary Waller (Eds.), *Metacognition, cognition, and human performance: Vol. 1. Theoretical perspectives.* Orlando, FL: Academic Press.

Bloom, D., & Green, J. (1984). Directions in the sociolinguistic study of reading. In P. D. Pearson (Ed.), *Handbook of reading research* (pp. 395–422). New York: Longman.

Brown, A. L., Armbruster, B. B., & Baker, L. (1986). The role of metacognition in reading and studying. In J. Orasanu (Ed.), *Reading comprehension: From research to practice* (pp. 49–76). Hillsdale, NJ: Lawrence Erlbaum Associates.

Brown, G., & Yule, G. (1983). *Discourse analysis.* New York: Cambridge University Press.

Canale, M. (1983). From communicative competence to communicative language pedagogy. In J. C. Richards & R. Schmidt (Eds.), *Language and communication.* London: Longman.

Canale, M., & Swain, M. (1980). Theoretical bases of communicative approaches to second language teaching and testing. *Applied Linguistics, 1,* 1–47.

Celce–Murcia, M., & Larsen–Freeman, D. (1983). *The grammar book: An ESL/EFL teacher's course.* Rowley, MA: Newbury House.

Chang, F. R. (1984). *Reading and listening processes in bilinguals.* San Diego, CA: Navy Personnel Research and Development Center.

Clark, J. L. D. (Ed.). (1978). *Direct testing of speaking proficiency.* Princeton, NJ: Educational Testing Service.

Cohen, A. D. (1984). On taking language tests: What the students report. In A. Hughes & D. Porter (Eds.), *Language Testing, 1*(1), 70–81.

College Entrance Examination Board. (1981). *Degrees of reading power brings the students and the text together.* New York.

Collins, A., & Smith, E. E. (1982). Teaching the process of reading comprehension. In D. K. Detterman & R. J. Sternberg (Eds.), *How and how much can intelligence be increased* (pp. 173–186). Norwood, NJ: Ablex.

Durán, R. P. (1985). Influences of language skills on bilinguals' problem solving. In S. F. Chipman, J. W. Segal, & R. Glaser (Eds.), *Thinking and Learning Skills: Vol. 2. Research and open questions.* (pp. 187–207). Hillsdale, NJ: Lawrence Erlbaum Associates.

Durán, R. P. (in press, a). Metacognition in second language behavior. To appear in J. Langer (Ed.), *Language, literacy, and culture: Issues of society and schooling.* Norwood, NJ: Ablex.

Durán, R. P. (in press, b). Testing of linguistic minorities. In R. Linn (Ed.), *Educational Measurement* (3rd ed.). New York: Macmillan.

Durán, R. P., Canale, M., Penfield, J., Stansfield, C. W., & Liskin–Gasparro, J. E. (1985). *TOEFL from a communicative viewpoint on language proficiency: A working paper.* (Research Report No. 85–8) Princeton, NJ: Educational Testing Service.

Fillmore, C. J. (1983). *Ideal readers and real readers.* (Berkeley Cognitive Science Report No. 5). Berkeley, CA: Cognitive Science Program, Institute of Human Learning.

Frederiksen, J. R. (1987). *Final Report on the Development of Computer-based Instructional Systems for Training Essential Components of Reading.* BBN Laboratories, Report No. 6465, Cambridge, MA: Bolt Beranek and Newman.

Frederiksen, J. R., Warren, B. M., & Rosebery, A. S. (1985a). A componential approach to training reading skills (Pt. 1): Perceptual Units training. *Cognition and Instruction, 2*(2), 91–130.

Frederiksen, J. R., Warren, B. M., & Rosebery, A. S. (1985b). A componential approach to training reading skills (Pt. 2): Decoding and use of context. *Cognition and Instruction, 2*(3, 4), 175–205.

Frederiksen, N., Jensen, O., & Beaton, A. E. (1972). *Prediction of organizational behavior.* New York: Pergamon.

Frederiksen, N., & Ward, W. C. (1978). Measures for the study of creativity in scientific problem solving. *Applied Psychological Measurement, 2,* 1–24.

Freeman, D. (1987). A study of the degrees of reading power test. In R. Freedle & R. Durán (Eds.)., *Cognitive and linguistic analyses of test performance.* (pp. 245–297). Norwood, NJ: Ablex.

Glaser, R. (1985). The integration of instruction and testing. *Proceedings of the 46th ETS Invitational Conference* (pp. 45–58). Princeton, NJ: Educational Testing Service.

Interagency Language Roundtable (1983). Interagency Language Roundtable Language Skill Level Descriptions. Washington, DC.

Kay, P. (1987). Three properties of the ideal reader. In R. Freedle & R. P. Durán (Eds.), *Cognitive and linguistics analyses of test performance.* (pp. 208–224). Norwood, NJ: Ablex.

Langer, J. A. (1987). The construction of meaning and the assessment of comprehension: Analysis of reader performance on standardized test items. In R. Freedle & R. Durán (Eds)., *Cognitive and linguistic analyses of test performance.* (pp. 225–244). Norwood, NJ: Ablex.

Lowe, P., Jr. (1981). The essential elements in training oral interviewers. Central Intelligence Agency Language School. Paper presented at the Interagency Language Roundtable Presession to the Georgetown University Roundtable on Linguistics, March 1981, Washington, DC.

Mann, W. C., & Thompson, S. A. (1986). Relational propositions in discourse. *Discourse Processes, 9,* 57–90.

McLaughlin, B., Rossman, T., & McLeod, B. (1983). Second language learning: An information-processing perspective. *Language Learning, 33,*(2), 135–158.

Oller, J. W., Jr. (1979). *Language tests in school.* London: Longman Group.

Pellegrino, J. W. (this volume and 1986, October). *Mental models and mental tests.* Final draft of a paper presented at the conference on Test Validity for the 1990s and Beyond, held at the Educational Testing Service, Princeton, NJ.

Quirk, R., Greenbaum, S., Leech, G., & Svartvik, J. (1985). *A comprehensive grammar of the English language.* New York: Longman.

Rivera, C. (Ed.). (1984). *Communicative competence approaches to language proficiency assessment: Research and application.* Clevedon, England: Multilingual Matters.

Spolsky, B. (1979). Linguistics and language testers. In B. Spolsky (Ed.), *Advances in language testing* (Vol. 1). Washington, DC: Center for Applied Linguistics.

Spolsky, B. (1981). Some ethical questions about language testing. In C. Klein–Braley & D. K. Stevenson (Eds.), *Practice and problems in language testing*, Bern: Peter D. Lang.

Spolsky, B. (1985). What does it mean to know how to use a language? An essay on the theoretical basis of language testing. In A. Hughes & D. Porter (Eds.), *Language Testing*, (pp. 180–191). London: Edward Arnold.

APPENDIX A

General Outline of Communication Skills

COMPETENCE AREA	RELEVANT MODE(S)
A. *Grammatical competence*	
1. *Pronunciation:*	
1.1. Lexical items in connected speech (at normal rate of speech)	L, S, R (oral)
1.2. Modifications to normal pronunciation of lexical items at word boundaries (e.g., liaison and elision) and in unstressed syllables (e.g., vowel and consonant reduction)	L, S
1.3. Normal word stress in connected speech	L, S, R (oral)
1.4. Emphatic or contrastive word stress (e.g., *Mary is happy but Paul is unhappy.*)	L, S. R (oral)
1.5. Normal intonation patterns in connected speech (e.g., for imperatives, interrogatives, etc.)	L, S
1.6. Emphatic of contrastive intonation patterns for different clause types (e.g., *He has arrived?* with rising intonation to signal an interrogative)	L, S. R (oral)
1.7. Normal pauses, loudness, and rate of speech	L, S
1.8. Modifications to normal pauses, loudness, and rate of speech for emphatic or contrastive purposes	L, S
2. *Orthography:*	
2.1. Graphemes (individually and in sequence)	R, W
2.2. Spelling (including capitalization and diacritics) for individual lexical items	R, W
2.3. Spelling of compounds (e.g., use of hyphens, as in *lion-like, level-headed* and *vice-president*)	R, W
2.4. Spelling of contractions (e.g., *can't*)	R, W
2.5. Spelling of abbreviations (e.g., *cont'd.*)	R, W

2.6. Spelling of possessive noun forms (e.g., *John's*) R, W
2.7. Common punctuation conventions (e.g., capitalization at beginning of a sentence and use of commas, quotes, etc.) R, W
2.8. Conventions for marking emphasis (e.g., underlining, italics, boldface type, capitalization) R, W

3. *Vocabulary:*

3.1. Literal meaning of common content words, in context, related to academic and social topics L, S, R, W
3.2. Literal meaning of common function words in context (e.g., prepositions, articles) L, S, R, W
3.3. Meaning of idioms and formulaic expressions in context (e.g., *That test was her Little Big Horn; Take care!*) L, W, S, R, W
3.4. Extended or figurative meaning of words in context (e.g., metaphorical uses of words as in *Marriage is a business partnership*) L, S, R, W
3.5. Synonyms, antonyms, and homonyms of common content words in context L, S, R, W

4. *Word formation:*

4.1. Inflection, in context, of nouns for number L, S, R, W
4.2. Inflection, in context, of demonstrative and possessive adjective for number L, S, R, W
4.3. Inflection, in context, of verbs for person, number and tense L, S, R, W
4.4. Agreement, in context, of pronouns with nouns L, S, R, W
4.5. Agreement, in context, of demonstrative and possesive adjectives with nouns and pronouns L, S, R, W
4.6. Agreement, in context, of nouns and pronouns with verbs (person and number for verbs, case for pronouns) L, S, R, W
4.7. Derivational relationships (e.g., among *attacker* and *attack* as a verb or noun) in context L, S, R, W
4.8. Variation at word boundaries in context (e.g., *a* and *an*) L, S, R, W

5. *Sentence formation:*

5.1. Basic form of common sentence and subsentence structures, in context, relevant to academic and

social language-use situation (e.g., subject–verb–
complement word order for a simple declarative
sentence)   L, S, R, W

5.2. Literal meaning of a sentence having a given
structure (with vocabulary), in context   L, S, R, W

B. *Sociolinguistic competence*

1. In academic and social situations that vary according to sociolinguistic variables, such as number and
status of participants (e.g., peers, strangers, au-
thorities), setting (e.g., formal/informal, pub-
lic/private, familiar/unfamiliar), channel (e.g.,
face-to-face, radio, letter, telephone), purpose
(e.g., routine/unusual, open-ended/fixed) and
amount of shared information:

1.1. Grammatical forms (e.g., pronunciation, etc.) appropriate for different communicative functions,
such as supplying or requesting information, per-
suading, seeking approval, inviting, promising,
complaining, socializing   L, S, R, W

1.2. Formulaic expressions appropriate for different
communicative functions (e.g., *Hello/Goodbye*
on the telephone rather than in written commu-
nication)   L, S, R, W

1.3. Appropriate grammatical forms for signaling attitudes (e.g., politeness, sincerity, empathy, cer-
tainty, anger)   L, S, R, W

1.4. Grammatical forms as indicators of social and
geographical background (e.g., dialect features)   L, S, R, W

C. *Discourse competence*

1. Cohesion in genres of discourse relevant to academic and social language use:

1.1. Lexical cohesion devices for:
conciseness: e.g., pronouns, synonyms
continuity: e.g., repetition of a vocabulary item
transition: e.g., logical connectors such as *however*
emphasis: e.g., choice of unexpected vocabulary   L, S, R, W

1.2. Grammatical cohesion devices for:
conciseness: e.g., ellipsis
continuity: e.g., parallel structures, lists

transition: e.g., transitional sentences to introduce ideas

emphasis: e.g., focusing structures, such as *What is needed is* . . .   L, S, R, W

2. Coherence in genres of discourse relevant to academic and social language use:

2.1. Conversational discourse patterns: turn-taking rules (as in a telephone conversation)   L, S

2.2. conversational discourse patterns: acceptable organization of ideas (literal meanings and communicative functions) in conversation in terms of:

development: e.g., sequencing and direction of ideas

continuity: e.g., relevance and consistency of ideas

balance: e.g., treatment of main vs. supporting ideas

completeness: e.g., thorough discussion of a topic   L, S, R, W

2.3. nonconversational discourse patterns: acceptable organization of ideas (literal meanings and communicative functions) in terms of:

development
continuity
balance
completeness   L, S, R, W

3. Transposing information in nonverbal/graphic form to and from oral and written discourse (e.g., diagrams, graphs, and tables)   L, S, R, W

D. *Strategic competences*

1. *Compensatory strategies for grammatical difficulties:*

1.1. Reference books (e.g., dictionary, grammar book)   R, W

1.2. Reference centers (e.g., library, resource center), including use of index cards, knowledge of Dewey decimal system   R, W

1.3. Phonetic spelling as a guide to pronunciation (e.g., International Phonetic Alphabet)   S, R

1.4. Grammatical and lexical paraphrase (e.g., use of general vocabulary items such as *place, person, thing, way* followed by a descriptive phrase; use of structures such as *ask someone—infinitive* rather than *demand that—subjunctive*)   L, S, R, W

1.5. Form of requests for repetition, clarification, or slower speech   L, S

1.6. Use of nonverbal symbols (e.g., gestures, drawings)   L, S, R, W

1.7. Use of contextual clues for inferences about literal meaning of unfamiliar vocabulary and structures   L, S, R

1.8. Use of word formation rules to draw inferences about literal meaning of unfamiliar vocabulary and structures (e.g., coinage of *fish-house* to express *aquarium*)   L, S, R, W

1.9. Other (e.g., avoidance of unfamiliar topics, memorization of certain verbal repertoires)   L, S, R, W

2. *Compensatory strategies for sociolinguistic difficulties:*

2.1. Single grammatical form for different communicative functions (e.g., a declarative, such as *Dinner is at 5 o'clock* with varying intonation to signal a statement, a question, a promise, an order, an invitation—all depending on sociolinguistic context)   L, S, R, W

2.2. Use of sociolinguistically neutral grammatical forms when uncertain about appropriateness of other forms in a given sociolinguistic context (e.g., in meeting someone, omission of the person's name if unsure about using his or her first name, versus title)   S, W

2.3. Use of first language knowledge about appropriateness of grammatical forms or communicative functions in a given sociolinguistic context   L, S, R, W

2.4. Use of contextual clues for inferences about social meaning (communicative function, etc.) in unfamiliar sociolinguistic situations or when unfamiliar grammatical forms are used   L, S, R

3. *Compensatory strategies for discourse difficulties:*

3.1. Use of nonverbal symbols or of emphatic stress
    and intonation to indicate cohesion and coherence
    (e.g., use of drawings to indicate sequencing of
    actions/ideas)   L, S, R, W
3.2. Use of first language knowledge about oral/writ-
    ten discourse patterns when uncertain about such
    aspects of discourse in second language   L, S, R, W
3.3. Use of contextual clues for inferences about
    patterning of literal and social meanings in un-
    familiar discourse   L, S, R, W

4. *Compensatory strategies for performance
limitations:*

4.1. Coping with background noise, interruptions, fre-
    quent changes in topic/interlocutors, and other
    distractions   L, S, R, W
4.2. Use of pause fillers (e.g., *well, you know, my,
    my*) to maintain one's turn in conversation while
    searching for ideas or grammatical forms or
    while monitoring them)   L, S

5. *Rhetorical enhancement strategies (noncompensato-
ry):*

5.1. In oral and written discourse, use of structures
    and vocabulary for special effect (e.g., use of
    adverbial phrase preposing, as in *Out of the
    woods came . . .*)   L, S, R, W
5.2. In oral discourse, use of slow, soft, deliberate
    speech for special effect   L, S
5.3. In oral and written discourse, use of literary
    devices (sentence rhythm, alliteration, literary
    references)   L, S, R, W

Chapter 9

Differential Item Performance and the Mantel–Haenszel Procedure

Paul W. Holland
Dorothy T. Thayer
Research Statistics Group
Educational Testing Service

The Mantel-Haenszel procedure is a noniterative contingency table method for estimating and testing a common two-factor association parameter in a $2 \times 2 \times K$ table. As such it may be used to study "item bias," or differential item functioning, in two groups of examinees. This technique is discussed in this context and compared to other related techniques as well as to item response theory methods.

INTRODUCTION AND NOTATION

Holland (1985) proposed the use of the Mantel–Haenszel procedure as a practical and powerful way to detect test items that function differently in two groups of examinees. In this chapter we show how this use of the Mantel–Haenszel (MH) procedure is a natural outgrowth of the previously suggested chi-square procedures of Scheuneman (1979), Marascuilo and Slaughter (1981), Mellenbergh (1982), and others and we show how the MH procedure relates to methods based on item response theory (Lord, 1980).

The study of items that function differently for two groups of examinees has a long history. Originally called "item bias" research, modern approaches focus on the fact that different groups of examinees may react differently to the same test question. These differences are worth exploring since they may shed light both on the test question and on the experiences and backgrounds of the different groups of examinees. We prefer the more neutral terms, differential item performance or *differential item functioning*, (i.e., *dif*), to item bias since in many examples of items that exhibit *dif* the term "bias" does not accurately describe the situation. Early work at ETS on *dif* began with Cardall and Coffman (1964) and Angoff and Ford (1973). The book by Berk (1982) summarizes research to 1980.

The following notational scheme and terminology is used in the rest of this chapter. We will always be comparing two groups of examinees, of which the performance of one, *the focal group,* F, is of primary interest. The performance of the other group, *the reference group,* R, is taken as a standard against which we will compare the performance of the focal group. For example, the focal group might be all black examinees, while the reference group might consist of the white examinees. Typically, all test items in a given testing instrument will be analyzed for evidence of *dif,* and this will be done one item at a time. We will refer to the *item* that is being examined for evidence of *dif* in a given analysis as the *studied item.*

Basic to all modern approaches to the study of *dif* is the notion of comparing only *comparable members* of F and R in attempting to identify items that exhibit *dif.* Comparability means identity in those measured characteristics in which examinees may differ and that are strongly related to performance on the studied item. Important among the criteria used to define comparability are (a) measures of the ability for which the item is designed, (b) schooling or other measures of relevant experience, and (c) membership in other groups. In practice, the matching criteria will usually include test scores, since these are available, accurately measured, and usually measure the same ability as the studied item.

If both examinee ability and item characteristics are confounded by simply measuring the difference in the performance of an item between unmatched reference and focal group members, the result is a measure of *impact* rather than of differential item performance. For example, comparing the proportion of reference and focal group members who give correct answers to a given item is a measure of the item's impact on the focal group relative to the reference group. In this chapter we do not discuss impact, since the confounding of differences in examinee ability with characteristics of items is of little utility in attempting to identify items that may truly disadvantage some subpopulations of examinees.

Suppose that criteria for matching have been selected, then the data for the studied item for the examinees in R and F may be arranged into a series of 2×2 tables; one such table for each matched set of reference and focal group members. The data for the performance of the jth matched set on the studied item is displayed:

TABLE 9.1
Data for the jth Matched Set of Members
of *R* and *F*

		Score on Studied Item		
		1	*0*	*Total*
Group	R	A_j	B_j	n_{Rj}
	F	C_j	D_j	n_{Fj}
	Total	m_{1j}	m_{0j}	T_j

In Table 9.1, T_j is the total number of reference and focal group members in the jth matched set; n_{Rj} is the number of these who are in R; *and of these A_j* answered the studied item correctly. The other entries in Table 9.1 have similar definitions.

In order to state statistical hypotheses precisely, it is necessary to have a sampling model for the data in Table 9.1. It is customary to act as though the values of the marginal totals, n_{Rj} and n_{Fj}, are fixed and to regard the data for R and F as having arisen as random samples of size n_{Rj} and n_{Fj} from large matched pools of reference and focal group members. It follows that A_j and C_j are independent binomial variates with parameters (n_{Rj}, p_{Rj}) and (n_{Fj}, p_{Fj}), respectively. These population values can be arranged as a 2×2 table that is parallel to Table 9.1, i.e.:

TABLE 9.2
Population Parameters for Data from the jth
Matched Set

		Score on Studied Item		
		1	0	Total
Group	R	p_{Rj}	q_{Rj}	1
	F	p_{Fj}	q_{Fj}	1

The hypothesis of no *dif* corresponds to the null hypothesis.

$$H_O : p_{Rj} = p_{Fj} \text{ for all } j.$$

The hypothesis, H_O, is also the hypothesis of conditional independence of group membership and the score on the studied item, given the matching variable (Bishop, Fienberg, & Holland, 1975).

Under H_O, the "expected values" for the cell entries of Table 9.1 are well known to be obtained by the "product of margins over total" rule and are summarized:

$$E(A_j) = n_{Rj} m_{1j}/T_j \qquad E(C_j) = n_{Fj} m_{1j}/T_j$$

$$E(B_j) = n_{Rj} m_{0j}/T_j \qquad E(D_j) = n_{Fj} m_{0j}/T_j. \qquad (1)$$

All of these "expected values" are really *conditional expectations*, given n_{Rj}, n_{Fj}, m_{1j}, m_{0j}.

PREVIOUS CHI-SQUARE PROCEDURES

Scheuneman (1979) proposed a procedure to test the hypothesis, H_O, utilizing a specific type of matching criterion. Let S denote a score on a criterion test—e.g., an operational test score that may or may not include the studied item. The values of S are categorized into a few intervals. Scheuneman suggests that three to five intervals are satisfactory. The matched groups are defined by the categorized values of S so that members of R and F are considered matched if their scores on S fall into the same score interval. In terms of the notation of Sec. 1, the test statistic proposed by Scheuneman is given by

$$\text{SCHEUN} = \sum_{j=1}^{K} \left[\frac{(A_j - E(A_j))^2}{E(A_j)} + \frac{(C_j - E(C_j))^2}{E(C_j)} \right].$$ (2)

which is algebraically equal to

$$\text{SCHEUN} = \sum_{j=1}^{K} \left[\frac{(A_j - E(A_j))^2}{n_{Rj}\, n_{Fj}\, m_{1j}/T_j} \right].$$

It was originally thought that SCHEUN had an approximate chi-square distribution on $K - 1$ degrees of freedom when H_0 is true (Schueneman, 1979). This is not correct, as discussed in Baker (1981) and Scheuneman (1981). For example, under H_0, the expectation of SCHEUN, conditional on the four marginal values n_{Rj}, n_{Fj}, m_{1j}, m_{0j} in each 2×2 table, is given by

$$\text{E(SCHEUN)} = \sum_{j=1}^{K} \frac{m_{0j}}{(T_j - 1)}.$$ (3)

This value is sensitive to the total number of incorrect responses in each 2×2 table and can range from 0 up to K. If SCHEUN had an approximate chi-square distribution on K $-$ 1 degrees of freedom then the expected value in (3) would be approximately K $-$ 1 for any set of values of m_{0j}. Fortunately, a small correction to (2) does give the resulting statistic an approximate chi-square distribution under H_0. The corrected statistic is

$$\text{CHISQ-P} = \sum_{j=1}^{K} \frac{T_j}{m_{0j}} \left[\frac{(A_j - E(A_j))^2}{E(A_j)} + \frac{(C_j - E(C_j))^2}{E(C_j)} \right]$$ (4)

which can be shown to be algebraically identical to

$$\text{CHISQ-P} = \sum_{j=1}^{K} \left[\frac{(A_j - E(A_j))^2}{n_{Rj}\, n_{Fj}\, m_{0j}\, m_{1j}/T_j^3} \right].$$ (5)

This is well known to be the Pearson chi-square test statistic for testing H_0 and the proper degrees of freedom equals the number of matched groups, K, if the T_j are *all* large, Bishop, Fienberg, and Holland (1975). It is also called the "full" chi-square by some to distinguish it from SCHEUN.

The K 2×2 tables may be regarded as a single $2 \times 2 \times K$ table and the standard theory of log-linear models for three-way tables may be used to test H_0. This leads to the suggestion of Marascuilo and Slaughter (1981) and Mellenbergh (1982) to use the likelihood ratio chi-square statistics to test H_0 instead of (5).

The alternative hypothesis against which H_0 is tested by CHISQ-P (and its likelihood ratio versions) is simply the negation of H_0, i.e.,

$$\bar{H}_0 : p_{Rj} \neq p_{Fj} \text{ for some } j.$$

This is why CHISQ-P is a multi-degree of freedom chi-square test. It is not powerful against specific alternatives to H_0, but it will detect *any* such departure if the T_j are large enough. This fact leads to a tradeoff between bias and statistical power that is not well made, in our opinion, by procedures such as Scheuneman's or "methods 1, 2, 4, 5, and 6" of Marascuilo and Slaughter (1981). The tradeoff arises by the desire to increase the values of T_j in order to increase the power of the test. This degrades the quality of the matching (i.e., lumps together examinees whose scores are not equal) in order to increase the sample sizes in the matched groups, i.e., T_j. This is necessary in these procedures because of the goal of being able to detect *any* type of departure from H_0. An alternative approach, and one that we favor, is to reduce the types of alternatives to H_0 against which the test has good power and to concentrate this power into a few degrees of freedom that actually occur in test data. This occurs in Method 3 of Marascuilo and Slaughter (1981). Mellenbergh (1982) has moved in this direction by distinguishing "uniform" from "nonuniform bias." The MH procedure does this by concentrating on Mellenbergh's uniform bias and yet it does not degrade the quality of the matching. We will discuss this in the next section.

A separate problem with the chi-square procedures is that they are only *tests* of H_0 and do not produce a parametric measure of the amount of *dif* exhibited by the studied item. As is well known, tests will always reject the null hypothesis, provided that the relevant sample sizes are large enough. It is more informative to have a measure of the size of the departure of the data from H_0. The Mantel–Haenszel procedure, discussed next, provides such a measure.

THE MANTEL–HAENSZEL PROCEDURE

In their seminal paper, Mantel and Haenszel (1959) introduced a new procedure for the study of matched groups. The data are in the form of K 2×2 tables as in Table 9.1. They developed a chi-square test of H_0 against the specific alternative hypothesis

$$H_1 : \frac{p_{Rj}}{q_{Rj}} = \alpha \frac{p_{Fj}}{q_{Fj}} \qquad j = 1, \ldots, K \qquad (6)$$

for $\alpha \neq 1$. Note that $\alpha = 1$ corresponds to H_0, which can also be expressed as:

$$H_0 : \frac{p_{Rj}}{q_{Rj}} = \frac{p_{Fj}}{q_{Fj}} \qquad j = 1, \ldots, K. \tag{7}$$

The parameter α is called the common odds ratio in the K 2×2 tables because under H_1, the value of α is the odds ratio

$$\alpha = \frac{p_{Rj}}{q_{Rj}} \Big/ \frac{p_{Fj}}{q_{Fj}} = \frac{p_{Rj}\, q_{Fj}}{p_{Fj}\, q_{Rj}} \qquad \text{for all } j = 1, \ldots, K. \tag{8}$$

The Mantel–Haenszel (MH) chi-square test statistic is based on

$$\frac{\Sigma_j\, (A_j - \Sigma_i\, E(A_j))^2}{\Sigma_j\, \mathrm{Var}(A_j)} \tag{9}$$

where $E(A_j)$ is defined in (1) and

$$\mathrm{Var}(A_j) = \frac{n_{Rj}\, n_{Fj}\, m_{1j}\, m_{0j}}{T_j^2(T_j - 1)}. \tag{10}$$

The statistic in (9) is usually given a continuity correction to improve the accuracy of the chi-square percentage points as approximations to the observed significance levels. This has the form

$$\text{MH-CHISQ} = \frac{(|\, \Sigma_j\, A_j - \Sigma_j\, E(A_j)\, | - \tfrac{1}{2})^2}{\Sigma_j\, \mathrm{Var}(A_j)} \tag{11}$$

It may be shown, for example Birch (1964) or Cox (1970), that a test based on MH-CHISQ is the uniformly most powerful unbiased test of H_0 versus H_1. Hence no other test can have higher power somewhere in H_1 than the one based on MH-CHISQ unless the other test violates the size constraint on the null hypothesis or has lower power than the test's size somewhere else on H_1. Under H_0, MH-CHISQ has an approximate chi-square distribution with 1 degree of freedom. It corresponds to the single degree of freedom chi-square test given by Mellenbergh (1982) for testing no "bias" against the hypothesis of "uniform bias." It is not identical to the test proposed by Mellenbergh but in many practical situations they give virtually identical results even though Mellenbergh's proposal involves an iterative log linear model fitting process. The MH procedure is *not* iterative.

Mantel and Haenszel also provided an estimate of α, the common odds ratio across the 2×2 tables. Their estimator is given by

$$\hat{\alpha}_{MH} = \frac{\Sigma\, A_j\, D_j\, /T_j}{\Sigma\, B_j\, C_j/T_j}. \tag{12}$$

The odds ratio is on the scale of 0 to ∞ with $\alpha = 1$ playing the role of a null value of no *dif*. It is convenient to take logs of $\hat{\alpha}_{MH}$ to put it into a symmetrical scale in which 0 is the null value. Thus we have proposed that

$$\Delta_{MH} = -\frac{4}{1.7} \ln(\hat{\alpha}_{MH}) = -2.35 \ln(\hat{\alpha}_{MH}) \tag{13}$$

be used as a measure of the amount of *dif*. $\hat{\Delta}_{MH}$ has the interpretation of being a measure of *dif* in the scale of differences in item difficulty as measured in the ETS "delta scale," (Holland & Thayer, 1985).

When using $\hat{\alpha}_{MH}$ or $\hat{\Delta}_{MH}$ it is useful to have a simple interpretation of these values. The value of $\hat{\alpha}_{MH}$ is the average factor by which the odds that a member of R is correct on the studied item exceeds the corresponding odds for a *comparable* member of F. Values of $\hat{\alpha}_{MH}$ that exceed 1 correspond to items on which the reference group performed better on average than did comparable members of the focal group. The value of $\hat{\Delta}_{MH}$ is the average amount more difficult that a member of R found the studied item than did comparable members of F. Values of $\hat{\Delta}_{MH}$ that are negative correspond to items that the reference group found easier on average than did comparable focal group members. The parameters, α and $\ln(\alpha)$, are also called "partial association" parameters because they are analogous to the partial correlations used with continuous data. The matching variable is "partialed out" of the association between group membership and performance on the studied item, (Birch, 1964).

Mantel and Haenszel proposed both the test statistic MH-CHISQ and the parameter estimate $\hat{\alpha}_{MH}$. Since that initial work many authors have contributed to the study of these procedures; the main results are as follows.

1. The effect of the continuity correction is to improve the calculation of the observed significance levels using the chi-square table rather than to make the size of the test equal to the nominal value. Hence simulation studies routinely find that the actual size of a test based on MH-CHISQ is *smaller* than the nominal value. However, the observed significance level of a large value of MH-CHISQ is better approximated by referring MH-CHISQ to the chi-square tables than by referring the expression in (9) to these tables. The continuity correction is simply to improve the approximation of a discrete distribution (i.e., MH-CHISQ) by a continuous distribution (i.e., 1 degree-of-freedom chi-square).

2. $\hat{\alpha}_{MH}$ is a consistent estimator of the α in (8) and the variability of $\hat{\alpha}_{MH}$ is nearly optimal over the range $\frac{1}{3} < \alpha < 3$, which translates into $-2.6 < \Delta < 2.6$ under the log transformation in (13). Outside this range $\hat{\alpha}_{MH}$ or $\hat{\Delta}_{MH}$ are still reasonably efficient, but very large (or small) values of α are not as accurately estimated by $\hat{\alpha}_{MH}$ as they are by maximum likelihood. Since larger values of α are easy to detect using MH-CHISQ, this is not an important limitation.

3. Standard error formulas for $\hat{\alpha}_{MH}$ and $\hat{\Delta}_{MH}$ that work in a variety of circumstances have taken a long time to develop. Important contributions have

been Hauck (1979), Breslow and Liang (1982), and Flanders (1985). Recent joint work with A. Phillips suggests that the following approximate variance formula for $\ln(\hat{\alpha}_{MH})$ is valid whenever the numerator and denominator of $\hat{\alpha}_{MH}$ are both large:

$$\text{Var}(\ln(\hat{\alpha}_{MH})) = \frac{1}{2U^2}\sum_j [T_j^{-2} (A_j D_j + \hat{\alpha}_{MH} B_j C_j)$$
$$(A_j + D_j + \hat{\alpha}_{MH} (B_j + C_j))], \tag{14}$$

where

$$U = \sum_j A_j D_j / T_j.$$

This approximate variance formula agrees with well-known variance estimates for $\ln(\hat{\alpha}_{MH})$ in the few cases in which these are available. It is discussed more extensively in Phillips and Holland (1987), and is equivalent to the variance estimate in Robbins, Breslow, and Greenland (1986).

It is sometimes helpful to show how $\hat{\alpha}_{MH}$ is expressed as a weighted average of the sample cross-product ratios in each of the K 2×2 tables. These are the values

$$\hat{\alpha}_j = \frac{A_j D_j}{B_j C_j}. \tag{15}$$

Hence

$$\hat{\alpha}_{MH} = \frac{\sum w_j \hat{\alpha}_j}{\sum w_j} \tag{16}$$

where

$$w_j = B_j C_j / T_j.$$

In their discussion of chi-square techniques, Marascuilo and Slaughter consider Cochran's (1954) test. In this test, instead of using the odds ratio in each table as a measure of *dif* in the jth matched group, the difference in proportion is used, i.e.

$$\frac{A_j}{n_{Rj}} - \frac{C_j}{n_{Fj}}. \tag{17}$$

These are averaged together with the weights,

$$n_{Rj} n_{Fj} / T_j,$$

to get an overall average difference across all matched groups. More recently, Dorans and Kulick (1986) have suggested applying the weights n_{Fj} to the difference in (17) to get an overall standardized measure of *dif* for the item. Dorans and Kulick do not develop a test based on their measures, but it is evident that such a test, similar to Cochran's test, could be developed. Since Dorans and Kulick are primarily interested in a good descriptive measure of *dif* their choice of weights does not correspond to a statistically optimal test of H_0.

In summary, the Mantel–Haenszel procedure is a natural extension of the ideas behind the chi-square procedures of Scheuneman and others. It provides a single degree-of-freedom chi-square test that is powerful against realistic alternatives to H_0, it allows detailed and careful matching on relevant criteria, and it provides a single summary measure of the magnitude of the departure from H_0 exhibited by the studied item.

THE MH PROCEDURE AND IRT MODELS

It is generally believed that there is, at best, only a rough correspondence between the "chi-square" types of procedures for studying *dif* and the more "theoretically preferred" methods based on item response theory (IRT). For examples of this view see Scheuneman (1979), Marascuilo and Slaughter (1981) and Shepard, Camilli, and Williams (1984). In this section we show that the MH procedure highlights a close connection between these two important classes of procedures. Our observations on this point are strongly influenced by the work of our colleague, Paul Rosenbaum (1985, 1986).

We adopt the notation and terminology for discussing IRT models given in Holland (1981), Cressie and Holland (1983), Rosenbaum (1984), and Holland and Rosenbaum (1986). Thus x_k is the 0/1 indicator of a correct response in item k, $k = 1, \ldots, J$, and $x = (x_1, \ldots, x_J)$ denotes a generic response vector— there are 2^J possible values of x. In any population of examinees we let $p(x)$ denote the proportion of them who would produce the response vector x if tested. Then

$$p(x) \geqslant 0, \sum_x p(x) = 1.$$

An IRT model assumes that the value of $p(x)$ is specified by an equation of the form

$$p(x) = \int \prod_{k=1}^{J} P_k(\theta)^{x_k} Q_k(\theta)^{1-x_k} \, dG(\theta). \tag{18}$$

In (18), $P_k(\theta) = 1 - Q_k(\theta)$ is the item characteristic curve (ICC) for the item k and $G(\theta)$ is the distribution function of the latent ability, θ, across the population of examinees.

It is customary to restrict the ICCs and θ in various ways. For example, θ is usually a scalar (not a vector) and the P_k are assumed to be monotone increasing functions of θ. Holland and Rosenbaum (1986) pointed out that without some restriction to this type, IRT models are vacuous. Parametric assumptions such as the 1-, 2-, or 3-parameter logistic form for $P_k(\theta)$ may also be imposed.

If there are two subpopulations of examinees, R and F, then there are corresponding values $p_R(x)$ and $p_F(x)$. In general, each subpopulation will have its own ICCs, i.e.

$$P_{kR}(\theta) \text{ and } P_{kF}(\theta) \ k = 1, \ldots, J$$

as well as its own ability distribution,

$$G_R(\theta) \text{ and } G_F(\theta).$$

Lord (1980) states the hypothesis of no *dif* in terms of an IRT model. For item k it is

$$H_0(\text{IRT}) : P_{kR}(\theta) = P_{kF}(\theta) = P_k(\theta) \text{ for all } \theta.$$

Thus, if $H_0(\text{IRT})$ holds for all k then $p_R(x)$ and $p_F(x)$ have the representations:

$$p_R(x) = \int \prod_{k=1}^{J} P_k(\theta)^{x_k} Q_k(\theta)^{1-x_k} \ dG_R(\theta)$$

$$p_F(x) = \int \prod_{k=1}^{J} P_k(\theta)^{x_k} Q_k(\theta)^{1-x_k} \ dG_F(\theta). \tag{19}$$

Rosenbaum (1985) considers tests of the hypothesis that a representation like (19) exists for $p_R(x)$ and $p_F(x)$ in which R has a "higher" distribution of θ than does F.

The integrals in (18) and (19) are not easy to work with except in one special case, i.e., the Rasch model. For this model $P_k(\theta)$ has the logistic form

$$P_k(\theta) = e^{\theta - b_k}/(1 + e^{\theta - b_k}). \tag{20}$$

If (20) is inserted into (18) then Cressie and Holland (1983) showed that $p(x)$ may be expressed as

$$p(x) = p(0) \prod_{k=1}^{J} f_k^{x_k} \ \mu(x_+) \tag{21}$$

where

$$f_k = e^{-b_k}, \tag{22}$$

$$x_+ = \sum_k x_k$$

and

$$\mu(t) = E(U^t) \qquad t = 0, 1, \ldots, J. \tag{23}$$

In (23), U is a positive random variable whose distribution depends on the ICCs *and* on the ability distribution $G(\theta)$. Hence if we apply (21) to $p_R(x)$ and $p_F(x)$ without assuming $H_{0(IRT)}$ we get

$$p_R(x) = p_R(0) \prod_{k=1}^{J} f_{kR}{}^{x_k} \ \mu_R(x_+) \tag{24}$$

and

$$p_F(x) = p_F(0) \prod_{k=1}^{J} f_{kF}{}^{x_k} \ \mu_F(x_+). \tag{25}$$

Now suppose that we wish to apply the MH procedure in this situation and that we take as the matching variable the total score on the test X_+. If item 1 is the studied item then the relevant population probabilities for R are of the form

$$p_{Rj} = P(X_1 = 1 | X_+ = j, R).$$

Using (24) this can be expressed as

$$p_{Rj} = \frac{P(X_1 = 1, X_+ = j)}{P(X_+ = j)} = \frac{f_{1R} \, S_{J-1,j-1} \, (f_R^*)}{S_{J,j} \, (f_R)} \tag{26}$$

where

$$f_R = (f_{1R}, \ldots, f_{JR}) = (f_{1R}, f_R^*)$$

and

$$S_{J,j}(f) = \sum_{x:x_+=j} \ \prod_{k=1}^{J} f_k^{x_k}$$

(i.e., the symmetric function of J-variables of degree j). Similarly,

$$q_{Rj} = \frac{S_{J-1,j} \, (f_R^*)}{S_{J,j} \, (f_R)} \tag{27}$$

Hence the odds for success on item 1 in R in the jth matched set are:

$$\frac{p_{Rj}}{q_{Rj}} = f_{1R} \frac{S_{J-1,j-1} \, (f_R^*)}{S_{J-1,j} \, (f_R^*)} \tag{28}$$

Similar equations hold for p_{Fj} and q_{Fj} and the corresponding odds are

$$\frac{p_{Fj}}{q_{Fj}} = f_{1F} \frac{S_{J-1,j-1} \, (f_F^*)}{S_{J-1,j} \, (f_F^*)}. \tag{29}$$

Now suppose that for items 2 through J there is no *dif*, i.e.,

$$f_{kF} = f_{kR} \quad k = 2, \ldots, J,$$

so that

$$f_F^* = f_R^*.$$

Then the population odds ratio in each 2×2 table is

$$\frac{p_{Rj}}{q_{Rj}} \Big/ \frac{p_{Fj}}{q_{Fj}} = \frac{f_{1R}}{f_{1F}} = e^{b_{1F} - b_{1R}}. \tag{30}$$

Equation (30) is a statement of H_1 in (6) with $\alpha = e^{b_{1F} - b_{1R}}$, so that for the Rasch model the hypothesis for which the MH procedure was developed holds exactly in the population under the following conditions.

1. The items $2, 3, \ldots, J$ exhibit no *dif*, but the studied item *may* exhibit *dif*,
2. The criterion for matching, X_+, includes the studied item,
3. The data are random samples from R and F.

This result is a little surprising since the inclusion of the studied item in the criterion seems to go against the traditional uses of the MH procedures in medical applications. However, it can be shown that if the studied item is excluded from the criterion then the null hypothesis H_0 is not satisfied even though $H_{0(\text{IRT})}$ is satisfied for every item.

For example, when the criterion for matching is $X_* = \sum_{k=2}^{J} X_k$ and item 1 is the studied item, the relevant population probabilities are

$$p_{Rj} = p(X_1 = 1 \mid X_* = j, R)$$

and

$$p_{Fj} = p(X_1 = 1 \mid X_* = j, F)$$

It is easy to show that the equations that correspond to (28) and (29) are

$$\frac{p_{Rj}}{q_{Rj}} = f_{1R} \frac{\mu_R(j + 1)}{\mu_R(j)} \tag{31}$$

$$\frac{p_{Fj}}{q_{Fj}} = f_{1F} \frac{\mu_F(j + 1)}{\mu_F(j)}. \tag{32}$$

Hence the odds ratio in the jth matched set is

$$\alpha_j = \frac{f_{1R}}{f_{1F}} \left[\frac{\mu_R(j + 1)}{\mu_R(j)} \Big/ \frac{\mu_F(j + 1)}{\mu_F(j)} \right]. \tag{33}$$

Thus the α_j are not constant across the 2×2 tables. The ratio of moments in (33) is related to order relationships between the distributions of the random variable U, from (23), in R and F. For example, if the distribution of U for F is "lower" than that for R then we will have

$$\frac{\mu_R(j + 1)}{\mu_R(j)} \Big/ \frac{\mu_F(j + 1)}{\mu_F(j)} \geq 1, \text{ for all } j = 1, 2, \ldots .$$

This analysis raises the issue of whether the studied item should be included or not in the matching criterion. If it is not included, then the MH procedure will not behave correctly when there is no *dif* according to an IRT model. However the Rasch analysis suggests that the inclusion of the studied item in the matching criterion does not mask the existence of *dif*, rather it is the inclusion of *other* items exhibiting *dif* in the criterion that could lead to the finding that no *dif* exists for the studied item when in fact it does. This idea leads to two steps

Step 1: Refine the matching criterion by eliminating items based on a preliminary *dif* or impact analysis (Kok, Mellenberg, & van der Flier, 1985, make a similar suggestion).

Step 2: Use as the matching criterion the total score on all items left in the refined criterion plus the studied item—even if it is then omitted from the criterion of all other items when they are studied in turned.

It is possible that we have drawn too heavily on the analysis of the Rasch model and a good deal of simulation work may be necessary before we know for sure if our suggestions hold in greater generality. We have begun some of that work and will report on it later. However, to date the results of the simulation study corroborates our proposal regarding the inclusion or exclusion of the studied item in the criterion.

The issue of including and excluding an item from the criterion shows the need for making these adjustments in the computational formulas for $\hat{\alpha}_{MH}$ and MH-CHISQ. These are as follows.

If the K 2×2 tables have been assembled for a number right score S as the matching criterion that does not include the studied item and we wish to include it in the score, then the 2×2 tables need to be altered to these.

Score on Studied Item

	1	0	Total
R	A_{j-1}	B_j	n_{Rj}
F	C_{j-1}	D_j	n_{Fj}
	m_{1j-1}	m_{0j}	T_j

The values of MH-CHISQ and $\hat{\alpha}_{MH}$ are then computed from these tables.

Similarly, if S contains the score of the studied item and we wish to eliminate it this is done by using these 2×2 tables.

Score on Studied Item

	1	0	Total
R	A_{j+1}	B_j	n_{Rj}
F	C_{j+1}	D_j	n_{Fj}
	m_{1j+1}	m_{0j}	T_j

Thus it is a simple matter to compute either $\hat{\alpha}_{MH}$ or MH-CHISQ including or excluding the studied item from a number-right score matching criterion. If the matching criterion is a formula score or a grouped, number-right score then it is not easy to adjust for the inclusion of the studied item into the criterion, without recalculating the entire set of 2×2 tables.

DISCUSSION

There are many procedures that have been proposed for the study of *dif* over the last 20 years, and the introduction of a new one, associated with names that are unfamiliar to psychometricians, is likely to be regarded skeptically. However, we have tried to show that the MH procedure, drawn from the field of bio-statistics, fits squarely into the network of ideas developed by previous workers in the field of "item bias." In addition, standard statistical concepts, such as tests, hypotheses, error of type I and II, estimates, and standard errors, all fit neatly into the package. Connections between chi-square methods and IRT-based methods are made evident by studying the Mantel–Haenszel procedure.

We believe that the view that IRT-based approaches to *dif* are "theoretically preferred" over chi-square based procedures is not a very precise way of describing the situation. It is certainly true that likelihood ratio tests of $H_{0(IRT)}$ in the context of specific parametric IRT models (i.e., 3PL ICCs and Normal θ-distributions) are statistically optimal (or very nearly so) in the sense of power and efficiency *when these models actually hold*. If the data really are generated by such models, as they would be in a simulation, then no other test of the equality of two ICCs for the same item, at the given significance level can have larger power than these likelihood ratio tests. However, it is only the procedures based on marginal maximum likelihood, as advocated by Bock and Aitkin (1981), that can yield true likelihood ratio tests (e.g., see Thissen, Wainer, & Steinberg, 1985). IRT-based procedures that depend on multiple LOGIST calibrations do not automatically result in tests of $H_{0(IRT)}$ and estimates of ICC differences that are optimal. Furthermore, even the marginal maximum likelihood procedures are *not* optimal when the assumed model is wrong.

In our view, parametric IRT models provide an important testing ground for evaluating *dif* procedures. Under $H_{0(IRT)}$, test statistics ought to achieve significance levels that are close to the nominal values *regardless* of the choices of G_R, G_F, and the ICCs, $P_k(\theta)$. Against alternatives to $H_{0(IRT)}$, the likelihood ratio procedure will set the upper bounds on the power and efficiency of *any* test procedure, including the LOGIST-based procedures or chi-square procedures such as the Mantel–Haenszel. Our use of a specific IRT model (the Rasch model) to evaluate the Mantel–Haenszel procedure resulted in a new conception of the importance of including or excluding the studied item in the criterion. This shows the advantage of a theoretical analysis. We were led to that analysis by the empirical finding that including the studied item in the test score used as a matching criterion had a measurable and consistent effect on the values of $\hat{\alpha}_{MH}$ and $\hat{\Delta}_{MH}$ computed in real data. The $\hat{\Delta}_{MH}$ values will shift by an amount that is nearly independent of the studied item and that depends on the overall differences in performance on the criterion test between R and F.. The bigger the difference the bigger the shift. This is exactly what is predicted by equation (33) when there are large differences between the θ-distributions, G_F and G_R.

Our conjecture is that it is correct to *include* the studied item in the matching criterion when it is being analyzed for *dif,* but if it has substantial *dif* then that item should be *excluded* from the criterion used to match examinees for any *other* studied item. The first "inclusion" is to control the size of the test given by MH-CHISQ while the second "exclusion" is to prevent large *dif* items from degrading the power of this test. Such an approach is independent of the MH procedure and can be incorporated into other chi-square techniques, or into the iterative logit technique discussed by Kok, Mellenbergh, and van der Flier, (1985).

A final note on costs. The MH procedure is very inexpensive to use compared with IRT analyses. For example, runs that involve 50 items and 2,500 examinees cost about $10 on a typical mainframe computer.

REFERENCES

Angoff, W. H., & Ford, S. F. (1973). Item-race interaction on a test of scholastic aptitude. *Journal of Educational Measurement, 10,* 95–106.

Baker, F. B. (1981). A criticism of Scheuneman's item bias technique. *Journal of Educational Measurement, 18,* 59–62.

Berk, R. A. (Ed.). (1982). *Handbook of methods for detecting test bias.* Baltimore: Johns Hopkins University Press.

Birch, M. W. (1964). The detection of partial association, I: The 2×2 case. *Journal of the Royal Statistical Society, Ser. B, 26,* 313–324.

Bishop, Y. M. M., Fienberg, S. E., & Holland, P. W. (1975). *Discrete multivariate analysis: Theory and practice.* Cambridge, MA: MIT Press.

Bock, R. D., & Aitkin, M. (1981). Marginal maximum likelihood estimation of item parameters: Application of the EM algorithm. *Psychometrika, 46,* 443–460.

Breslow, N. E., & Liang, K. Y. (1982). The variance of the Mantel–Haenszel Estimator. *Biometrics, 38,* 943–952.

Cardall, C., & Coffman, W. E. (1964). A method for comparing the performance of different groups on the items in a test. Princeton, NJ: Educational Testing Service, Research Bulletin RB–64–61.

Cochran, W. G. (1954). Some methods for strengthening the common χ^2 test. *Biometrics, 10,* 417–451.

Cox, D. R. (1970). *Analysis of binary data.* London: Methuen.

Cressie, N., & Holland, P. W.. (1983). Characterizing the manifest probabilities of latent trait models. *Psychometrika, 48,* 129–141.

Dorans, N. J., & Kulick, E. M. (1986). Demonstrating the utility of the standardization approach to assessing unexpected differential item performance on the Scholastic Aptitude Test. *Journal of Educational Measurement 23,* 355–368.

Flanders, W. D. (1985). A new variance estimator for the Mantel–Haenszel odds-ratio. *Biometrics, 41,* 637–642.

Hauck, W. W. (1979). The large sample variance of the Mantel–Haenszel estimator of a common odds ratio. *Biometrics, 35,* 817–819.

Holland, P. W. (1981). When are item response models consistent with observed data? *Psychometrika, 46,* 79–92.

Holland, P. W. (1985). On the study of Differential Item Performance without IRT. *Proceedings of the Military Testing Association,* October.

Holland, P. W., & Rosenbaum, P. R. (1986). Conditional association and unidimensionality in monotone latent variable models. *Annals of Statistics, 14,* 1523–1543.

Holland, P. W., & Thayer, D. T. (1985). *An alternative definition of the ETS delta scale of item difficulty.* Princeton, NJ: Educational Testing Service, Research Report RR–85–43.

Kok, F. G., Mellenbergh, G. J., & van der Flier, H. (1985). Detecting experimentally induced item bias using the iterative logit method. *Journal of Educational Measurement, 22,* 295–303.

Lord, F. M. (1980). *Applications of item response theory to practical testing problems.* Hillsdale, NJ: Lawrence Erlbaum Associates.

Mantel, N., & Haenszel, W. (1959). Statistical aspects of the analysis of data from retrospective studies of disease. *Journal of the National Cancer Institute, 22,* 719–748.

Marascuilo, L. A., & Slaughter, R. E. (1981). Statistical procedures for identifying possible sources of item bias based on χ^2 statistics. *Journal of Educational Measurement, 18,* 229–248.

Mellenbergh, G. J. (1982). Contingency table models for assessing item bias. *Journal of Educational Statistics, 7,* 105–118.

Phillips, A., & Holland, P. W. (1987). Estimators of the variance of the Mantel–Haenszel log-odds-ratio estimate. *Biometrics, 43,* 425–431.

Robbins, J., Breslow, N., & Greenland, S. (1986). Estimation of the Mantel–Haenszel variance consistent in both sparse data and large-strata limiting models. *Biometrics, 42,* 311–324.

Rosenbaum, P. R. (1984). Testing the conditional independence and monotonicity assumptions of item response theory. *Psychometrika, 49,* 425–435.

Rosenbaum, P. R. (1985). Comparing distributions of item responses for two groups. *British Journal of Mathematical and Statistical Psychology, 38,* 206–215.

Rosenbaum, P. R. (1986). *Comparing item characteristic curves.* (Unpublished manuscript).

Scheuneman, J. D. (1979). A method of assessing bias in test items. *Journal of Educational Measurement, 16,* 143–152.

Scheuneman, J. D. (1981). A response to Baker's criticism. *Journal of Educational Measurement, 18,* 63–66.

Shepard, L. A., Camilli, G., & Williams, D. M. (1984). Accounting for statistical artifacts in item bias research. *Journal of Educational Statistics, 9*, 93–128.

Thissen, D., Wainer, H., & Steinberg, L. (1985). *Studying differential item performance with item response theory.* Paper presented at the Military Testing Association meeting, San Diego, CA, October 21.

Chapter 10

Use of Item Response Theory in the Study of Group Differences in Trace Lines

David Thissen
University of Kansas

Lynne Steinberg
Stanford University

Howard Wainer
Educational Testing Service

Differential Item Functioning is an expression which describes a serious threat to the validity of tests used to measure the aptitude, ability, or proficiency of members of different populations or groups. Some test items may simply function differently for examinees drawn from one group or another or they may "measure different things" for members of one group as opposed to members of another. Tests containing such items may have reduced validity for between-group comparisons, because their scores may be indicative of a variety of attributes other than those the test is intended to measure.

Dorans (1986) described an analogy item which functioned very differently for males and females:

DECOY:DUCK:: (A) net:butterfly (B) web:spider (C) lure:fish
(D) lasso:rope (E) detour:shortcut

on this item, the proportion of male examinees responding correctly within each particular score group in the lower half of the score distribution was .15 to .2 higher than the corresponding proportion for female examinees. The source of differential functioning for this item, knowledge of hunting and fishing, is so obvious that statistical procedures are probably not required to detect the problem. Contemporary "sensitivity review" of the item content would lead to its rejection. The example nevertheless provides a clear prototype of an item exhibiting differential functioning.

In the past, differential functioning has been called "item bias" in the literature because there are senses in which an item such as the DECOY:DUCK example is "biased" (in this case, against women in the majority American culture). However, the relationship of "item bias" to bias in complete tests (in a legal sense or otherwise) is complex; the phrase is more evaluative than descriptive. Therefore, it has been replaced by the term "differential item functioning" *dif*. Some recent literature also uses the phrases *differential item performance* and *unexpected* differential item performance.

Dif is most frequently defined in the context of *Item Response Theory* (IRT). In conventional unidimensional IRT, a test is presumed to measure a single unobservable latent variable θ (representing some dimension of ability, proficiency, etc.); the probability of a correct response to an item is represented by a line "tracing the probability" (Lazarsfeld, 1950) of that response as a function of θ. Using these concepts, the IRT definition of *dif* is straightforward: an item functions similarly in two groups if it has the same trace line for both groups; there is evidence of *dif* if the item has different trace lines for the two groups.

Any pair of groups may be considered; it is convenient to use "generic" terms in the description of the analysis. Here we use the terms *focal group* and *reference group* to refer to the group of particular interest and the comparison group, respectively. Fig. 10.1 shows trace lines for the correct response for an item which functions differently in two groups: at any particular value of θ, it is less likely that a member of the focal group will respond correctly than for an examinee at the same level of θ in the reference group. It is important to note that

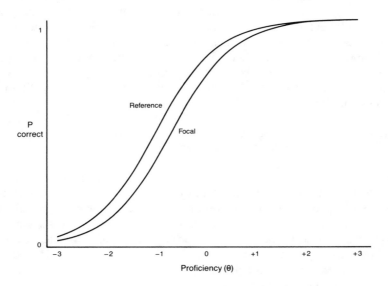

FIG. 10.1. Trace lines for an item which functions differently in two groups: a "biased" item ($a = 1$, $c = 0$ for both groups; $b_R = -1$, $b_F = -0.7$).

this definition of *dif* does not mean that the proportions responding correctly in the two groups will follow any particular pattern; that depends on the distribution of θ in each group.

Many approaches to detecting *dif* have been proposed in the past 15 years. While there was some earlier work on "group by item interaction," the contemporary explosion of methods for *dif* analysis began with Angoff and Ford's (1973) description of the "transformed item difficulty" or "delta plot" method. In an effort to provide reasonable tests of significance of *dif,* a number of subsequent investigators have proposed chi-square indexes of *dif;* these have been based on some three-way table of counts: score level by group by item (correct-incorrect). Scheuneman (1979), Marascuilo and Slaughter (1981), Mellenbergh (1982) and Kok, Mellenbergh, and van der Flier (1985) all described somewhat different methods. Holland and Thayer (1986) provided an integrative review of the earlier contingency table based chi-square indexes in the context of their description of the Mantel–Haenszel procedure. Some of these methods may be described as testing implications of an item response model; Holland and Thayer (1986) were especially clear about the relationship of the Mantel–Haenszel procedure with the one-parameter logistic. In general, these procedures are not obvious developments of item response theory.

Within the context of item response theory, Lord (1977, 1980) proposed a procedure for studying item bias based on tests of the parameters of the three-parameter logistic model. Linn and Harnisch (1981) and Linn, Levine, Hastings, and Wardrop (1981) suggested several procedures based on the analysis of differences between the fitted trace lines themselves, as opposed to their parameters; in a similar vein, Dorans and Kulick (1983) examined differences in empirical trace lines between groups, using very large samples. More recently, Muthén and Lehman (1985) have described a method of *dif* analysis which tests the significance of the difference between IRT parameters using an item factor-analysis procedure. We also make use of direct tests of the equality of IRT parameters between groups (Thissen, Steinberg & Gerrard, 1986; Thissen & Wainer, 1985).

Ironson and Subkoviak (1979), Shepard, Camilli, and Averill (1981) and Shepard, Camilli, and Williams (1984) compared the performance of some of the earlier IRT and chi-square approaches to the assessment of *dif*. The remainder of this chapter will examine two procedures based on direct tests of hypotheses concerning the parameters of IRT models, emphasizing our work with likelihood ratio tests. The goal of these procedures is to assess the magnitude and significance of group differences in trace lines (or *Item Characteristic Curves,* attributed to Tucker by Lord, 1952). In IRT, the item parameters provide the numerical summary of the trace lines; thus, parameter estimation and hypothesis tests involving the parameters are equivalent to estimation and hypothesis tests concerning the trace lines themselves.

THE 3-PARAMETER LOGISTIC MODEL

The application of IRT in educational measurement has generally made use of the three-parameter logistic (3PL) model (Birnbaum, 1968; Lord, 1980) to describe the trace line representing the probability of a correct response to a multiple-choice item. For a particular item, the equation for the trace line is

$$T = c + (1-c)/\{1 + \exp[-1.7a(\theta-b)]\} \tag{1}$$

in which θ is the latent (ability, proficiency) variable, and $\{a, b, c\}$ are the item parameters. The parameter b is sometimes called a "threshold" parameter and represents the point on the θ scale at which examinees have a 50% chance of "really knowing" the correct answer (Thissen & Steinberg, 1986). The slope of the trace line at that point, which indicates the strength of the relationship between the item response and θ, is proportional to a, and the probability of responding correctly (presumably, by chance) for examinees very low on the θ scale is given by c. The constant 1.7 is frequently included for historical reasons related to the use of the normal ogive function in some of the original IRT literature. The parameters of the trace lines in Fig. 10.1 are $a = 1$ and $c = 0$ (for both groups) and $b_R = -1.0$ and $b_F = -.7$.

A central aspect of IRT is that the item responses given by an examinee to a set of items are independent, *conditional on* θ; this is usually called "local independence." This means that the probability of any response vector $\mathbf{x}$ ($x_1 = 1$ if item i correct, 0 otherwise) is given by

$$P(\mathbf{x}) = \int \prod_i T_i^{x_i} (1 - T_i)^{(1 - x_i)} \ \phi(\theta) \ d\theta \tag{2}$$

in which $\phi(\theta)$ is the population distribution of θ. The data used for parameter estimation are the counts $r(\mathbf{x})$ observed for each response vector $\mathbf{x}$. *Marginal maximum likelihood* parameter estimation is based on locating estimates of the parameters $\{a, b, c\}$ for each item which maximize the likelihood (marginal with respect to θ) proportional to

$$L = \prod_k P(\mathbf{x}_k)^{r(\mathbf{x}_k)} \tag{3}$$

in which k is an index for the response patterns. The algorithm we use for obtaining the MML parameter estimates was described by Bock and Aitkin (1981). When all three parameters of the 3PL model are to be estimated, we frequently include a *prior density* for one or more of the parameters (usually c), and maximize

$$L' = L\ h(p), \tag{4}$$

where $h(p)$ represents the prior density for parameter (vector) p.

In principle, MML estimation and the procedures we describe for assessing *dif* may use any parametric item response model; in this chapter we discuss only applications of the 3PL model and constrained versions of that model. We will consider data simulated under the IRT model, in an effort to describe the performance of our IRT procedure for assessing *dif*.

METHODS OF ASSESSING *DIF* BASED ON TESTS OF EQUALITY OF ITEM PARAMETERS

IRT-D²

Lord (1977, 1980) introduced tests of *dif* based on tests of the significance of differences between estimated item parameters for the reference and focal groups. Lord (1980, p. 212) stated that "if . . . an item has a different item response function for one group than another, it is clear that the item is biased." Since item response functions (trace lines) are characterized by their parameters in parametric IRT, Lord proposed that a test of the significance of the difference between the parameters of the IRT model estimated for the two groups would provide a test of "item bias," or *dif*.

To test the hypothesis that a single parameter, for example *b*, differs between two groups, Lord's test is quite simple. He proposed comparing, for a given item, the difference between the estimated *b*s with its estimated standard error

$$SE(b_R - b_F) = \sqrt{var\ (b_R) + var\ (b_F)}.$$

Second-derivative approximations of the standard errors of estimated item parameters are a routine by-product of ML parameter estimation with Newton–Raphson procedures such as those commonly used for IRT models. The sample sizes involved in IRT calibration are usually so large that the degrees of freedom for these estimates are effectively infinite, so a test statistic such as

$$z = (b_R - b_F)\ /\ SE(b_R - b_F)$$

may be referred to a table of the standard normal distribution. Alternatively, z^2 may be referred to a table of the chi-square distribution with 1 degree of freedom; that procedure will be used in our illustration for direct comparability with other methods which are based on single-degree-of-freedom chi-square tests.

Lord further proposed that the same asymptotic normal theory could be used to produce a simultaneous test of the hypothesis that $a_R = a_F$ and $b_R = b_F$. The procedure is based on the Mahalanobis distance (D^2) between the parameter vectors for the two groups:

$$D^2 = \mathbf{v}'\Sigma^{-1}\mathbf{v},$$

in which $\mathbf{v}$ is the vector of differences between the parameter estimates

$[a_R - a_F, b_R - b_F]$, and Σ is the corresponding covariance matrix. Under the assumptions that:

1. The likelihood for the data is (approximately) Gaussian in the parameter space, and
2. Accurate estimates of Σ derived from that likelihood are available,

D^2 is distributed as chi-square on 2 degrees of freedom under the null hypothesis of no difference between parameters for the two groups.[1] In general, the number of degrees of freedom is equal to the number of parameters being tested. The univariate test for the difference between two bs is a special case of this bivariate test, and a trivariate test for all three parameters of the 3PL model is an obvious extension. Thus we will refer to the family of methods proposed by Lord as IRT-D^2 methods.

Lord (1977, 1980) specified a number of additional procedures to facilitate useful computation of these test statistics from estimates then available from the computer program LOGIST; those additional procedures were mostly concerned with "standardization" (setting the same scale for θ for the two groups) and the treatment of the asymptote in the three-parameter logistic model. With the advent of MML estimation procedures which permit simultaneous estimation of item parameters in two or more groups arising from different populations, the need for these additional procedures is eliminated. But Lord's central proposal of a strategy for statistical tests of *dif* remains useful.

IRT-LR

We have been using likelihood ratio chi-squares (IRT-LR tests) to test the same hypotheses defined by Lord in our recent work on *dif* (Thissen, Steinberg, & Gerrard, 1986; Thissen & Wainer, 1985). Mislevy (1985) has described IRT-LR procedures for testing differences between population distributions in the context of IRT; and Muraki and Bock (1986) use such tests in his analysis of "item drift." It is interesting to note that the problem of "item drift" is formally identical to *dif*; specifically, the question in *dif* is "does an item's performance characteristics differ between groups?", whereas in "item drift" the question is "does an item's performance characteristics change over time?" For both research questions, the investigation concerns the equivalence of item parameters or trace lines, over time or across groups.

In IRT-LR analysis, the null hypothesis of no group differences in trace lines

---

[1]We use the nomenclature "Mahalanobis distance" and the notation D^2 following Anderson (1984, p. 219) and Bock (1975 p. 399), referring to early work by Mahalanobis (1930, 1936). Anderson (1984, p. 73) notes that Pearson (1900) first proved that D^2 is distributed as chi-square under the null hypothesis. Wald (1943) provided an extensive development of the properties of this statistical test, so it is sometimes also called the "Wald statistic."

is tested using information obtained in three steps; for instance, consider the hypothesis that $b_R = b_F$:

1. The IRT model is fitted simultaneously to the data for both groups with an "anchor" item or items constrained to have the same parameters for both groups; there are no between-group equality constraints placed on the item under investigation (i.e., $b_R \neq b_F$).

$$G_1^2 = -2(\text{loglikelihood})$$

   is computed for the ML estimates of the parameters.
2. The IRT model is refitted under the constraint that $b_R = b_F$;

$$G_2^2 = -2(\text{loglikelihood})$$

   is computed.
3. The likelihood ratio test (Neyman & Pearson, 1928) of the significance of the difference between b_R and b_F is

$$G^2(1) = G_2^2 - G_2^2.$$

Simultaneous tests of group differences on more than one parameter of the IRT model are straightforward generalizations of the procedure described above; if k parameters are constrained to be equal between groups in Step 2, the simultaneous test is given by G^2 on k degrees of freedom. For example, the IRT-LR test of Lord's (1977, 1980) hypothesis that $[a, b]_F = [a, b]_R$ has 2 degrees of freedom. Statistical tests constructed in this way may also be used to test joint hypotheses in designed experiments: If k items are constructed to be more difficult in one group than another as a test of some theory of difficulty, a joint k degree of freedom test may be used.

The null hypothesis being tested in IRT-LR and IRT-D^2 analyses is the same: that the specified item parameters do not differ between the groups. Wald (1943) and Rao (1973, pp. 416–418) showed that the two tests are asymptotically equivalent. Both statistical tests make equal use of the (assumed asymptotic) normality of the likelihood when they obtain p-values from the chi-square distribution; if the likelihood is (multivariate) normal, the probability of obtaining parameter estimates for the two groups which differ as much or more than those observed is given by the chi-square tail area. The difference between the two procedures lies in the use of the estimated covariance matrix in IRT-D^2: when second-derivative approximations to that covariance matrix are used, the procedure uses the (estimated) curvature at the mode of the likelihood to define the distance in standard units between the item parameters or vectors being tested. IRT-LR does not make use of estimated error variances and covariances; instead, it computes the likelihoods at the overall mode and at the mode under the equality constraints and then uses the assumed normality of the likelihood to compute the probability under the null hypothesis.

Thus, both procedures rely crucially on the (multivariate) normality of the likelihoods; IRT-D^2 further depends on the accuracy of the estimate of Σ. In practical IRT estimation programs, the second derivative approximation to Σ (which is itself an approximation which is only asymptotically valid) is usually further approximated, because the complete matrix of second-derivatives and cross-derivatives among the parameters is extremely difficult to compute. Bock and Lieberman (1970) give some idea of the difficulties involved. Therefore, to the extent that the likelihood is normal and Σ is estimated well, both methods should perform identically. However, the need to estimate Σ well, combined with the actual difficulties of doing so, is a weakness of IRT-D^2 methods.

An Illustration.   The simplest case which will serve as an illustration of the performance of IRT-LR and IRT-D^2 includes two groups (reference and focal) and two items; one of the items is designated the "anchor" because it is presumed to function similarly for members of both groups, and the other is designated the "candidate" item because it is the item to be tested for possible *dif*. From a purely statistical point of view, these designations are arbitrary; for two items, with no collateral information to distinguish between them, *dif* could not reasonably be assigned to one item or the other. We assume that there exists some mechanism for selecting the anchor item.

The data, drawn from a simulation performed by Holland and Thayer (personal communication, March 1986), are presented at the top of Table 10.1. There are two 2×2 tables, one for each of the two groups, in which the numbers responding correctly (1) and incorrectly (0) to the anchor and candidate items are recorded. There are 2,000 "simulees" in the reference sample, and 500 in the focal sample; the distribution of θ in both groups is unit normal with a mean of zero for the reference group and a mean of -1 for the focal group. The true values of the item parameters are also shown in Table 10.1; the item slopes are equal (and the asymptotes are zero); that is, the 1PL model is an accurate representation of the simulated item-response process. The true trace lines for this candidate item are shown in Fig. 10.1. The candidate item does have different trace lines for the two groups. However, without the formal analysis, it is very difficult to interpret the data in the table; *dif* is obscured by the obviously visible effect of the difference between the two means: there are many fewer correct responses to both items in the focal group.

For this illustration we assume that the correct structure of the IRT model is known a priori: the slopes are equal (to a), there are (potentially) three thresholds to be estimated (b for the anchor, b_R and b_F), and the mean of the focal group is also estimated. The mean of the reference groups is fixed at zero, so the estimated mean of the focal group is actually the estimate of the difference between the two means. Both population distributions are assumed (correctly) to be unit normal. The five parameters $\{a, b, b_R, b_F, \mu_F\}$ estimated by MML (Thissen, 1982; using the computer program MULTILOG; Thissen, 1986) are also listed in

TABLE 10.1
Item 26 Anchor, Item 6 Candidate, dif4A

Data

		Reference Group					Focal Group	
		Candidate Item					Candidate Item	
		0	1				0	1
Anchor Item	0	368	661			0	278	125
	1	91	880			1	27	70

True parameters: $\mu_R = 0$ $\mu_F = -1$
(Candidate item:) $b_R = -1$ $b_F = -.7$
(Anchor item:) $b = .04$
                                $a = 1$
                                $\sigma = 1$

MML estimates: $\mu_R = 0$ (fixed) $\mu_F = -1.09$ (.06)
(Candidate item:) $b_R = -.99$ (.05) $b_F = -.72$ (.09)
(Anchor item:) $b = .05$ (.04)
                            $a = 1.13$ (.05)
G^2 (1) = 0.1 $\sigma = 1$ (fixed)
(Approximate standard errors in parentheses near parameters)

IRT-D^2 test, $b_R = b_F$: $z^2 = [-.99 - (-.72)]^2/0.1 = 7.3$

Constrained, $b_R = b_F$:

MML estimates: $\mu_R = 0$ (fixed) $\mu_F = -1.26$ (.06)
(Candidate item:) $b_R = -.97$ (.05) $b_F = -.97$ (equal b_R)
(Anchor item:) $b = .03$ (.04)
                            $a = 1.12$ (.05)
G^2 (1) = 5.7 $\sigma = 1$ (fixed)
(Approximate standard errors in parentheses near parameters)

IRT-LR test, $b_R = b_F$: G^2 (1) = 5.7 - 0.1 = 5.6.

Table 10.1. Figs. 10.2 and 10.3 illustrate the fitted trace lines, and the fit of the model to the data.

The fit of the model to the data is excellent (the model is correct, after all!), G^2 (1) = 0.1. Recovery of the true values of the parameters is quite good. It should be noted that these items were chosen for illustration in part because everything works very well; neither the fit nor the parameter recovery is always this good. Note that when the thresholds for the candidate item are (incorrectly) constrained to be equal for the two groups, the estimate of the mean for θ for the focal group drops from −1.09 to −1.26; that is the "effect" of a single biased item in a two-item test.

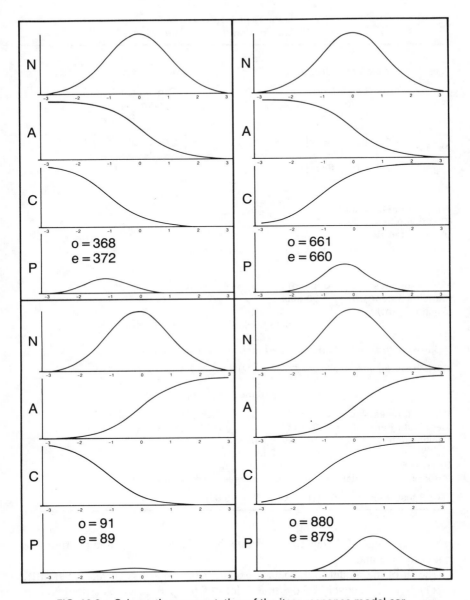

FIG. 10.2. Schematic representation of the item response model corresponding to the reference group 2 × 2 table in Table 10.1. Each quadrant corresponds to a response pattern, or a cell in the 2 × 2 table. Within each quadrant, the appropriate trace lines for the two items follow the population distribution; the product of the top three is the posterior, equivalent to the integrand of equation 2.

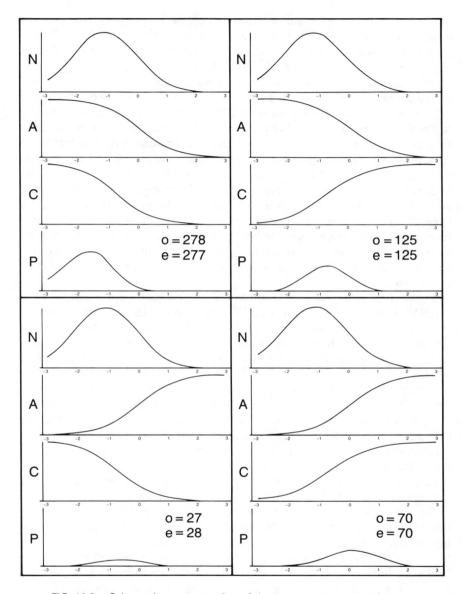

FIG. 10.3. Schematic representation of the item response model corresponding to the focal group 2 × 2 table in Table 10.1. Each quadrant corresponds to a response pattern, or a cell in the 2 × 2 table. Within each quadrant, the appropriate trace lines for the two items follow the population distribution; the product of the top three is the posterior, equivalent to the integrand of equation 2.

There is sufficient information in the tabulated data from the correct model to perform the IRT-D^2 test of the equality of the bs: $z = 2.7$, so $z^2 = 7.3$ on 1 degree of freedom. Parameters from the constrained estimation for the IRT-LR test are given near the bottom of Table 10.1; $G^2(1) = 5.6$. Both tests are significant at the $p = .05$ level, and they are not as different as they appear in the chi-square metric. The IRT-D^2 estimate is that the difference between the two bs is 2.7 times its standard error, while the IRT-LR estimate is that the difference is $\sqrt{5.6} = 2.4$ times its standard error. The standard errors used here for the IRT-D^2 procedure are approximations to the "true" second-derivative standard errors from the MML estimation procedure. Specifically, they are based on the standard errors from the "M step" of the Bock–Aitkin (1981) algorithm and the rate of convergence of the EM-like algorithm, using a procedure shown to be valid only for univariate problems (Dempster, Laird, & Rubin, 1977). Inaccuracy in those standard error estimates may well account for the relatively small difference; alternatively, it may be that the likelihood is not quite multivariate normal. In any event, both procedures are quite straightforward and give the correct decision in this case at $\alpha = .05$: the candidate item functions differently in the two groups.

Figure 10.4 is a Perozzo (1880) plot of the contours of the loglikelihood involved in both the IRT-LR and IRT-D^2 tests. Contours of the increase in twice-the-loglikelihood are plotted over the (b_F, b_R) surface, normed so that the level at the unconstrained MML estimate $(b_F, b_R) = (-.72, -.99)$ is zero. At each point on the (b_F, b_R) plane, the contour plot indicates the value of LR G^2, given that the other three parameters $(a, b_{Anchor}, \text{ and } \mu_F)$ are chosen to maximize the likelihood for that value of (b_F, b_R). Thus, although the plot is a two-dimensional surface derived from a five-dimensional likelihood, it is not "marginal" and it is not "conditional" on any particular values of (a, b_{Anchor}, μ_F); the values of (a, b_{Anchor}, μ_F) are those which maximize the likelihood at (b_F, b_R), so it is a "maximum" plot. The apparent "nonsmoothness" of the plotted contours is due to the fact that they are constructed from a relatively coarse grid in the five-dimensional space; plots like this are computationally intensive: Figure 10.4 required more than 14,000 evaluations of the loglikelihood.

Fig. 10.4 illustrates the meaning of the test statistics involved in IRT-LR and IRT-D^2. The unconstrained MML estimate of (b_F, b_R) is $(-.72, -.99)$. The hypothesis of no *dif* constrains the estimate of (b_F, b_R) to lie on the line $b_F = b_R$, and the constrained estimate is located at the highest point on the likelihood surface on that line, at $(-.97, -.97)$. To the extent that the contours plotted in Fig. 10.4 correspond to the contours of a bivariate normal loglikelihood, the probability (area under the likelihood surface in the direction $b_R - b_F$) between the unconstrained estimate $(-.72, -.99)$ and points as far away as $(-.97, -.97)$ is given by tabulated value for the chi-square of 5.6. IRT-LR evaluates the loglikelihood at two points, with and without the equality constraint; normal theory is used to infer the probability.

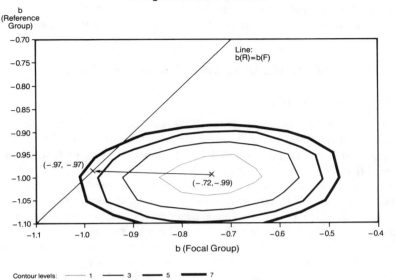

FIG. 10.4. Perozzo plot of the maximized loglikelihood over the $b_F - b_R$ surface for the data in Table 10.1; the values of a, b_{anchor}, and μ_F are those which maximize the likelihood for each value $[b_F, b_R]$. The contour levels are associated with increases in the LR G^2, from zero at the MLE $(-.72, -.99)$.

IRT-D^2 uses the estimated curvature of the surface at $(-.72, -.99)$ to estimate the distance, in the same chi-square/probability metric, to the point on the surface which is the ML estimate given $b_R = b_F$. In this case, IRT-D^2 overestimates that distance slightly, giving 2.7 standard units as opposed to the IRT-LR estimate of 2.4 standard units. The difference is small, and as noted, may be due either to the nonnormality of the surface (it appears to be slightly asymmetrical, and may not have Gaussian curvature everywhere) or inaccurate estimation of the variances from the approximated curvature at $(-.72, -.99)$.

Either statistical test seems reasonable given the contours plotted in Fig. 10.4.[2] Due to the difficulties involved in accurately computing (or evaluating) the estimates of Σ required for the IRT-D^2 test, we will not pursue IRT-D^2

----

[2]As Rubin points out in his discussion, a strict frequentist justification of the use of the probabilities associated with these test statistics is not based on the surface plotted in Fig. 10.4 at all, but rather on a surface describing the relative frequency of parameter estimates from *samples* arising from the model with the parameters specified. Fig. 10.4 illustrates the likelihood of a *single sample* as a function of the parameters, not the distribution of a sample of samples. Fig. 10.4 does illustrate a Bayesian interpretation of the use of these statistics; and the (hypothetical) frequentist surface would probably be quite similar.

further. Instead, we will concentrate on the performance of IRT-LR on simulated data for which we know the true model and parameters, or the "right answer"; we will see under what circumstances IRT-LR recovers that right answer.

SOME RESULTS WITH SIMULATED DATA

One-item Anchor, 1PL

Table 10.2 summarizes the results of IRT-LR *dif* analysis of simulated data for several candidate items using the same single item as an anchor as was used in the extended illustration in Fig. 10.4.[3] At three levels of b_R (-1, 0, and 1), b_F differed from b_R by .05, .15, and .30. For all of these items, $a = 1$ and $c = 0$. Differences between b_R and b_F of .05 and .15 were never detected; these correspond to differences of no more than .5 and 1.5 standard errors, which are difficult to detect in any event. The standard errors are similar to those reported in the extended illustration. But the standard error for b_F *increases as* b_F moves away from the mean of the focal group; differences are more difficult to detect at higher levels of b, near which there are few simulees. *dif* was detected for two of the three items where the true difference was 0.3. Item 9 in these simulated data is something of an anomaly: The true model may be rejected at $\alpha = 0.01$. The difference between the true model and the model with equality constraints is not significant, but it is likely that the data happened to be quite atypical.

50-item Anchor, 1PL

Table 10.3 summarizes IRT-LR *dif* analyses with the same structure as those described; however, the 1-item anchor is replaced by a 50-item anchor. The 50 items used as the anchor all had $a = 1$ and $c = 0$; their b values were equally spaced between -2 and $+2$. The candidate items are the same as those in Table 10.2. The analysis was directly parallel to those described above. The results were similar: Differences between the bs or .05 and .15 were not detected. Differences of .30 were detected: two of the three at $\alpha = .01$, the third at $\alpha = .05$. The much longer anchor increased computing time a great deal (from a few minutes on an IBM-PC class machine for the 1-item anchor to many minutes on a mainframe for the 50-item anchor), and appeared to increase power somewhat less.

---

[3]Practical considerations permitted the analysis of only a subset of the data simulated by Holland and Thayer. The subsets analyzed here were chosen to be theoretically sensible, and span the range of reasonable conditions in the larger sample of available data. With 1PL anchors, we considered only candidate items which fell within the 1PL framework. In a model-fitting approach such as IRT-LR analysis, it is not clear how to analyze simulated 3PL candidate items with a 1PL anchor; although such 3PL candidate items were included in the simulated data, they were not analyzed. Where several replications were available, we analyzed only the first for our illustrative purposes here.

TABLE 10.2
IRT-LR *dif* Analysis Results, One-item Anchor, 1PL

dif4A Item	Reference Group		Focal Group		
	True b_R	Estimated b_R	True b_F	Estimated b_F	G^2
4	−1.00	−1.04	−0.95	−1.14	1.2
5	−1.00	−1.02	−0.85	−1.03	0.0
6	−1.00	−0.99	−0.70	−0.72	5.6*
7	0.00	−0.03	0.05	0.00	0.0
8	0.00	0.03	0.15	0.02	0.0
9	0.00	0.04	0.30	0.11	0.2
10	1.00	1.00	1.05	0.78	2.4
11	1.00	1.04	1.15	0.97	0.3
12	1.00	0.99	1.30	1.36	5.0*

*$p < .05$

50-item Anchor, 3PL

The results reported in Table 10.4 use a different set of simulated data than those described above, also generated by Holland and Thayer. All three parameters of both the anchor and the candidate items were estimated. The true values of the anchor item parameters were $c = 0.2$ for all 50 items, and the as and bs were randomly sampled from a bivariate distribution. Therefore, the parameterization

TABLE 10.3
IRT-LR *dif* Analysis Results, 50-item Anchor, 1PL

dif4A Item	Reference Group		Focal Group		
	True b_R	Estimated b_R	True b_F	Estimated b_F	G^2
4	−1.00	−1.02	−0.95	−1.01	0.0
5	−1.00	−0.98	−0.85	−0.88	1.9
6	−1.00	−1.03	−0.70	−0.62	29.8**
7	0.00	−0.01	0.05	0.13	2.9
8	0.00	0.04	0.15	0.16	1.8
9	0.00	0.05	0.30	0.23	4.8*
10	1.00	0.97	1.05	0.89	0.4
11	1.00	1.04	1.15	1.12	0.4
12	1.00	0.99	1.30	1.52	14.8**

*$p < .05$
**$p < .01$

TABLE 10.4
IRT-LR *dif* Analysis Results, 50-item Anchor, 3PL

| dif7A Item | Reference Group | | Focal Group | | |
	True b_R	Estimated b_R	True b_F	Estimated b_F	G^2
4	−1.00	−0.85	−0.95	−0.84	0.0
5	−1.00	−0.86	−0.85	−0.72	2.4
6	−1.00	−0.88	−0.70	−0.61	9.8**
7	0.00	0.11	0.05	0.21	1.7
8	0.00	0.06	0.15	0.22	2.9
9	0.00	0.02	0.30	0.23	5.1*
10	1.00	1.00	1.05	0.95	0.3
11	1.00	1.14	1.15	1.32	1.5
12	1.00	1.10	1.30	1.79	14.1**
	(For items 4–12, $a = 1$ and $c = 0$ for both groups)				
13	−1.00	−1.18	−0.95	−1.01	2.4
14	−1.00	−0.98	−0.85	−0.77	4.4*
15	−1.00	−1.14	−0.70	−0.68	17.3**
16	0.00	−0.04	0.05	0.13	1.8
17	0.00	−0.06	0.15	0.13	2.0
18	0.00	0.12	0.30	0.32	2.5
19	1.00	1.12	1.05	0.84	2.0
20	1.00	1.05	1.15	1.18	0.3
21	1.00	1.06	1.30	1.55	4.3*
	(For items 15–21, $a = 1$ and $c = 0.2$ for both groups)				

| dif7A Item | Reference Group | | Focal Group | | |
	True c_R	Estimated c_R	True c_F	Estimated c_F	G^2
22	0.20	0.16	0.15	0.19	1.4
23	0.20	0.22	0.10	0.13	13.6**
24	0.20	0.17	0.05	0.08	12.7**
	(For item 24, $a = 1$ and $b = 0.5$ for both groups)				

$*p < .05$
$**p < .01$

of the anchor differed from the 1PL parameterization used in the preceding examples: All three parameters of the 3PL were estimated for each of the anchor items. It is well known (Lord, 1980; Thissen & Wainer, 1982) that there is very little information about the value of the parameter c in data from relatively easy items; therefore, as suggested by Lord (1986), a prior density for c was included making estimation *maximum a posteriori* (MAP). The program used (MULTI-LOG) estimates logit[c]; the prior for c (for each item) was $N(-1.4, 0.5)$ for logit[c]. Fig. 10.5 shows the prior. Except for the additional parameters and the prior, the treatment of the anchor was exactly as we have described. The population distributions for θ for the reference and focal groups were the same as those described above: the reference group was $N(0,1)$ and the focal group was $N(-1,1)$.

For Items 4–12 in Table 10.4, the true parameters were the same as for Items 4–12 in the preceding tables. Although the values of c are really zero, we are treating these data as though they came from an actual multiple-choice test. Under these circumstances, we have no advance "warning" about the functioning of the items. Therefore, we estimated all three parameters of the 3PL model for the candidate items, including the prior (centered at 0.2 for c). To obtain the single-degree-of-freedom test for the b-difference, we included equality constraints for a and c between groups for the candidate items in the "unconstrained" model, and then added the single constraint that $b_F = b_R$ to obtain the single-degree-of-freedom tests in Table 10.4. Only items with b-differences of .30 showed significant *dif;* the pattern of results is similar to that with the 1PL anchor.

The "easy" Items (4–6) exhibit substantial bias in the estimates of b. This is due to the use of the (incorrect) 3PL parameterization and the prior on c. Since there is very little information about the value of c for these items, the estimates of c remain near the prior mean of 0.2, instead of approaching the correct value of zero; the estimates of b are shifted to the right to compensate. However, the estimate of the *difference* between the bs, which is being tested for significance, appears to be relatively unaffected.

Simulated Items 13–21 are similar to Items 4–12, except that the true value of c in the generating model is 0.2. We detect only two of the three b-differences of .30 under these circumstances (nonzero "guessing") at $\alpha = .05$, and one of

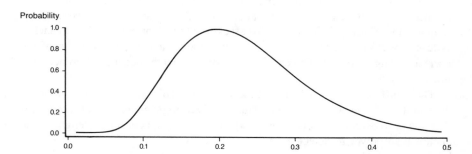

FIG. 10.5. The prior density for c used for all items when the 3PL model is used; the parameter actually estimated is logit[c], and the prior is $N(-1.4, 0.5)$ for logit[c]

the items for which the b-difference is .15. Only one of the chi-squares is significant at the .01 level.

Simulated candidate Items 22–24 are different: The focal and reference groups had the same as and bs, and different cs. So the IRT-LR tests were done slightly differently from those concerned with b-differences: the LR test is the single-degree-of-freedom test for the equality of the c parameters between the groups. Differences of .1 and .15 were easily detectable by the IRT-LR method, even though the estimated c for the focal group was required to "pull away" from a prior centered on a value equal to the value of c for the reference group. The prior introduced some bias in the estimate of c; but it is not large. Items 22–24 were set up to be highly discriminating, difficult items: the kind for which the parameter c can be estimated reasonably accurately.

4-item Anchor, 3PL

In some situations, such as those arising with the very short "experimental sections" which may be included in operational computerized adaptive tests, it may be desirable to assess *dif* using only a very few items as the anchor. To consider the performance of IRT-LR in such a situation, we constructed a 4-item anchor by selecting items from those in the 50-item 3PL anchor described. The results of IRT-LR *dif* analysis for several of the same candidate items described above are reported in Table 10.5, and a list of the true parameters for the 4-item anchor and estimates for one of the candidate items are shown in Table 10.6.

The four items of the anchor were chosen to be roughly equally spaced, with bs ranging from about -1 to about 1 in steps of about .7; they have as of about 1. Only candidate items for which the true b-difference was 0.3 or c-difference was 0.15 were considered because these were the items for which *dif* was easily detectable using the 50-item anchor. As shown in Table 10.5, all such b-differences were detected at $\alpha = .05$, and four of the six at $\alpha = .01$, using the 4-item anchor. While it is likely that the assessment of *dif* based on a 4-item anchor is less powerful than that based on a much longer anchor, comparison of the corresponding results in Tables 10.4 and 10.5 indicate that the difference may not be large.

The c-difference was not detected at $\alpha = .05$. This is in marked contrast to the results with the 50-item anchor. This is only a single example; but it indicates that power to detect differences in c may be more dependent on the length of the anchor than power to detect b-differences.

Table 10.6 shows that parameter estimates for an illustrative case with the four-item anchor, as fitted with the "true" model. Recovery of the generating parameters for both the anchor and the candidate item is quite good. As tested by the LR G^2 against the general multinomial alternative, the true model fits: $G^2(45) = 52.8$. Indeed, in all seven cases reported in Table 10.5, the LR test against the general multinomial alternative was within the central 90% region for chi-square

TABLE 10.5
IRT-LR *dif* Analysis Results, 4-item Anchor, 3PL

dif7A Item	Reference Group True b_R	Estimated b_R	Focal Group True b_F	Estimated b_F	G^2
6	−1.00	−0.79	−0.70	−0.44	7.1**
9	0.00	0.10	0.30	0.48	7.8**
12	1.00	0.98	1.30	1.82	11.4**
(For items 6–12, $a = 1$ and $c = 0$ for both groups)					
15	−1.00	−1.20	−0.70	−0.69	10.5**
18	0.00	0.10	0.30	0.49	4.8*
21	1.00	0.99	1.30	1.54	3.9*
(For items 15–21, $a = 1$ and $c = 0.2$ for both groups)					

dif7A Item	Reference Group True c_R	Estimated c_R	Focal Group True c_F	Estimated c_F	G^2
24	0.20	0.16	0.05	0.09	3.3
(For item 24, $a = 1$ and $b = 0.5$ for both groups)					

*$p < .05$
**$p < .01$

TABLE 10.6
Parameter Recovery, 4-item Anchor, 3PL

Item		a	b	c
30	true	1.02	−.84	.20
	est.	0.92	−.97	.15
39	true	1.08	−.34	.20
	est.	1.01	−.32	.22
6	true	1.07	0.40	.20
	est.	1.25	0.37	.20
48	true	1.19	0.92	.20
	est.	1.20	0.92	.18
Cand. 15	true(R)	1.00	−1.00	.20
	est.	1.20	−1.20	.19
Cand. 15	true(F)	"	−.70	"
	est.	"	−.69	"

Note: Focal Group mean: true = −1.00;
est. = −1.03

Goodness-of-fit G^2 (45) = 52.8, $p = .2$

with 45 d.f. It appears that MML estimation and the IRT-LR chi-square tests may be used quite effectively with very small sets of items, such as the five used here, given these sample sizes and values of a.

IRT-LR and Mantel–Haenszel: An Aside

For the results tabulated in Table 10.4, Holland and Thayer (personal communication, April 1986) have also computed the Mantel–Haenszel (M–H) test (Holland & Thayer, 1986) with the same 50-item anchor used as the matching criterion. Both M–H and IRT-LR provide single-degree-of-freedom chi-square tests of *dif;* the tests are of different null hypotheses against different alternatives, but in both cases the null hypothesis reflects no *dif* while the alternative indicates *dif.*

Fig. 10.6 plots the square root of the M–H chi-square values for the 21 items in Table 10.4 against the square root of the IRT-LR chi-squares. The square roots of the single-d.f. chi-squares may be considered "parameter-being-tested over its standard error." While the *dif* in the simulation was so small that neither procedure detected it frequently, the agreement between the two procedures is striking: The square roots of the chi-squares never differ by more than 1. In principle, since IRT-LR tested exactly the difference simulated in the data, and M–H does not, IRT-LR should exhibit more power: a tendency to produce larger chi-squares. No such tendency shows in this set of 21 items; whatever difference

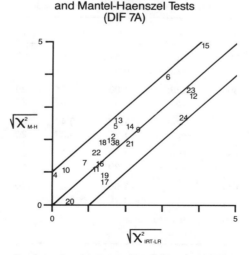

FIG. 10.6.   Scatter plot of the square root of the M–H chi-square against the square root of the IRT-LR chi-square for the 21 items tabulated in Table 10.4. The numbers are the item numbers (for identification), and the lines show the location of the identity line ±1.

may exist between the two procedures using the same 50-item anchor is probably quite small with the parameters used to simulate these data.

CONCLUSIONS

In analysis of simulated test data, IRT-LR assessment of *dif* readily detected differences between *b*s of 0.3 and differences between *c*s of 0.1, using a focal group sample of 500 and both very short and very long sets of anchor items. Smaller differences were not readily detected. Since IRT-LR is the "theoretically preferred" test, which is optimal for the model that generated the data, it is likely that detection of smaller differences can be done reliably only with larger sample sizes.

Throughout our analyses, we assume that the anchor consists of items which do not exhibit *dif*. Stated differently, *dif* detected by IRT-LR as described here is differential functioning *relative to* the differences between groups on the anchor items: *dif* is detected if the group difference on the candidate item is different from the group difference on the anchor item(s). "Uniform" group differences are not detected by such analyses. The hypotheses tested in *dif* analyses are essentially group-by-item *interaction hypotheses;* overall differences, or "main effects" are not tested. Methods of selecting the anchor item(s), or testing overall "bias" in tests, remain topics for future research.

With anchors comprising relatively few items, IRT-LR *dif* analysis is straightforward and practical, and may be done at relatively low cost; the computation required is well within the capacity of a personal computer. With long anchors, the computational burden increases rapidly. The similarity of the results obtained with IRT-LR and the Mantel–Haenszel procedure (Holland & Thayer, 1986) suggests that M–H may provide useful assessment in the context of very long tests; or M–H may be used as a "screening device" for items to be examined later, using IRT-LR.

IRT-LR examination is useful for item analysis; the results provide information concerning whether the differential item functioning is due to group differences related to guessing, difficulty, or the relationship of the item to the attribute measured by the test. Such information may facilitate an understanding of variables associated with differential item functioning. Such understanding is necessary to reduce the incidence of *dif*, and improve the validity of measurement with psychological tests.

ACKNOWLEDGMENTS

The research described in this chapter was supported, in part, by an NIMH Individual Research Service Award to L. Steinberg, and by the Research Statistics Program of ETS. We are grateful to Paul Holland for encouragement and helpful discussions on these and related topics over the past several years, and to Paul Holland and Dorothy Thayer for generously providing the simulated data.

REFERENCES

Anderson, T. W. (1984). *An introduction to multivariate statistical analysis*. New York: Wiley.

Angoff, W. H., & Ford, S. F. (1973). Item-race interaction on a test of scholastic aptitude. *Journal of Educational Measurement, 10,* 95–106.

Birnbaum, A. (1968). Some latent trait models and their uses in inferring an examinee's ability. In F. M. Lord & M. R. Novick, *Statistical theories of mental rest scores (Pt. 5,* pp. 397–479). Reading, MA: Addison–Wesley.

Bock, R. D. (1975). *Multivariate statistical methods in behavioral research*. New York: McGraw-Hill.

Bock, R. D., & Aitkin, M. (1981). Marginal maximum likelihood estimation of item parameters: An application of an EM algorithm. *Psychometrika, 46,* 443–459.

Bock, R. D., & Lieberman, M. (1970). Fitting a response model for *n* dichotomously scored items. *Psychometrika, 35,* 179–197.

Dempster, A. P., Laird, N. M., & Rubin, D. B. (1977). Maximum likelihood from incomplete data via the EM algorithm with discussion. *Journal of the Royal Statistical Society, Ser. B, 39,* 1–38.

Dorans, N. (1986, April). *Two new approaches to assessing unexpected differential item performance: Standardization and the Mantel–Haenszel method*. Paper presented at the annual meeting of the National Council on Measurement in Education, San Francisco.

Dorans, N., & Kulick, E. (1983). *Assessing unexpected differential item performance of female candidates on SAT and TSWE forms administered in December, 1977: An application of the standardization approach*. ETS Research Report (RR–83–9). Princeton, NJ: Educational Testing Service.

Holland, P. W. & Thayer, D. T. (1986, April). *Differential item performance and the Mantel–Haenszel procedure*. Paper presented at the annual meeting of the American Educational Research Association, San Francisco.

Ironson, G. H., & Subkoviak, M. (1979). A comparison of several methods of assessing item bias. *Journal of Educational Measurement, 16,* 209–225.

Kok, F. G., Mellenbergh, G. J., & van der Flier, H. (1985). Detecting experimentally induced item bias using the iterative logit method. *Journal of Educational Measurement, 22,* 295–303.

Lazarsfeld, P. F. (1950). The logical and mathematical foundation of latent structure analysis. In S. A. Stouffer, L. Guttman, E. A. Suchman, P. F. Lazarsfeld, S. A. Star, & J. A. Clausen, *Measurement and Prediction* (pp. 362–472). New York: Wiley.

Linn, R. L. & Harnisch, D. L. (1981). Interactions between item content and group membership on achievement test items. *Journal of Educational Measurement, 18,* 109–118.

Linn, R. L., Levine, M. V., Hastings, C. N. & Wardrop, J. L. (1981). Item bias on a test of reading comprehension. *Applied Psychological Measurement, 5,* 159–173.

Lord, F. M. (1952). A theory of test scores. *Psychometric Monographs,* Whole No. 7.

Lord, F. M. (1977). A study of item bias using item characteristic curve theory. In Y. H. Poortinga (Ed.), *Basic problems in cross-cultural research* (pp. 19–29). Amsterdam: Swets & Zeitlinger.

Lord, F. M. (1980). *Applications of item response theory to practical testing problems*. Hillsdale, NJ: Lawrence Erlbaum Associates.

Lord, F. M. (1986). Maximum likelihood and Bayesian estimation in item response theory. *Journal of Educational Measurement, 23,* 157–162.

Mahalanobis, P. C. (1930). On tests and measures of group divergence. *Journal and Proceedings of the Asiatic Society of Bengal, 26,* 541–588.

Mahalanobis, P. C. (1936). On the generalized distance in statistics. *Proceedings of the National Institute of Science of India, 12,* 49–55.

Marascuilo, L. A., & Slaughter, R. E. (1981). Statistical procedures for identifying possible sources of item bias based on chi-square statistics. *Journal of Educational Measurement, 18,* 229–248.

Mellenbergh, G. J. (1982). Contingency table models for assessing item bias. *Journal of Educational Statistics, 7,* 105–118.

Mislevy, R. J. (1985). Estimation of latent group effects. *Journal of the American Statistical Association, 80,* 993–997.

Muraki, E., & Bock, R. D. (1986, April). *An item maintenance system with provision for item parameter drift.* Paper presented at the ONR contractors' meeting on model based psychological measurement, Gatlinburg, TN.

Muthén, B., & Lehman, J. (1985). Multiple group IRT modeling: Applications to item bias analysis. *Journal of Educational Statistics, 10,* 133–142.

Neyman, J., & Pearson, E. S. (1928). On the use and interpretation of certain test criteria for purposes of statistical inference. *Biometrika, 20A,* 174–240, 263–294.

Pearson, K. (1900). On the criterion that a given system of deviations from the probable in the case of a correlated system of variables is such that it can be reasonably supposed to have arisen from random sampling. *Philosophical Magazine, 50,* 157–175.

Perozzo, L. (1880). Della rapresentazione graphica di una collettivita di individui successione del tempo. *Annali di Statistica, 12,* 1–16.

Rao, C. R. (1973). *Linear statistical inference and its applications.* New York: Wiley.

Scheuneman, J. D. (1979). A method of assessing bias in test items. *Journal of Educational Measurement, 16,* 143–152.

Shepard, L., Camilli, G., & Averill, M. (1981). Comparison of six procedures for detecting test item bias using both internal and external ability criteria. *Journal of Educational Statistics, 6,* 317–375.

Shepard, L., Camilli, G., & Williams, D. M. (1984). Accounting for statistical artifacts in item bias research. *Journal of Educational Statistics, 9,* 93–128.

Thissen, D. (1982). Marginal maximum likelihood estimation for the one-parameter logistic model. *Psychometrika, 47,* 201–214.

Thissen, D. (1986). *Multilog: A user's guide.* Mooresville, IN: Scientific Software.

Thissen, D., & Steinberg, L. (1986). A taxonomy of item response models. *Psychometrika, 51,* 567–577.

Thissen, D., Steinberg, L., & Gerrard, M. (1986). Beyond group mean differences: The concept of item bias. *Psychological Bulletin, 99,* 118–128.

Thissen, D., & Wainer, H. (1982). Some standard errors in item response theory. *Psychometrika, 47,* 397–412.

Thissen, D., & Wainer, H. (1985, July). *Studying item bias with item response theory.* Paper presented at the fourth European meeting of the Psychometric Society, Cambridge, England.

Wald, A. (1943). Tests of statistical hypotheses concerning several parameters when the number of observations is large. *Transactions of the American Mathematical Society, 54,* 426–482.

STATISTICAL INNOVATIONS
IN VALIDITY ASSESSMENT

Meta-analysis is concerned with quantitative methods for combining evidence from different studies. In this section, methods of meta-analysis for assessing the validity of tests through the study of data collected in a number of different settings are explored. The opening chapter by Frank Schmidt deals with that particular area of meta-analysis termed validity generalization. Focusing primarily on employment testing, he reviews the findings obtained principally by himself and his colleagues on the criterion-related validity of cognitive tests. The key result is that a very substantial portion of the variation in test-criterion correlations across a broad variety of employment settings appears to be due to "artifactual" differences in the settings: differences in sample sizes, restriction of range, etc. Schmidt goes further by asserting that all such variation is essentially artifactual and concludes by making predictions about the role validity generalization, and meta-analysis methods generally, will play both in employment selection and in research on the cognitive demands of different jobs.

In the next chapter, Larry Hedges describes how empirical Bayes methods can be used in a meta-analysis to develop a more comprehensive approach to the problem of criterion validity. Specifically, using the empirical Bayes approach a researcher can not only estimate the true variance among correlations across studies but also can obtain improved estimates of the validity in each constituent study. Hedges shows how corrections for unreliability

171

in test score or criterion and restriction of range can be made, even in the presence of missing data. This chapter, as well as those studies cited in the references, indicate that the empirical Bayes paradigm will play an increasingly important role in this area of meta-analysis.

The last chapter, by Bengt Muthén, introduces an important extension of both classical Item Response Theory (IRT) models and LISREL-type analyses. He proposes a multilevel model in which observed responses to test questions are tied to latent traits and these, in turn, are tied to observed external variables such as class type, socioeconomic status, etc. Interestingly, the mathematical formalism of Muthén's model is reminiscent of that of empirical Bayes. Using multigroup versions of the model, Muthén shows how a number of questions relating to the validity of tests can be addressed. These include differential item functioning and the impact of instruction on achievement. It is particularly noteworthy that these methods facilitate the examination of measurement models in a social context. While the approach can be applied to many problems, their impact on the quantitative assessment of test validity is potentially very great.

Rubin, in his discussion (pp. 241–256) urges extreme caution in the use of those complex statistical models and procedures that can distance investigators from their data. However, he does strongly support the notion of meta-analysis, particularly the empirical Bayes approach espoused by Hedges.

Chapter 11

Validity Generalization and the Future of Criterion-Related Validity

Frank L. Schmidt
University of Iowa

In terms of the number of people affected, the two major areas of test use in the U.S. have traditionally been education and employment. This chapter is concerned primarily with employment testing, although the methods described can be and have been applied in educational testing (Linn, Harnisch, & Dunbar, 1981). In the employment area, research on selection utility has shown that use of valid employment tests of cognitive abilities in place of less valid selection methods can yield large economic gains in the form of increased output, reduced personnel costs, or both (Cascio & Ramos, 1986; Hunter & Schmidt, 1982a; Schmidt, Hunter, McKenzie, & Muldrow, 1979; Schmidt, Hunter, Outerbridge, & Trattner, 1986). The research findings in validity generalization that are the focus of this presentation bear strongly on the two important questions in this area: (1) The question of how valid cognitive ability tests and other selection procedures generally are, and (2) The question of what is required to demonstrate their validity for particular applications in particular organizations. Briefly, what research over the last 10 years has demonstrated is that (1) The mean level of validity of cognitive tests for the prediction of job performances is higher than previously believed and (2) These validities are much less variable, and much more generalizable, across settings, organizations, geographical areas, jobs, and time periods than previously believed. These findings set the stage for an increase in the validity of employment selection procedures, with consequent economic gains in worker productivity.

Validity generalization (VG) research is based on the application of a particular set of meta-analytic methods (Hunter, Schmidt, & Jackson, 1982) to criterion-related validities of tests. We initially developed our meta-analysis methods not as general research integration methods, but as a way of attacking a critically important problem in personnel psychology: the problem of "situational specificity" of employment test validities. For more than 50 years, most personnel psychologists had believed that employment test validities were specific to situations and settings, and that, therefore, every test had to be revalidated anew in every setting in which it was considered for use. This belief was based on the empirical fact that considerable variability was present from study to study in observed validity coefficients even when the jobs and tests studied appeared to be similar or identical. The explanation developed for this variability was that the factor structure of job performance was different from job to job and that the human observer or job analyst was too poor an information receiver and processor to detect these subtle but important differences. The conclusion was that validity studies must be conducted—typically at considerable expense—in every setting. That is, the conclusion was that validity evidence could not be generalized across settings. Lawshe (1948) stated:

> A given test may be excellent in connection with one job and virtually useless in connection with another job. Furthermore, job classifications that seem similar from plant to plant sometimes differ significantly; so it becomes essential to test the test in practically every new situation. (p. 13)

And in the words of Albright, Glennon, and Smith (1963):

> If years of personnel research have proven anything, it is that jobs that seem the same from one place to another often differ in subtle but important ways. Not surprisingly, it follows that what constitutes job success is also likely to vary from place to place. (p. 18)

The fact that our point of departure was the problem of situational specificity explains why our methods of meta-analysis are focused strongly on estimation of the true (i.e., nonartifactual) *variance* of study correlations and effect sizes. We hypothesized that most or all of the variance in test validity coefficients across studies and settings was due to artifactual sources, such as sampling error, and not to real differences between jobs. This focus on the variance of effect sizes and correlations is the primary difference between our methods and those of Glass and his associates (Glass, McGaw, & Smith, 1981) or those of Rosenthal (1984; Rosenthal & Rubin, 1978). In validity generalization, merely showing that the mean is substantial is not sufficient to demonstrate generalizability. One must be able to show that the standard deviation of true validities is small enough to permit generalization of the conclusion that the test has positive validity in the great majority of situations. Figs. 11.1 and 11.2 illustrate this point. Fig. 11.3 is a counter example.

None of this means that we were unconcerned with accurate estimation of the mean. Accurate estimation of mean true validities is critical because the mean affects both generalizability (by affecting the lower credibility value) and ex-

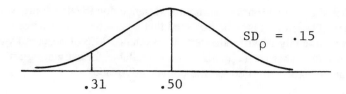

FIG. 11.1   Typical validity generalization results for cognitive abilities in predicting job performance. The mean is .50 and the 10th percentile (90% credibility value) is .31.

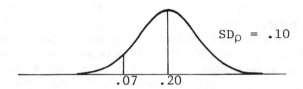

FIG. 11.2.   Example of validity generalization results with relatively low mean and low variance. Despite lower mean, validity is still generalizable; this is representative of results obtained for sales clerks.

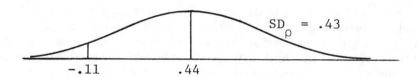

FIG. 11.3.   Validity generalization results for performance tests used with clerical workers. Substantial mean but large variance; 90% credibility value is negative. Performance tests are a heterogeneous group of predictors.

pected practical utility. Practical utility is a direct multiplicative function of the expected operational validity, other things equal (Brogden, 1949; Schmidt, Hunter, McKenzie, & Muldrow, 1979). Therefore, we introduced methods for correcting the mean observed validity for attentuation due to mean levels of range restriction and mean levels of measurement error in the measures of job performance. These corrections also differentiate our methods from those of Glass and his associates.

Artifacts other than sampling error and differences between studies in measurement error and in range restriction can cause variance in study outcomes. Computational, typographical, transcriptional, and computer program errors may be important sources of artifactual variance in many validity coefficient sets. No method or equation for estimating variance due to such sources has yet been devised. Therefore it is to be expected that even when all variance is in fact artifactual, meta-analysis will indicate that less than 100% of observed variance is due to artifacts. That is, the methods now available for estimating artifactual variance can be expected to err on the conversative side.

APPLICATIONS AND IMPACT

To date, the validity generalization procedure has been applied to more than 500 research literatures in employment selection, each one representing a predictor-job performance combination. Most of these predictors have been cognitive ability tests, but they have also included nontest procedures, such as evaluations of education and experience (McDaniel & Schmidt, 1985) and the interview (Whetzel, McDaniel, & Schmidt, 1985). In many cases, artifacts accounted for all variance across studies; for cognitive tests, the average amount of variance accounted for by artifacts has been approximately 80%. As an example, consider the relation between quantitative ability and overall job performance in clerical jobs (Pearlman, Schmidt, & Hunter, 1980). This substudy was based on 453 correlations computed on a total of 39,584 individuals. Seventy-seven percent of the variance in observed validities was traceable to artifacts, leaving a neglible variance of .019. The mean effect size was .47. Thus, integration of this massive amount of data leads to the general and generalizable principle that the correlation between quantitative ability and clerical performance is .47, with very little, if any, true variation around this value. Findings like this show the old belief that validities are situationally specific to be false and show that cumulative, generalizable knowledge about validities *is* possible.

Today many organizations—including the federal government, the U.S. Employment Service, and some large corporations—use validity generalization findings as the basis of their selection-testing programs. Validity generalization has been included in standard texts (e.g., Anastasi, 1982) and in the *Standards for Educational and Psychological Tests* (APA, AERA, NCME, 1985). Proposals have been made to include validity generalization in the federal government's Uniform Guidelines on Employee Selection Procedures (U.S. Equal Employment Opportunity Commission et al., 1978) when this document is next revised. In recent litigation in Canada, the use of validity generalization findings as the basis for the use of a group intelligence test in selecting tax collectors was upheld (Maloley et al., v. Department of National Revenue, 1986).

Early in 1978, Lee J. Cronbach suggested in correspondence that our validity generalization methods could be applied to research literatures in many different areas of the social and behavioral sciences (Cronbach, personnel communication, February 15, 1978). Our book on general meta-analysis methods was published in 1982 (Hunter, Schmidt, & Jackson, 1982), 1 year after the Glass, McGaw, and Smith (1981) book.

Our meta-analysis procedures go beyond the Glass methods in providing methods for correcting both variances and means of correlations or effect sizea for the distorting effects of the artifacts of sampling error, measurement error, and range restriction. Steps in this procedure are (Hunter, Schmidt & Jackson 1982):

1. Effect sizes are expressed as correlations or d-values and the (sample-size-weighted) average effect size is computed across studies. This mean effect size is then corrected for the attenuating effects of instrument unreliability and range restriction (if any). This latter is a step not included in Glassian meta-analysis. (Where the data allow, these corrections are made to each effect size individually prior to calculating the mean.)

2. One then determines whether the variance in effect sizes across studies is due solely to statistical and measurement artifacts. This step is likewise not included in Glassian meta-analysis. If one can reject the hypothesis that the observed variance of effect sizes is greater than the variance expected from artifacts, one concludes that the mean corrected effect size estimates the true effect size, and a general principle has been established. The mean corrected effect size then incorporates and summarizes the results of all previous studies.

3. If one *cannot* reject the hypothesis that the variance of effect sizes is greater than that expected from artifacts, one then determines whether any of the study characteristics are correlated with effect size. Here the focus should be on theoretically meaningful moderators. In areas outside of employment testing, there are often sound theoretical reasons for expecting moderators. This step we borrowed from Glass and his associates (while recognizing and warning against the severe problems of capitalization on change and low statistical power).

4. If the remaining variance is still too large to be accounted for by artifacts, it is adjusted for the effects of these artifacts, and this adjusted variance is used to set confidence or credibility intervals around the mean effect size. Again, this is a step not included in Glassian meta-analysis.

Our meta-analysis procedures have now been applied to numerous topics outside the area of validity generalization in employment selection. Some examples include:

1. Correlates of role conflict and role ambiguity (Fisher & Gittelson, 1983; Jackson & Schuler, 1985).
2. Effects of realistic job previews (McEvoy & Cascio, 1985; Premack & Wanous, 1985).
3. Evaluation of Fieldler's theory of leadership (Peters, Harthe, & Pohlman, 1985).
4. Accuracy of self-ratings of ability and skill (Mabe & West, 1982).
5. Relation of LSAT scores to performance in law schools (Linn, Harnisch, & Dunbar, 1981).

6. Relation of job satisfaction to absenteeism (Hackett & Guion, 1985; Terborg & Lee, 1982).
7. The relation between job satisfaction and job performance (Iaffaldono & Muchinsky, 1985; Petty, McGee, & Cavender, 1984).
8. The relation of job characteristics to job satisfaction (Loher, Noe, Moeller, & Fitzgerald, 1985).
9. The effectiveness of different techniques for changing attitudes and beliefs (Dillard, Hunter, & Burgoon, 1984).
10. Race effects in job performance ratings (Kraiger & Ford, 1985).
11. Relation between employee tenure intentions and actual turnover (Steele & Ovalle, 1984).
12. The effects of nonselection psychological interventions on employee output and productivity (Guzzo, Jette, & Katzell, 1985).
13. Ability of financial analysts to predict stock growth (Coggin & Hunter, 1983).
14. Premorbid functioning and recidivism in schizophrenia (Stoffelmeyr, Dillavou, & Hunter, 1983).

In some of these nonemployment selection applications, the results have been similar to those for employment tests: Most or all of the observed between-study variance in effect sizes or correlations has been found to be due to statistical artifacts (principally sampling error). However, in other cases, considerable variance has remained after correcting for the effects of artifacts, indicating the appropriateness of moderator analyses. In many of these cases, the subsequent moderator analysis has provided evidence for theoretically predicted and meaningful moderators.

Applications to data other than test validities—and the results of such analyses—have generated little, if any controversy. However, the results and conclusions produced by application of these same methods to test validities provoked reaction and criticism from some. Conclusions in the area of validity generalization can take two forms: a weak form and a strong form. The weak conclusion states that while artifacts cannot account for all the observed variance of validities across studies, the mean true validity is large enough, and the remaining variance is small enough, that one can conclude that validity will be positive in virtually all new settings (e.g., 90% or 95%). Figs. 11.1 and 11.2 illustrate such outcomes. In contrast to the conclusion that the *presence* of some level of validity is generalizable, a stronger conclusion would be that there is *no* real (i.e., nonartifactual variance), and therefore, true validity is constant across settings and is best estimated by the mean true validity. This conclusion holds that there is no situational specificity at all; i.e., that there is not even minor variation across studies or settings in positive validities. This situation is illustrated in Fig. 11.4. Evidence for the weaker conclusion of generalizability was

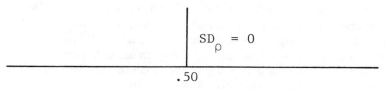

$$SD_\rho = 0$$

.50

FIG. 11.4. Example of validity generalization results when artifacts account for all variance in validities.

developed first. Strong evidence for the second conclusion developed only after numerous validity generalization studies become available. Even then, this evidence was limited (and still is) to tests of cognitive abilities. Initially, even the weaker conclusion of generalizability was controversial. It flew in the face of more than 50 years of belief to the contrary in personnel psychology. In addition, it was based on methods that seemed complex and esoteric to some. It was therefore difficult initially for many to accept. We have long since moved past this point.

Today, the generalizability of validity is widely accepted; as noted earlier, these methods are even included in the 1985 *Standards*. Today the focus of remaining criticism seems to be on the conclusion that there is no situational specificity (no situational variance) at all in the true validities of cognitive tests (James, Demaree, & Mulaik, 1986; Sackett et al., 1985). In this connection, it is important to note that, even if they were successful, such challenges would have no implications for the practical use of validity generalization; such use depends only on a demonstration of generalizability. It does not require a demonstration that there is no situational variance at all in validities.

Over a number of years, we collected in a single document most of the objections to, and reservations about, validity generalization methods, findings, and conclusions and provided our responses (Schmidt, Hunter, Pearlman, & Hirsh, 1985). Publication of this document was accompanied by commentary on our responses by five personnel psychologists (Sackett, Schmitt, Tenopyr, Kehoe, & Zedeck, 1985) and our responses to their commentary. The commentators, chosen by the editor for their knowledge in this area (Hakel, 1985), took no issue with the major practical conclusion of meta-analytical research in personnel selection: that validities, particularly of cognitive tests, have been shown to be widely generalizable across settings, jobs, populations, organizations, geographical areas, time periods, etc. Most of the commentary was in the nature of attempts to "fine tune" statistical methods or applications. While the commentators accepted validity generalization, they appeared on balance to reject (or at least question) the conclusion that the evidence was now sufficient to reject all situational variation in cognitive test validities.

In questioning our conclusions about situational specificity, Sackett et al. (1985) focused on single validity generalization studies. Just as earlier researchers focused on the individual test-validation study, failing to realize that single studies cannot be interpreted in isolation, the commentators focused on single meta-analyses—in particular, on the statistical power of single meta-analyses to detect variation in true validities—(Sackett, Harris, & Orr, 1986) failing to see it is the overall pattern of findings from many meta-analyses that is important in revealing the underlying reality. The same can be said of a similar critique offered by James, Demaree, & Mulaik (1986).

The overall pattern of evidence against the theory of situational variance in true validities of cognitive tests includes the following. When the most accurate quantitative procedures are employed, the average percentage of variance accounted for across traditional VG studies is approximately 85% (Schmidt, Hunter, Pearlman & Hirsh, 1985, Q & A 27). Traditional VG studies are those that include individual validity studies from a wide variety of sources and conducted by a variety of different researchers. When all studies going into a VG analysis are conducted by the same well-trained research team, there can be better control of the "other" sources of artifactual variance. For example, differences between studies in criterion contamination and deficiency are controlled because the same criterion measures are used in all studies. The small differences that might exist between studies in the factor structure of the predictor (e.g., for different arithmetic reasoning tests) are controlled, because the same predictor is used in all studies. And it is possible to set up strong controls to check for and eliminate computational, programming, and transcriptional errors. In three recent large-scale, nationwide, well-controlled consortium studies (Dunnette et al., 1982; Dye, 1982; Peterson, 1982), it was found the average percentage of variance accounted for was essentially 100%. (For example, in Dye, 1982, it was 99%.) Thus the better the methods and data used, the larger the percentage of a validity variance that is accounted for. And when this control is at the highest level yet attained (the consortium studies), all variance is accounted for. This is strong evidence against the existence of situational variance.

Further, it has been found that in a data set in which there could be no situational specificity—because all data were gathered in the same organization, at the same time, using the same test and criterion, and using subjects drawn from the same group—the amount of observed variance in validity coefficients across studies was about the same as that typically found across studies conducted in entirely different settings and organizations (Schmidt, Ocasio, Hillery, & Hunter, 1985). All of this variance was accounted for by sampling error. This finding indicates that the between-setting variance typically observed is artifactual. These and other lines of evidence are discussed in more detail in Schmidt, Hunter, Pearlman & Hirsh (1985) and in the studies cited therein. In light of this general pattern of evidence, the fact that statistical power to detect validity variation is less than perfect in individual validity generalizational analyses (in particular, those with small numbers of studies based, in turn, on small Ns) is not of critical significance.

Recently, James, Demaree, & Mulaik (1986) have advanced the proposition that validity generalization research should not be conducted on correlations but rather on the Fisher's z transformation of the correlation. The basis for this position is the well-known fact that there is a slight downward bias in the correlation coefficient (r) as an estimator of the population correlation (ρ).

This downward bias creates a small covariance between ρ and e, the random sampling error term. Linn and Dunbar (1982) showed that the bias in the estimated sampling error created by this small covariance is trivial and concluded, "it is unlikely that the missing covariance term creates any serious difficulty in practice" (p. 15). This leaves the question of bias in mean validities estimated using r and using Fisher's z. We have now completed a study that investigates this question in some detail (Hunter, Schmidt, & Coggin, 1986). This investigation found that when there is no variation in the population correlations (ρ_i), r has a small negative bias that is less than rounding error (i.e., less than .005) unless N is smaller than 40. With sample sizes less than 40, the downward bias can be reduced to below rounding error by multiplying each r by the linear correction factor $(2N - 1)/(2N - 2)$. For Fisher's z, when the ρ_i do not vary, the bias is in the opposite direction—a positive bias—and is always larger than the bias in r. When there is variation in ρ_i, this variation introduces an additional bias component into both r and Fisher's z. This bias component is positive. For the average correlation, this positive bias acts in a direction opposite to the initial negative bias, reducing the overall bias. Further, both bias components and total bias decrease for r as N increases. For Fisher's z the story is different. The additional positive bias resulting from variation in the ρ_i (the transformational bias) is added to the previously existing positive bias, producing a larger positive bias. Furthermore, the transformational bias is independent of sample size; it does not decrease as sample size increases. For further details, formulas, derivations, and tables of bias values, see Hunter, Schmidt, and Coggin (1986). The discovery of a transformational bias in Fisher's z that is independent of sampling error is an additional reason for not employing that statistic in validity generalization methods. Further, the z transformation is often employed in the averaging of correlations outside of VG analyses. These findings indicate that Fisher's z should probably not be used for that purpose either. Its use can lead to inflation of obtained averages by substantial amounts—up to .06 or more under extreme circumstances (Hunter, Schmidt, & Coggin, 1986).

FUTURE TRENDS AND IMPLICATIONS

It is likely that practical applications of validity generalization methods and findings in organizational selection and placement will expand in the future. As applications currently in place gain increasing exposure, many organizations and personnel psychologists now studying and evaluating validity generalization will probably follow suit. The two largest users of validity generalization are currently in the public sector—the U.S. Employment Service (USES) and the federal government. Based on recent developments, it appears that there will also be significant usage by the military in the future (Foley & Swanson, 1985; Hunter, Crosson, & Friedman, 1985). Based on validity generalization analyses that included 515 validity studies conducted by USES psychologists over the last 40 years (Hunter, 1983a, b, c, d), the USES has adopted validity generalization as the basis for its nationwide job-testing program that operates through state employment services and uses the General Aptitude Test Battery (GATB). This new program, which involves changes in *how* the GATB scores are used, was pilot-tested in North Carolina (McKinney, 1984) and has since been introduced into a dozen states. The federal government is currently implementing validity generalization as the basis for selection in a wide variety of civilian jobs. It has been used for some years now as the basis for selection in clerical occupations (Pearlman, 1979; Pearlman, Schmidt, & Hunter, 1980), a very numerous employment category in the government. Other government agencies (e.g., the CIA) have conducted research on validity generalization independently and have employed the findings.

Validity generalization is now used by large groups in the private sector also. For example, in the petroleum industry, validity generalization research sponsored by the American Petroleum Institute has led to an industry-wide program for the selection of refinery operations, maintenance workers and lab technicians (Schmidt, Hunter, & Caplan, 1981a, b; Wunder & Herring, 1980; Wunder, Herring, & Carron, 1982). Similar programs have been set up in the insurance (Peterson, 1982) and utilities (Dunnette et al., 1982) industries. Sears and Armco have also conducted VG research. My associates and I believe that such applications will expand in number and scope over the next decade. We believe also that the following VG-related trends will be evident over the next 10 years:

1. The federal government will revise its Uniform Guidelines For Employee Selection Procedures (U.S. EEOC et al., 1978), and the revision will incorporate VG, as do the current AERA–APA–NCME testing *Standards*. The *Principles for the validation and use of personnel selection procedures,* published by the Society for Industrial and Organizational Psychology are currently undergoing revision. The revision—the third Edition—will contain a greatly expanded treatment of validity generalization. These developments will further encourage use of VG methods and findings.

2. Impetus will be given to applications of VG findings by the increasing use of decision-theoretic, regression-based methods for determining the economic value of selection procedures (Boudreau, 1983; Cascio, 1982; Cascio & Ramos, 1986; Cronshaw & Alexander, 1985; Hunter & Schmidt, 1982a,b,1983; Schmidt, Hunter, McKenzie, & Muldrow, 1979; Schmidt, Hunter, Outerbridge, & Trattner, 1986; Schmidt, Mack, & Hunter, 1984). Research along these lines is increasingly making it clear that the economic implications of selection methods are quite substantial.

3. There will be increasing optimism about the possibility of establishing cumulative knowledge and general principles in personnel psychology (and in other areas of industrial/organizational psychology as well) as a result of application of meta-analysis methods. The belief will become increasingly strong that the phenomona that we study are lawful, rather than capricious, and are subject to systematic scientific study. Some of the epistimological pessimism of earlier years (e.g., see Cronbach, 1975) will dissipate. Ironically, this will take us back to the more optimistic epistimological beliefs and orientations that were dominant in the 1920s, before the reification of sampling error and other statistical artifacts distorted our interpretations of our research (Hunter, 1980). This will accelerate as current graduate students and young Ph.D.s—who have consistently reacted the most positively to these developments—assume increasingly important roles in their fields. VG research will be seen in historical context as the first of many areas in which systematic application of meta-analysis led to surprising new findings and rapid progress in understanding.

4. There will be some continuing criticisms of validity generalization methods and findings, but none will prove to be of consequence. In particular, the attempt to argue that application of meta-analysis to validity coefficients is fundamentally different from application of meta-analysis to other correlations will fail. Criticisms will increasingly be directed to suggestions for fine tuning details of the statistical and measurement procedures involved (as in James, Demaree, & Mulaik, 1986). These efforts will have little implication for the actual findings or conclusions.

5. The findings in VG research will stimulate an increasing emphasis on the importance of general mental ability, relative to specific aptitudes and abilities. Validity generalization methods applied to large empirical data bases have allowed for systematic control of sampling error, measurement error, and range variation. Elimination of these distortions has allowed improved applications of confirmatory factor analysis and path analysis. (Hunter, 1983a, e, 1984, 1985). In particular, Hunter's (1983e) analysis of three large sample (Ns from 16,618 to 21,032) military data bases has shown that factors specific to abilities below the level of general mental ability generally contribute nothing to the prediction of performance in job training. In all three data bases, the only path models that fit the data were models in which general ability is the cause of both more specific abilities and of job-training performance itself. Models with direct causal paths from specific abilities (e.g., quantitative ability or verbal ability) to job-training performance were disconfirmed. In further analyses (Hunter, 1985), he found that the general mental ability composite predicted job-training performance in specific occupational areas (e.g., electronics) as well or better than the regression-based composite of specific abilities designed expressly for that occupational area (e.g., the electronics composite). The only exception was the clerical occupational area, where perceptual speed made an incremental contribution to validity of .02 over the validity of general ability. Similar findings revealing the overwhelming importance of general ability were reported in the analysis of the

USES data base (Hunter, 1983b). Thus an indirect result of VG methods and research appears to be support for the importance of general mental ability. These findings add to the empirical evidence and theoretical arguments advanced by Jensen, among others (e.g., Jensen, 1980).

6. VG and meta-analysis methods are strengthening the trend, begun earlier by the introduction of LISREL (Jöreskog & Sörbom, 1979) for researchers to focus their work on latent variables rather than observed scores on single measures or tests, or even true scores on single tests. This trend has also been spurred by the increasing skepticism about, and rejection of, logical positivism as a philosophy of science (Glymour, 1980; Schlagel, 1979; Suppe, 1977) and behaviorism (Mackenzie, 1972, 1977) as a philosophical guide to the conduct of research. Like LISREL, VG and meta-analysis methods contain built-in corrections for measurement error. VG and meta-analysis methods also emphasize the importance of correcting for sampling error and range variation, bringing researchers closer to the underlying latent variables. Also, as we have noted, these methods yield estimates of latent variable correlations that are well suited to the conduct of confirmatory factor analysis and path analysis (Hunter & Gerbing, 1982).

7. Finally, VG findings are overturning some more specific but long-held beliefs. These beliefs are perhaps less broadly important than the belief in the situational specificity of test validities, but nevertheless they have been strongly held and the emerging evidence that they may be false appears to be surprising to many. One such belief is that validities of cognitive ability tests tend to be substantially smaller for criteria of performance on the job than for criteria of performance in training. It now appears that there may be no such difference when job performance is measured using objective job sample measures, rather than supervisory ratings of job performance. VG studies have shown that validities against job sample measures are of essentially the same magnitude (.50–.60) as validities against training performance measures, while validities against supervisory ratings are lower (.40–.50) (Hunter, 1983f; Nathan, 1985; Schmidt, Hunter et al., 1985, Q & A 1 & 4). Our traditional use of supervisory ratings as criterion measures may have led to systematic underestimates of validity. A related belief is that cognitive tests valid for predicting training performance may be invalid for predicting performance on the job, and vice versa. The cumulative data from VG studies suggest that a test valid for predicting one of these criteria is valid for predicting the other. Further, looking across measures of different abilities, the relative sizes of mean validities appear to be similar for the two types of criterion measures ($r = .77$; Pearlman, Schmidt, & Hunter, 1980). Another long-held belief that has been disconfirmed by VG research findings is the proposition that differences between jobs and between job families in task composition moderate cognitive test validities. Even large differences between jobs in task composition have now been shown to have little or no effect on test validities so long as the level of information processing demands are similar

(Schmidt, Hunter, & Pearlman, 1981). The erroneous notion that task differences per se would moderate validities appears to have developed in reaction to behavioristic influences in personnel psychology. Finally, another belief challenged by VG findings is the belief that cognitive ability tests are sometimes—or even often—invalid for particular jobs. The evidence is now substantial that cognitive ability tests have at least some positive validity for predicting performance in training and on the job for virtually all jobs (Hunter, 1983b; Pearlman, 1982; Schmidt & Hunter, 1981). The evidence indicates that as the information-processing demands (that is, "complexity") of the job decline, validity declines. However, it never declines to zero; in Hunter (1983b), even the least complex job family—machine-tending jobs—showed a validity of .23 for general cognitive ability against performance on the job.

ACKNOWLEDGMENTS

The author would like to thank John E. Hunter and Hannah Rothstein Hirsh for their helpful comments on earlier versions of this chapter.

REFERENCES

American Psychological Association, American Educational Research Association, & National Council on Measurement in Education (1985). *Standards for educational and psychological testing*. Washington, DC: American Psychological Association.

Albright, L. E., Glennon, J. R., Smith, W. J. (1963). *The use of psychological tests in industry*. Cleveland: Howard Allen.

Anastasi A. (1982). *Psychological testing* (5th ed.). New York: Macmillan.

Boudreau, J. W. (1983). Economic considerations in estimating the utility of human resource productivity improvement programs. *Personnel Psychology, 36*, 551–576.

Brogden, H. E. (1949). When testing pays off. *Personnel Psychology, 2*, 171–183.

Cascio, W. F. (1982). *Costing human resources: The financial impact of behavior in organizations*. Boston: Kent.

Cascio, W. F., & Ramos, R. A. (1986). Development and application of a new method for assessing job performance in behavioral economic terms. *Journal of Applied Psychology, 71*, 20–28.

Coggin, T. D., & Hunter, J. E. (1983). Problems in measuring the quality of investment information: The perils of the information coefficient. *Financial Analysts Journal*, May/June, 1–10.

Cronbach, L. J. (1975). Beyond the two disciplines of scientific psychology revisited. *American Psychologist, 30*, 116–127.

Cronshaw, S. F., & Alexander, R. A. (1985). One answer to the demand for accountability: Selection utility as an investment decision. *Organizational Behavior and Human Performance, 35*, 102–118.

Dillard, J. P., Hunter, J. E., & Burgoon, M. (1984). Sequential requests, persuasive message strategies: A meta-analysis of foot-in-door and door-in-the-face. *Human Communication Research, 10*, 461–488.

Dunnette, M. D., & Borman, W. C. (1979). Personnel selection and classification. In *M. R. Rosenzweig & L. W. Porter (Eds.), Annual review of psychology* (Vol. 30). Palo Alto, CA: Annual Reviews.

Dunnette, M. D., Houston, J. S., Hough, L. M., Toquam, J., Lamnstein, S., King, K., Bosshardt, M. J., & Keys, M. (1982). *Development and validation of an industry-wide electric power plant operator selection system.* Minneapolis, MN: Personnel Decisions Research Institute.

Dye, D. (1982). *Validity generalization analysis for data from 16 studies participating in a consortium study.* Unpublished manuscript, Department of Psychology, George Washington University, Washington, DC.

Fisher, C. D. & Gittelson, R. (1983). A meta-analysis of the correlates of role conflict and ambiguity. *Journal of Applied Psychology, 68,* 320–333.

Foley, P. P., & Swanson, L. (1985). An investigation of validity generalization of Navy selector composites Technical Report, Navy Personnel Research and Development Center, San Diego, CA.

Glass, G. V., McGaw, B., & Smith, M. L. (1981). *Meta-analysis in social research.* Beverly Hills, CA: Sage.

Glymour, C. (1980). The good theories do. In *Construct validity in psychological measurement: Proceedings of a colloquium on theory and application in education and employment,* Educational Testing Service, Princeton, NJ.

Guzzo, R. A., Jette, R. D., Katzell, R. A. (1985). The effects of psychologically based intervention programs on worker productivity: A meta-analysis. *Personnel Psychology, 38,* 275–292.

Hakel, M. D. (1985). Editorial note. *Personnel Psychology, 38,* 697–699.

Hackett, R. D., & Guion, R. M. (1985). A re-evaluation of the absenteeism–job satisfaction relationship. *Organizational Behavior and Human Decision Processes, 35,* 340–381.

Hunter, J. E. (1980). Validity generalization and construct validity. In *Construct validity in psychological measurement: Proceedings of a colloquium on theory and application in education and measurement,* Educational Testing Service, Princeton, NJ.

Hunter, J. E. (1983a). *The dimensionality of the General Aptitude Test Battery and the dominance of the general factors over specific factors in the prediction of job performance for USES,* Test Research Report No. 44, U.S. Department of Labor, U.S. Employment Services, Washington, DC.

Hunter, J. E. (1983b). *Test validation for 12,000 jobs: An application of job classification and validity generalization analysis to the General Aptitude Test Battery,* Test Research Report No. 45, U.S. Employment Service, U.S. Department of Labor, Washington, DC.

Hunter, J. E. (1983c). *Fairness of the General Aptitude Test Battery: Ability differences and their impact on minority hiring rates,* Test Research Report No. 46, U.S. Employment Service, U.S. Department of Labor, Washington, DC.

Hunter, J. E. (1983d). *The economic benefits of personnel selection using ability tests: A state of the art review including a detailed analysis of the dollar benefit of U.S. employment service placements and a critique of the low cut off method of test use,* Test Research Report No. 47, U.S. Employment Service, U.S. Department of Labor, Washington, DC.

Hunter, J. E. (1983e). The prediction of job performance in the military using ability composites: The dominance of general cognitive ability over specific aptitudes. Report for Research Applications, Inc., in partial fulfillment of DOD contract No. F41689–83–C–0025.

Hunter, J. E. (1983f). A causal analysis of cognitive ability, job knowledge, job performance, and supervisory ratings. In F. Landy, S. Zedeck, & J. Cleveland (Eds.), *Performance Measurement and theory* (pp. 257–266), Hillsdale, NJ: Lawrence Erlbaum Associates.

Hunter, J. E. (1984). The validity of the Armed Forces Vocational Aptitude Battery (ASVAB) High School Composites. Report for Research Applications, Inc., in partial fulfillment of DOD contract No. F41689–83–C–0025.

Hunter, J. E. (1985). Differential validity across jobs in the military. Report for Research Applications, Inc., in partial fulfillment of DOD contract No. F41689–83–C–0025.

Hunter, J. E., Crosson, J. J., & Friedman, D. H. (1985). The validity of the Armed Services Vocational Aptitude Battery (ASVAB) for civilian and military job performance. Final report by Research Applications, Inc., in fulfillment of contract No. F41689–83–C–0025.

Hunter, J. E., & Gerbing, D. W. (1982). Unidimensional measurement, second order factor analysis and causal models. In B. M. Staw & L. L. Cummings (Eds.), *Research in organizational behavior* (Vol. 4). Greenwich, CT: JAI Press.

Hunter, J. E., & Schmidt, F. L. (1982a). Fitting people to jobs: Implications of personnel selection for national productivity. In E. A. Fleishman & M. D. Dunnette (Eds.), *Human performance and productivity, Vol. I: Human capability assessment* (pp. 223–284). Hillsdale, NJ: Lawrence Erlbaum Associates.

Hunter, J. E., & Schmidt, F. L. (1982b). Ability tests: Economic benefits versus the issue of fairness. *Industrial Relations, 21*(3), 293–308.

Hunter, J. E., & Schmidt, F. L. (1983). Quantifying the effects of psychological interventions on employee job performance and work force productivity. *American Psychologist, 38,* 473–478.

Hunter, J. E., Schmidt, F. L., & Coggin, T. D. (1986). Meta-analysis of correlations: The issue of bias and misconceptions about the Fisher *z* transformation. Department of Psychology, Michigan State University, East Lansing.

Hunter, J. E., Schmidt, F. L., & Jackson, G. B. (1982). *Meta-analysis: Cumulating research findings across studies.* Beverly Hills, CA: Sage.

Iaffaldono, M. T., & Muchinsky, P. M. (1985). Job satisfaction and job performance: A meta-analysis. *Psychological Bulletin, 97,* 251–273.

Jackson, S. E., & Schuler, R. S. (1985). A meta-analysis and conceptual critique of research on role ambiguity and role conflict in work settings. *Organizational Behavior and Human Decision Processes, 36,* 16–78.

James, L. R., Demaree, R. G., & Mulaik, S. A. (1986). A note on validity generalization procedures. *Journal of Applied Psychology, 71,* 440–450.

Jensen, A. R. (1980). *Bias in mental testing.* New York: Free Press.

Jöreskog, K. G., & Sörbom, D. (1979). *Advances in factor analysis and structural equation models.* Cambridge, MA: Abt Books.

Kraiger, K., & Ford, J. K. (1985). A meta-analysis of race effects in performance ratings. *Journal of Applied Psychology, 70,* 56–65.

Lawshe, C. H. (1948). *Principles of personnel testing.* New York: McGraw–Hill.

Linn, R. L., & Dunbar, S. B. (1982, November). Validity generalization and predictive bias. In *Performance assessment: The state of the art.* The fourth Johns Hopkins University National Symposium on Educational Research, Washington, DC.

Linn, R. L., Harnisch, D. L., & Dunbar S. B. (1981). Validity generalization and situational specificity: an analysis of the prediction of first year grades in law school *Applied Psychological Measurement, 5,* 281–289.

Loher, B. T., Noe, R. A., Moeller, N., & Fitzgerald, M. P. (1985). A meta-analyis of the relationship of job characteristics to job satisfaction. *Journal of Applied Psychology, 70,* 280–289.

Mabe, P. A., III, & West, S. G. (1982). Validity of self evaluations of ability: a review and meta-analysis. *Journal of Applied Psychology, 67,* 280–296.

Mackenzie, B. D. (1972). Behaviorism and positivism. *Journal of the History of the Behavioral Sciences, 8,* 222–231.

———. (1977). *Behaviorism and the limits of scientific method.* Atlantic Highlands, NJ: Humanities Press.

Maloley et al. v. Department of National Revenue.(1986, February). Canadian Civil Service Appeals Board, Ottawa.

McDaniel, M. A., & Schmidt, F. L. (1985). *A meta-analysis of the validity of training and experience ratings in personnel selection.* Paper submitted for publication.

McEvoy, G. M., & Cascio, W. F. (1985). Strategies for reducing employee turnover: A meta-analysis. *Journal of Applied Psychology, 70,* 342–353.

McKinney, M. W. (1984). Final report: Validity generalization pilot study. Submitted to the USES Southern Test Development Field Center, Raleigh, NC.

Nathan, B. R. (1985). *The predictability of criteria for clerical workers: A meta-analytic investigation.* Department of Psychology, University of Missouri–St. Louis.

Pearlman, K. (1979). *The validity of tests used to select clerical personnel: A comprehensive summary and evaluation.* Washington, DC: U.S. Office of Personnel Management.

Pearlman, K. (1982). *The Bayesian approach to validity generalization: A systematic examination of the robustness of procedures and conclusions.* Doctoral dissertation, Department of Psychology, George Washington University, Washington, DC.

Pearlman, K., Schmidt, F. L., & Hunter, J. E. (1980). Validity generalization results for tests used to predict job proficiency and training success in clerical occupations. *Journal of Applied Psychology, 65,* 373–406.

Peters, L. H., Harthe, D., & Pohlman, J. (1985). Fiedler's contingency theory of leadership: An application of the meta-analysis procedures of Schmidt and Hunter. *Psychological Bulletin, 97,* 274–285.

Peterson, N. G. (1982, October). *Investigation of validity generalization in clerical and technical/professional occupations in the insurance industry.* Paper presented at the Conference on Validity Generalization, Personnel Testing Council of Southern California, Newport Beach, CA.

Petty, M. M., McGee, G. W., & Cavender, J. W. (1984). A meta-analysis of the relationship between individual job satisfaction and individual performance. *Academy of Management Review, 9,* 712–721.

Premack, S., & Wanous, J. P. (1985). Meta-analysis of realistic job preview experiments. *Journal of Applied Psychology, 70,* 706–719.

Rosenthal, R. (1984). *Meta-analysis procedures for social research.* Beverly Hills, CA: Sage.

Rosenthal, R., & Rubin, D. B. (1978). Interpersonal expectancy effects: The first 345 studies. *Behavioral and Brain Sciences, 3,* 377–415.

Sackett, P. R., Schmitt, N., Tenopyr, M. L., Kehoe, J., & Zedeck, S. (1985). Commentary on Forty Questions about validity generalization and meta-analysis. *Personnel Psychology, 38,* 697–798.

Sackett, P. R., Harris, M. M., & Orr, J. M. (1986). On seeking moderator variables in the meta-analysis of correlational data: A Monte Carlo investigation of statistical power and resistance to Type 1 error, *Journal of Applied Psychology.*

Schlagel, R. H. (1979). *Revaluation in the philosophy of science: Implications for method and theory in psychology.* Address at the meeting of the American Psychological Association, New York.

Schmidt, F. L., & Hunter, J. E. (1981). Employment testing: Old theories and new research findings. *American Psychologist, 36,* 1128–1137.

Schmidt, F. L., Hunter, J. E., & Caplan, J. R. (1981a). Validity generalization results for two job groups in the petroleum industry. *Journal of Applied Psychology, 66,* 261–273.

Schmidt, F. L., Hunter, J. E., & Caplan, J. R. (1981b). *Selection procedure validity generalization (transportability) results for three job groups in the petroleum industry.* American Petroleum Institute, Washington, DC.

Schmidt, F. L., Hunter, J. E., McKenzie, R. C., & Muldrow, T. W. (1979). The impact of a valid selection procedures on work-force productivity. *Journal of Applied Psychology, 64,* 609–626.

Schmidt, F. L., Hunter, J. E., Outerbridge, A. M., & Trattner, M. H. (1986). The economic impact of job selection methods on the size, productivity, and payroll costs of the Federal workforce: An empirical demonstration. *Personnel Psychology, 39,* 1–29.

Schmidt, F. L., Hunter, J. E., & Pearlman, K. (1981). Task difference and validity of aptitude tests in selection: A red herring. *Journal of Applied Psychology, 66,* 166–185.

Schmidt, F. L., Hunter, J. E., Pearlman, K. and Hirsh, H. R. (1985). Forty questions about validity generalization and meta-analysis. *Personnel Psychology, 38,* 697–798.

Schmidt, F. L., Mack, M. J., & Hunter (1984). Selection utility in the occupation of United States Park Ranger. Part three modes of test use. *Journal of Applied Psychology, 69,* 490–497.

Schmidt, F. L., Ocasio, B. P., Hillery, J. M., & Hunter, J. E. (1985). Further within-setting empirical tests of the situational specificity hypothesis in personnel selection. *Personnel Psychology, 38,* 509–524.

Steele, R. P., & Ovalle, N. K. (1984). A review and meta-analysis of research on the relationship between behavioral intentions and employee turnover. *Journal of Applied Psychology, 69,* 673–686.

Stoffelmeyr, B. E., Dillavou, D., & Hunter, J. E. (1983). Premorbid functioning and recidivism in schizophrenia: A cumulative analysis. *Journal of Consulting and Clinical Psychology, 51,* 338–352.

Suppe, F. (Ed.). (1977). *The structure of scientific theories.* Urbana: University of Illinois Press.

Terborg, J. R., Lee, T. W. (1982). Extension of the Schmidt-Hunter validity Generalization procedure to the prediction of absenteeism behavior from knowledge of job satisfaction and organizational commitment. *Journal of Applied Psychology, 67,* 280–296.

U. S. Equal Employment Opportunity Commission, U. S. Civil Service Commission, U. S. Department of Labor, & U. S. Department of Justice. (1978). Uniform guidelines on employee selection procedures. *Federal Register,* 1978, *43*(166), 38295–38309.

Whetzel, D. L., McDaniel, M. A., & Schmidt, F. L. (1985). The validity of employment interviews: A review and meta-analysis. In H. R. Hirsh (Chair), *Meta-analysis of alternative predictors of job performance,* Symposium at the 93rd annual convention of the American Psychological Association, Los Angeles.

Wunder, R. S., & Herring, J. W. (1980). *Interpretive guide for the API test validity generalization project.* Human Resources Series, American Petroleum Institute, Publication 755.

Wunder, R. S., Herring, J. W., & Carron, T. J. (1982). *Interpretive guide for the API test validity generalization project.* Human Resources Series, American Petroleum Institute, Publication 755.

Chapter 12

The Meta-Analysis
of Test Validity Studies:
Some New Approaches

Larry V. Hedges
The University of Chicago

There has recently been a great deal of interest in the use of quantitative methods for combining evidence from different studies yielding correlation coefficients as measures of association. One reason for this interest is that the correlation coefficient is often seen as a natural and easily interpretable index of effect magnitude for meta-analytic work. Consequently many investigators with a general interest in meta-analysis have examined the problem of combining estimates of correlation coefficients.

Much of the interest in combining estimates of test validity has been focused on the problems of combining evidence on the validity of tests used in personnel selection. The central question in the literature on personnel test validity is whether the true (population) test validity is reasonably constant across studies. Personnel psychologists have noted considerable variability in validity coefficients derived from studies using tests and jobs that appeared to be very similar (Ghiselli, 1966, p. 28). The traditional interpretation of this variability in observed validity coefficients was that validity coefficients were influenced by situational (contextual) factors that are hard to determine completely. A consequence of this situational specificity is that it is difficult or impossible to make generalizations about validity and that new validation studies are required in each new situation (Albright, Glennon, & Smith, 1963, p. 18; Ghiselli, 1966, p. 28; Guion, 1965, p. 126).

In the last 10 years, several researchers have investigated the traditional wisdom that variation in observed validity coefficients makes validity generalization impossible (Callender & Osburn, 1980; Callender, Osburn, Greener, & Ashworth, 1982; Pearlman, Schmidt, & Hunter, 1980; Schmidt, Gast–Rosenburg, & Hunter, 1980; Schmidt & Hunter, 1977; Schmidt, Hunter, & Caplan,

1981; Schmidt, Hunter, & Pearlman, 1982). The results of these meta-analyses of test validity studies, often called validity generalization studies, challenged the notion that test validities are highly situation-specific.

These investigators were stimulated by a recognition that variability among observed validities may arise from several sources even if the true (population) validity is constant. Since each observed validity coefficient is a sample statistic, some of the variability among observed validities is due to sampling fluctuations. Sampling variability is, of course, particularly a problem among studies that have small samples. Unreliability in the variables that are correlated to yield the validity coefficient attenuates the correlation. If reliabilities vary across studies, then some of the variation in observed validity coefficients is attributable to this differential attenuation. Finally, restriction of the range of the independent variable is also known to attenuate correlations. Validity coefficients in personnel selection studies are typically based on applicants selected. Therefore some degree of range restriction is a characteristic of these studies. When some studies involve a lower selection rate (greater restriction of range) than others, this differential range restriction will produce variability among the observed validities. The statistical methods used in recent studies of validity generalization involve attempts to estimate the contribution of sampling error, measurement error, and restriction of range, respectively, to the observed variability in a collection of validity coefficients. Each author has used slightly different methods, but the principle in each case is to compare the variability in the observed validities with the variability attributable to the "artifacts" of sampling error, (differential) measurement error, and (differential) restriction of range. If a large proportion of the observed variability is attributable to the "artifactual sources," then the researchers conclude that the variability in the true (population) validities is negligible and validity coefficients can be safely generalized across situations.

The work of Hunter, Schmidt, and their associates has contributed a great deal to the proper interpretation of validity studies. Although their "sources of artifactual variance" were well known prior to work on validity generalization, reviewers had paid very little attention to their implications for research reviews. The use of these "artifacts" to explain some of the variability in the validities observed in a series of studies is therefore a contribution to methodology for research reviewing. Methods in the spirit of those proposed by Hunter, Schmidt and their associates are likely to be useful in research reviews that attempt to combine evidence from any studies that yield correlation coefficients. Despite the intuitive appeal of the methods used in validity generalization studies, there are some statistical problems with these methods.

This chapter has three purposes. The first is to describe the statistical models underlying methods for the study of validity generalization. The second purpose is to expose some potential problems with the methods that are most frequently used in the validity generalization studies. The third purpose is to suggest a new method for studying validity generalization incorporating empirical Bayes methods. This method of studying test validities is consistent with the idea that test validities are partly situation-specific but are also partly generalizable across situations. It provides for estimation of the mean and variance of the distribution of test validities as well as for improved estimates of validity in particular situations. This new method is a slight generalization of that employed by Rubin (1980) to study estimation of treatment effects in replicated experiments and by Rubin (1981) to study the estimation of regression coefficients in law school validity studies. The generalization is in the adaptation of Rubin's method to handle estimation of the correlation variance component in the presence of missing data on test reliability, criterion reliability, or range restriction. The chapter begins with an explication of notation. Statistical models underlying procedures for validity generalization are then considered. The first case is that in which there are no corrections for unreliability or restriction of range. The second case involves corrections for unreliability and restriction of range under the assumption that there are no missing data on the correction factors for these artifacts. The third case involves the more realistic situation in which corrections for restriction of range and unreliability are desired, but there are some missing data on the correction factors for some of these artifacts. Finally an example is provided.

NOTATION AND STATISTICAL MODELS

This chapter is concerned entirely with methods for the study of test validity from several validity studies each of which measures test validity via a correlation coefficient between a test and a criterion. Although much of the literature in applied psychology involves correlations as indexes of test validity, note that not all studies of test validity utilize this index. Another index of test validity used in some investigations is the regression coefficient (see Raju & Burke, 1983; Rubin, 1980).

Notation

Consider a series of k independent validity studies. Let $X_1, \ldots, X_k$ be k random variables, each of which represents the test scores in one of the k studies. Let $Y_1, \ldots, Y_k$ be random variables representing the scores on k criterion measures and assume that (X_i, Y_i) has a multivariate normal distribution for $i = 1, \ldots, k$. The population validity (parameter) in the ith validity study is the population product-moment correlation ρ_i, and the sample size in the ith study is n_i. Thus the observed data are the sample validity coefficients $r_1, \ldots, r_k$ derived from k studies with population validities $\rho_1, \ldots, \rho_k$ and sample size $n_1, \ldots, n_k$.

Corrections for Unreliability & Restriction of Range

Measurement error in either the test or the criterion is known to attenuate correlations. Similarly restriction of range on either test or criterion is known to attenuate correlations. Consequently if (test or criterion) reliability or the degree of range restriction varies across studies, the validity coefficient ρ will also tend to vary across the studies. Because variation in population validities due to unreliability and range restriction may occur even when all studies would have yielded the same correlation of true scores in the unrestricted population, Hunter and Schmidt call this variation *artifactual*.

For the purposes of studying nonartifactual variation in the population validities, Hunter and Schmidt consider the variation in validities that would be obtained in a reference population of known variability when there is no measurement error in either test or criterion. That is, they consider the variation among the correlations between true scores on X_i and Y_i in the reference population. Denote the ith population and sample validities corrected for the effects of unreliability and range restriction by $\tilde{\theta}_i$ and $\tilde{T}_i$ respectively.

It is easy to correct an individual correlation for the artifacts of measurement error and restriction of range. Let η_{1i} and η_{2i} be the population reliability coefficients of the test (X_i) and criterion (Y_i) in unrestricted population of the ith study, and let h_{1i} and h_{2i} be the corresponding sample reliabilities. Let u_i be the ratio of the standard deviation of X_i in the unrestricted (reference) population to the standard deviation of X_i in the restricted (observed) population in the ith study. That is,

$$u_i = \frac{\sigma \ (X_i \text{ in the reference or unrestricted population})}{\sigma \ (X_i \text{ in the restricted or observed population})} .$$

Assuming that both reliabilities are obtained in the unrestricted population, the corrected population and sample validity coefficients for the ith study are

$$\tilde{\theta}_i = \frac{\rho_i \ u_i}{\{\eta_{1i}\eta_{2i} \ [1 \ + \ (u_i^2 \ - \ 1) \ \rho_i^2]\}^{1/2}}, \tag{1}$$

and

$$\tilde{T}_i = \frac{r_i \ u_i}{\{h_{1i}h_{2i} \ [1 \ + \ (u_i^2 \ - \ 1) \ r_i^2]\}^{1/2}} . \tag{2}$$

It will sometimes be useful to think of $\tilde{\theta}_i$ and $\tilde{T}_i$ as arising from three separate "corrections" of ρ_i and r_i. We can write

$$\tilde{T} = a_{1i}a_{2i}a_{3i}r_i$$

and

$$\tilde{\theta}_i = \alpha_{1i}\alpha_{2i}\alpha_{3i}\rho_i$$

194

where

$$\alpha_{1i} = 1/\sqrt{\eta_{1i}} \cdot \alpha_{2i} = 1/\sqrt{\eta_{2i}},$$

$$\alpha_{3i} = \frac{u_i}{[1 + (u_i^2 - 1)\rho_i^2]^{1/2}}, \tag{3}$$

$$a_{1i} = 1/\sqrt{h_{1i}}, \ a_{2i} = 1/\sqrt{h_{2i}}, \text{ and}$$

$$a_{3i} = \frac{u_i}{[1 + (u_i^2 - 1)r_i^2]^{1/2}}.$$

For statistical purposes it is also easier to work in the metric of the Fisher z-transformed correlations. Therefore we write θ_i and T_i, the z-transforms of $\tilde{\theta}$ and $\tilde{T}_i$ as

$$\theta_i = z(\alpha_{1i} \, \alpha_{2i} \, \alpha_{3i} \, \rho_i) \tag{4}$$

and

$$T_i = z(a_{1i} \, a_{2i} \, a_{3i} \, r_i), \tag{5}$$

where $z(x) = \log[(1 + x)/(1 - x)]/2$ is Fisher's z-transform.

Statistical Models in Meta-analysis

Several different statistical-modeling approaches have emerged in meta-analysis generally. Fixed effects approaches treat the underlying effect magnitude parameters as if they were functions of known between-study variables. The object of fixed effects analyses is typically to determine which study characteristics are related to effect magnitude (see Hedges, 1982; Hedges & Olkin, 1985; Rosenthal & Rubin, 1982).

Random effects approaches treat the underlying effect magnitude parameters as if they have a sampling distribution (see DerSimonian & Laird, 1983; Hedges, 1983; Hedges & Olkin, 1985; Hunter, Schmidt, & Jackson, 1982; Rubin, 1981). One object of random effects analyses is to quantify between-study variation of effect magnitude parameters via an estimate of the parameter variance component. Typically, random effects analyses employ a hyperparameter model and a corresponding sampling scheme. The model is usually that the values $\rho_1, \ldots,$ ρ_k are sampled from a universe of possible values characterized by its mean $\tilde{\mu}_*$ and variance $\tilde{\sigma}_*^2$. The ith "sample" correlation r_i is then sampled from a distribution conditional on ρ_i.

Mixed effects models combine the attributes of fixed and random effects models. Mixed effects models treat some of the variation in effect magnitude parameters as if it is a function of known between-study variables, but the remainder of the between-study variation is treated as stochastic (see Raudenbush & Bryk, 1985).

Procedures for fixed effects models involving correlations have been developed and could be used in the study of validities, but they typically have not been used in this context. Similarly there seems to be little or no use of mixed effects models in the study of validity.

CASE I: RANDOM EFFECTS MODELS
WITH NO CORRECTIONS FOR THE EFFECTS
OF UNRELIABILITY OR RESTRICTION OF RANGE

The description of the random effects procedure usually used in validity generalization studies (e.g., by Hunter, Schmidt, & Jackson, 1982) begins with the explanation that

$$r = \rho + e, \tag{6}$$

where e is a random variable defined as

$$e = r - \rho.$$

This first step is simply a tautology. The asymptotic distribution of r as $n \to \infty$ with ρ fixed is given by

$$\sqrt{n}(r - \rho) = \sqrt{n}\, e \sim N[0,(1 - \rho^2)^2]. \tag{7}$$

Therefore in large samples the conditional variance of e is approximately

$$\sigma^2(e|\rho) = \frac{(1 - \rho^2)^2}{n}. \tag{8}$$

The next step in the argument is to declare that, as is customary in classical test theory, ρ and e are independent of one another. Thus if $\sigma^2(r)$ is the (unconditional) variance of r and $\tilde{\sigma}_*^2$ is the variance of ρ,

$$\sigma^2(r) = \tilde{\sigma}_*^2 + \sigma^2(e|\rho). \tag{9}$$

Strictly speaking, it is not true that ρ and e are independent. Moreover, since r is a biased estimator of ρ, there can be a nonzero covariance between ρ and e. This covariance is of the same order $(1/n)$ as $\sigma^2(e|\rho)$ and need not be negligible in comparison with $\sigma^2(e|\rho)$. Thus the variances of ρ and e are not strictly additive and (9) may be incorrect by a substantial fraction of $\sigma^2(e|\rho)$ in some cases. In most applications (where n is moderate to large) there seems little reason for concern, however, since the *absolute magnitude* of the bias caused by the departure from additivity is small.

The partitioning of the variance of r given in (9) is typically used (e.g., by Hunter, Schmidt, & Jackson, 1982) to obtain an estimate of $\tilde{\sigma}_*^2$. Since $\sigma^2(r)$ can be estimated empirically from a sample of observed correlations, and $\sigma^2(e|\rho)$ may be estimated by substituting the consistent estimator for r for ρ in (8).

Hunter, Schmidt, and Jackson also use $n - 1$ in place of n in (8) when estimating $\sigma^2(e|\rho)$. The usual estimate of $\tilde{\sigma}^2_*$ is therefore given by

$$\hat{\sigma}^2_* = S^2_r - \frac{1}{k} \sum_{i=1}^{k} (1 - r_i^2)^2/(n_i - 1), \tag{10}$$

where S^2_r is the usual sample variance of $r_1, \ldots, r_k$. The usual estimate of $\tilde{\mu}_*$ is the weighted mean given by

$$\sum_{i=1}^{k} \omega_i r_i \bigg/ \sum_{i=1}^{k} \omega_i \tag{11}$$

where $\omega_i = [\hat{\sigma}^2_* + (1 - r_i^2)^2/(n_i - 1)]^{-1}$.

An Unbiased Estimator of the Correlation Variation Component

An unbiased estimator of the variance component $\tilde{\sigma}^2_*$ for the population correlation can be obtained by using procedures that are analogous to those used by Hunter, Schmidt, and Jackson (1982) but which make use of an unbiased estimator of ρ. The statistical argument required is identical to that used to obtain estimates of variance components in the one factor random effects analysis of variance.

Recall that the reason that the variances of ρ and e may not be strictly additive is that the expectation of e, or alternatively the bias of r, is nonzero. A natural strategy for dealing with the problem of the covariance term is to use an unbiased estimator of ρ. Such an estimator was obtained by Olkin and Pratt (1958). One representation for their minimum variance unbiased estimator q of ρ is

$$q = r\, F(\tfrac{1}{2}, \tfrac{1}{2}; (n - 2)/2; 1 - r^2), \tag{12}$$

where $F(a, b; c; x)$ is Gauss's hypergeometric function

$$F(a, b; c; x) = \sum_{j=0}^{\infty} \frac{\Gamma(a + j)\,\Gamma(b + j)\,\Gamma(c)}{\Gamma(a)\,\Gamma(b)\,\Gamma(c + j)} \frac{x^j}{j!}. \tag{13}$$

Olkin and Pratt also suggest an approximation to q which is unbiased to order $1/n$ and has bias smaller than .01 if $n \geq 8$. The expression for this approximation is

$$q \doteq r + \frac{r(1 - r^2)}{2(n - 3)}. \tag{14}$$

It is easy to show that the covariance of the unbiased estimator q with ρ is zero and that this covariance is zero (to order $1/n$) for the approximate unbiased estimator (14).

Since ρ and $e' = r - q$ are uncorrelated, the variances of ρ and e' are additive and the unconditional variance of q is

$$\sigma^2(q) = \tilde{\sigma}_*^2 + \sigma^2(q|\rho).$$

It therefore seems sensible to estimate $\tilde{\sigma}_*^2$ as the difference between estimates of $\sigma^2(q)$ and $\sigma^2(q|\rho)$.

Specifically, the sample variance of the unbiased estimates $q_1, \ldots, q_k$ is an unbiased estimator of $\sigma^2(q)$. A direct calculation using a well-known theorem on the expectation of quadratic forms (see e.g., Searle, 1971) shows that the expected value of S_q^2 is

$$E(S_q^2) = \tilde{\sigma}_*^2 + \frac{1}{k} \sum_{i=1}^{k} \sigma^2(q_i|\rho_i).$$

Consequently an estimate of $\tilde{\sigma}_*^2$ can be obtained if estimates of the $\sigma^2(q_i|\rho_i)$ are available. An estimator of $\sigma^2(q_i|\rho_i)$ is given by

$$q_i^2 - Q_i, \tag{15}$$

where

$$Q_i = 1 - \frac{(n_i - 3)\,(1 - r_i^2)\,F(1, 1;\, n_i/2;\, 1 - r_i^2)}{(n_i - 2)} \tag{16}$$

is the minimum variance unbiased estimator of ρ_i^2 given by Olkin and Pratt, and $F(a, b;\, c;\, x)$ is the hypergeometric function given by (13). Because

$$E(q_i^2 - Q_i|\rho_i) = E(q_i^2|\rho_i) - \rho_i^2 = \sigma^2(q_i|\rho_i),$$

$q_i^2 - Q_i$ is an unbiased estimator of $\sigma^2\,(q_i|\rho_i)$.

Therefore an unbiased estimator of $\tilde{\sigma}_*^2$ is

$$\hat{\sigma}_*^2 = S_q^2 - \frac{1}{k} \sum_{i=1}^{k} (q_i^2 - Q_i). \tag{17}$$

Example. The results of 12 studies of the validity of student ratings of achievement are presented in Table 12.1. These studies are a subset of the studies reported by Cohen (1981, 1983). In each of the studies class mean ratings of the instructors are correlated with the class mean achievement scores to obtain a validity coefficient. Each of these studies was conducted in a multisection college course and consequently the sample size is the number of sections, which is typically small. Table 12.1 presents for each study, the sample size, observed

TABLE 12.1
Data from 12 Studies of the Validity of Student Ratings
of Instruction

Study	n	r	q	$q^2 - Q$	$(1 - r^2)^2/(n - 1)$
1	10	.68	.71	.032	.032
2	7	.61	.66	.067	.066
3	7	.60	.65	.071	.068
4	8	.87	.89	.006	.008
5	16	.34	.35	.061	.052
6	40	.40	.40	.019	.018
7	9	.57	.60	.062	.057
8	14	.42	.44	.061	.052
9	6	.55	.62	.105	.097
10	7	.79	.82	.019	.024
11	12	−.75	−.76	.017	.017
12	33	.26	.26	.030	.027

validity coefficient, the unbiased estimate q_i of ρ_i, and an unbiased estimate $q_i^2 - Q_i$ of $\sigma^2(q_i|\rho_i)$.

The sample variance of the q_i values is .187 and the average of the $q_i^2 - Q_i$ values is .046. Consequently the unbiased estimator (17) of $\tilde{\sigma}_*^2$ is

$$\hat{\sigma}_*^2 = .187 - .046 = .141.$$

The last column of Table 12.1 presents $(1 - r_i^2)/(n_i - 1)$, the estimate of the conditional variance of $r - \rho$ recommended by Hunter, Schmidt, and Jackson (1982). The average of the values in the last column is .043, which gives the usual estimator (10) of $\hat{\sigma}_*^2$ as

$$.187 - .043 = .144.$$

Note that these estimates of $\tilde{\sigma}_*^2$ are very similar.

Problems with Conventional Approaches
to Studying the Generalization of Test Validities

The general object of most validity generalization studies is to examine the situational specificity hypothesis. That is, the analysis is designed to examine the extent to which test validities are generalizable across situations (i.e., across studies). Statistical methods are used to study the variation of the observed validity coefficients across situations and to examine the extent to which this variation is the result of "artifacts," such as within-study sampling error of the observed validity coefficients about the true validities, variations in test or criterion reliability, and variations in range restrictions on tests or criterion measures. Analyses in the tradition of the work by Hunter and Schmidt attempt to estimate a variance component for the population validities across studies. They then typically argue that because the variance component is small, it can be treated as zero. In essence they argue that a small variance component demonstrates that there is *no* situational specificity and that the validity in any situation is best represented by the overall average validity.

Yet research in this tradition acknowledges the fact that tests of homogeneity of validities (essentially tests that the variance component is zero) often soundly reject the hypothesis that the variance component is *exactly zero*. One way this research has acknowledged the possibility of small but nonzero variance components associated with situational specificity is to compute confidence intervals for the average validity. The estimated variance component is usually used to establish a 2-standard-error confidence interval around the mean test validity (ignoring the contribution of within-study sampling error to the variability of the estimate of the average test validity). If this confidence interval does not contain zero, the test validity is assumed to be essentially always positive. For example, Hunter, Schmidt, and Jackson (1982) state that "if the mean is more than two standard deviations large than 0, then it is reasonable to conclude that the relationship considered [the validity] is always positive" (p. 28).

This research tradition reflects an extreme position on the existence of situational specificity of test validities. The assumption that between-study variance components are exactly zero and that all studies yield homogeneous results is clearly an extreme position that is often contradicted by empirical results from tests of homogeneity of validities across studies. In part this research tradition arose as a reaction to the earlier (and equally extreme) research tradition that treated test validities as entirely situationally specific. In this earlier tradition, validities were seen as very heavily influenced by situational (contextual) factors so that a new validity study was needed in each new situation. One interpretation of this tradition is that the results of previous validity studies provide essentially no information about test validity in new, but similar situations.

The work of Hunter, Schmidt, and their associates has clearly demonstrated that the variability of validities across situations is much smaller than was previously believed. They have not, however, convincingly demonstrated that the variability in validities due to situational specificity is zero. Nor is this a particularly sensible proposition. The arguments advanced for situational specificity *do* have an intuitive appeal and it is hard to believe that context has no effect on test validity other than that which arises as purely technical artifacts of measurement.

Clearly an approach to the study of situational specificity is needed that makes possible a compromise between the two extremes. Such a compromise approach would acknowledge the possibility of some degree of situational specificity but would also acknowledge that there is some consistency of results across studies. The analysis procedures in such a compromise approach should recognize that neither the group mean validity nor the validity estimated from a single study alone is the most intuitively satisfying indicator of the validity in a given situation. Rather it should reflect the scientific intuition that if results are similar across situations there is some, but probably imperfect, degree of predictability across situations.

Fortunately such an analysis procedure exists. Empirical Bayes methods provide analyses with precisely the sort of properties mentioned herein. Such analyses permit rigorous estimation of the mean population validity and the variance component. Thus the methods permit the empirical analysis of the size of the effect due to situational specificity. Empirical Bayes analyses also permit improved estimation of the population validity in any *particular* situation by supplementing the information provided by an individual validity coefficient with the information provided by validity coefficients in other situations. Moreover such analyses can also be used to explore the sensitivity of inferences to variations in the size of situational specificity effects (variance components).

In addition to these clear conceptual advantages, empirical Bayes methods also have statistical advantages. Of course Bayesian methods have the advantage that they are always optimal in terms of minimizing mean squared error. Empirical Bayes methods share this advantage to the extent that they approximate true Bayesian methods. When the prior distribution is uninformative and the likelihood is very peaked, using the maximum likelihood estimates of the hyperparameters (in place of integrating over the whole posterior distribution as in true Bayesian estimation) should give results similar to true Bayesian methods.

Empirical Bayes methods can also be justified from the perspective of classical statistics. Deeley and Lindley (1981) and Morris (1983) have shown that empirical Bayes methods can also be viewed as asymptotically optimal classical methods.

Because empirical Bayes methods seem well suited to the problem of studying validity generalization, the rest of this chapter is an examination of the application of empirical Bayes methods to the study of validity generalization. Conventional methods are discussed only for the purposes of comparison.

CASE II: PROCEDURES WITH CORRECTIONS FOR THE EFFECTS OF UNRELIABILITY OR RESTRICTION OF RANGE WITH NO MISSING DATA

Now consider the problem of estimating the variance of the population validities corrected for the effects of unreliability and restriction or range. That is, we seek to estimate the mean and variance of the validities that would be obtained in the reference (unrestricted) population with a perfectly reliable test and criterion. In this situation the correction factors $a_{11}, \ldots a_{1k}, a_{21}, \ldots a_{2k}, a_{31}, \ldots a_{3k}$ are known (and usually treated as if they are the population values $\alpha_{11}, \ldots \alpha_{1k}, \alpha_{21}, \ldots \alpha_{2k}, \alpha_{31}, \ldots \alpha_{3k}$), the sample correlations $r_1, \ldots, r_k$ are also observed, and the object is to estimate the mean μ_* and σ_*^2 of the distribution from which $\sigma_1 \ldots \ldots ,\sigma_k$ are sampled. I first review procedures in the spirit of those suggested by Hunter, Schmidt, and Jackson (1982). Then I present an analogous procedure using empirical Bayes methodology.

Conventional Estimation Procedures

There are several variations in the procedures that have been suggested for estimating μ_* and σ_*^2, but the following treatment is consistent with the spirit of this work (see Hunter, Schmidt, & Jackson, 1982). The usual procedure is to start by calculating the estimates $T_1, \ldots , T_k$ of $\theta_1, \ldots \theta_k$. The variance σ_*^2 is then estimated via an estimator of the form

$$\hat{\sigma}_*^2 = S_T^2 - \sum_{i=1}^{k} \sigma^2 \, (T_i|\theta_i), \qquad (18)$$

where S_T^2 is the usual sample estimate of the variance of $T_1, \ldots T_k$ and

$$\sigma^2(T_i|\theta_i) = \alpha_{1i}^2\alpha_{2i}^2\alpha_{3i}^2/(n_i - 3). \qquad (19)$$

This estimate $\hat{\sigma}_*^2$ is then used to estimate μ_* via a weighted mean of the form

$$\hat{\mu}_* = \sum_{i=1}^{k} \omega_i T_i \left/ \sum_{i=1}^{k} \omega_i \right. \qquad (20)$$

where

$$\omega_i = 1/[\sigma_*^2 + \sigma^2(T_i|\theta_i)].$$

The variance of $\hat{\mu}_*$ is then taken to be

$$\left[\sum_{i=1}^{k} \omega_i \right]^{-1}.$$

or just $\hat{\sigma}_*^2$ if the $\sigma^2(T_i|\theta_i)$ are considered to be negligible. Although estimates of the individual θ_i are not usually used, the estimate of the validity in the reference population in the ith study or situation would presumably be μ_* if σ_*^2 was considered to be negligible and T_i if σ_*^2 was not considered to be negligible.

Empirical Bayes Estimation Procedures

The estimation of μ_* and σ_*^2 by empirical Bayes methods is straightforward. One empirical Bayes approach begins with the specification that the θ_i have a normal distribution given by

$$\theta_i \sim N(\mu_*, \sigma_*^2).$$

The conditional distribution of each T_i given θ_i is approximately normal with a mean of θ_i and a variance of $\sigma^2(T_i|\theta_i)$ given in (19). Treating this approximate distribution as if it were exact, the hyperparameters μ_* and σ_*^2 can be estimated by the method of maximum likelihood.

The log likelihood $L(\mu_*, \sigma_*^2|T_i, \ldots, T_k)$ is proportional to

$$\prod_{i=1}^{k} [2\pi v_i]^{-1/2} \exp\left[-\sum_{i=1}^{k} (T_i - \mu_*)^2/2v_i\right], \tag{21}$$

where $v_i = \sigma_*^2 + \sigma^2(T_i|\theta_i)$. Although maximum likelihood estimators for μ_* and σ_*^2 do not exist in closed form, it is easy to maximize the likelihood (21) numerically. An alternative procedure for obtaining maximum likelihood estimates of μ_* and σ_*^2 is the use of the EM algorithm (Dempster, Laird, & Rubin, 1977). The EM algorithm is used here because this procedure has the advantage of generalizing readily to the case to be considered later where some of the correction factors needed to compute the T_i are missing.

The EM algorithm is used to estimate μ_* and σ_*^2 by treating the situation as a missing data problem in which $T_1, \ldots, T_k$ are observed but $\theta_1, \ldots, \theta_k$ are "missing." The basic idea is to start with initial estimates $\mu_{*(0)}$ and $\sigma_{*(0)}^2$ of μ_* and σ_*^2 (such as the conventional estimates given in the previous section) and to use the observed values of $T_1, \ldots, T_k$ to estimate $\theta_1, \ldots, \theta_k$. This is called the E-step of the EM algorithm. Then the estimates of $\theta_1, \ldots \theta_k$ are used to calculate improved estimates of μ_* and σ_*^2. This is called the M-step of the EM algorithm because the improved estimates are maximum likelihood estimates of μ_* and σ_*^2 given the E-step estimates of $\theta_1, \ldots, \theta_k$. The improved estimates of μ_* and σ_*^2 derived in the M-step are then used in another E-step, which is followed by another M-step and so on until the estimates (or the likelihood) do not change substantially with further iterations.

Use the notation $\mu_{*(j)}$, $\sigma_{*(j)}^2$, $\theta_{i(j)}$, for the estimates of μ_*, σ_*^2, and θ_i on the jth iteration. Note that $\sigma^2(T_i|\theta_i) = 1/(n_i - 3)$ does not change during the iteration process. A direct argument (see Box & Tiao, 1973) shows that the estimates of θ_i and $\hat{\sigma}^2(\theta_i)$ on the jth E-step are

$$\theta_{i(j)} = \frac{T_i \sigma_{*(j-1)}^2 + \mu_{*(j-1)} \sigma^2(T_i|\theta_{i(j-1)})}{\sigma_{*(j-1)}^2 + \sigma^2(T_i|\theta_{i(j-1)})},$$

$$\hat{\sigma}^2(\theta_{i(j)}) = [\sigma^{-2}(T_i|\theta_{i(j-1)}) + \sigma_{*(j-1)}^{-2}]^{-1}. \tag{22}$$

The maximum likelihood estimates of $\mu_{*(j)}$ and $\sigma_{*(j)}^2$ of μ_* and σ_*^2 the jth M-step are

$$\mu_{*(j)} = \sum_{i=1}^{k} \theta_{i(j)} k \tag{23}$$

and

$$\sigma^2_{*(j)} = \frac{1}{k} \sum_{i=1}^{k} [\theta^2_{i(j)} + \hat{\sigma}^2(\theta_{i(j)})] - k\mu^2_{*(j)} \quad . \tag{24}$$

Improved estimates of validities in specific situations

One particularly appealing aspect of empirical Bayes methods is that they provide improved estimates of the test validities $\theta_1, \ldots, \theta_k$ in particular situations. Unlike conventional procedures which would estimate the ith validity as either T_i (in the case of assumed situational specificity or heterogeneity among validities) or μ_* (in the case of perfect validity generalization), empirical Bayes methods estimate the ith validity as a linear combination of T_i and the estimate of the group mean μ_*. The improved estimates of $\theta_1, \ldots, \theta_k$ are those calculated in the last step of the EM algorithm and can be expressed as

$$\theta_i = \lambda_i T_i + (1 - \lambda)\mu_* \tag{25}$$

where

$$\lambda_i = \sigma^2_* / [\sigma^2_* + \sigma^2(T_i | \theta_i)], \tag{26}$$

which highlights the fact that θ_i is a weighted average of the estimate T_i from the ith study and μ_* the (estimated) mean validity from all of the studies. The implication of (25) is that the estimate T_i is "shrunken" toward the mean μ_* of all of the validities by an amount that is proportioned $1 - \lambda_i$, the shrinkage factor discussed by James and Stein (1961). The amount of shrinkage toward μ_* depends on the magnitude σ^2_* of the situational specificity effect relative to the within-situation sampling error $\sigma^2(T_i | \theta_i)$.

There is a great deal of evidence that "improved" estimators of the form (25) are actually superior to their alternatives such as T_i or $\bar{T}$. Theoretical considerations aside, such estimators usually prove to have smaller mean squared error in practical estimation situations (see e.g., Efron & Morris, 1977; Rubin, 1980).

The sensitivity of Empirical Bayes Estimates to Variation in the Situational Specificity Effect

It is clear from expression (25) that the improved estimates θ_i depend on σ^2_*, which must be estimated from the data. Since there is some degree of uncertainty in the estimate of σ^2_* there will be some uncertainty in our estimates of the individual validities. Consequently it may be wise to examine the sensitivity of our estimates θ_i to changes in σ^2_* throughout the range of values of σ^2_* that are plausible given the data. This is easily accomplished by plotting the values of θ_i given (25) for the range of σ^2_* values for which the likelihood of σ^2_* is not negligible (see Rubin, 1980).

CASE III: PROCEDURES WITH CORRECTIONS FOR THE EFFECTS OF RESTRICTION OF RANGE AND UNRELIABILITY WITH MISSING DATA

Now consider the more difficult problem of estimating μ_* and σ_*^2 when $r_1, \ldots, r_k$ are observed but some of the correction factors $a_{11}, \ldots, a_{1k}, a_{21}, \ldots, a_{2k}, a_{31}, \ldots, a_{3k}$ are missing. In this situation an estimate T_i of θ_i cannot be computed for every study. This situation is typical in the meta-analysis of validity studies of personnel selection tests, where the proportion of studies with missing data can be quite large. The presence of the missing data becomes a central methodological problem and a great deal of effort has gone into the study of procedures to make efficient use of the (partially incomplete) data that do exist.

Conventional Procedures

The procedures that are usually used to cope with missing data in studies of validity generalization are variations of a method suggested by Schmidt and Hunter (1977). The first step is to "correct the variance of $r_1, \ldots, r_k$ for sampling error" by estimating the variance component of $\rho_1, \ldots, \rho_k$ via (10). Of course the variance of $\rho_1, \ldots, \rho_k$ will not serve as an estimate of σ_*^2 since the former is partly a function of variation across studies in the artifacts of unreliability and restriction of range. The next step is to "correct" the variation of $\rho_1, \ldots, \rho_k$ for variation due to these artifacts.

This is done by observing that

$$\theta_i = \alpha_{1i}\alpha_{2i}\alpha_{3i}\,\rho_i,$$

and noting that *if* α_{1i}, α_{2i}, α_{3i}, and ρ_i are independent, the variance of θ_i is a function of the means and variances of α_{1i}, α_{2i}, α_{3i}, and ρ_i. Solving the equation for the variance of θ yields an expression for $\tilde{\sigma}_*^2$ in terms of the first two moments of α_{1i}, α_{2i}, α_{3i}, and ρ_i. The moments of the artifact corrections α_{1i}, α_{2i}, and α_{3i} are obtained from the empirical distributions the (so-called artifact distributions) of α_{1i}, α_{2i}, and α_{3i} derived from the studies that report this information. It is important to note that the assumption of independence of α_{1i}, α_{2i}, α_{3i}, and ρ_i is probably incorrect, particularly since α_{3i} is functionally related to ρ_i. Certainly α_{1i}, α_{2i}, α_{3i}, and ρ_i are correlated if they are computed from the same sample (see e.g., Anderson, 1958). Some researchers (e.g., Raju & Burke, 1983) have studied the problem of relaxing the assumptions of independence, and their methods yield somewhat different formulas, but the overall approach remains quite similar to that presented.

Problems with the Conventional Approach to Handling Missing Data

Although the conventional approaches to dealing with missing data are interesting, they have several deficiencies. First they make unrealistic assumptions (e.g., the assumption of independence) about the joint distribution of α_{1i}, α_{2i}, α_{3i}, and ρ_i. Although simulation studies (Callender & Osburn, 1980, 1982; Callender, Osburn, Greener, & Ashworth, 1982) have not identified serious problems with these methods, the use of methods requiring strong assumptions (that are likely to be false) is still disturbing. The methods are essentially attempts to infer properties (the variance of a particular function) of a joint distribution from the marginal distributions. This attempt can only succeed under independence or other very special situations.

There is, however, a more fundamental criticism of the method for handling missing data, namely that it implies that the studies with missing observations can be treated, for the purposes of estimating the means and variances of the artifact corrections, as a random sample of all studies actually conducted. This assumption is sometimes made in handling missing data in other contexts, but it seems particularly unrealistic here (see Rubin, 1976, for a discussion of the conceptualization of missing data). For example, since high validity is desirable, it seems likely that researchers who observed low validity coefficients would be more likely to investigate and report artifact corrections that have the effect of increasing the estimate of test validity than would researchers who observed high validity coefficients. It also seems quite plausible that situations in which there is greater selectivity, and therefore greater economic and legal risk in the use of personnel selection tests, researchers would be more likely to monitor reliability of criteria used in validity studies. Presumably they would also be likely to take steps to increase reliability of tests or criteria if they were found to be low. Thus situations in which selectivity is high are more likely to have high reliabilities and to report those reliabilities.

Empirical Bayes Approach

A different and more satisfactory approach to handling the missing data can be incorporated into the estimation of μ_* and σ_*^2 by empirical Bayes methods. This method is essentially the same as the empirical Bayes method described for complete data except that it employs a slight variant of the estimation procedure to handle cases in which T_i is not observed. The T_i are calculated as before for each study in which the a_{ij} are observed. In studies where at least one of the a_{ij} is missing, T_i is estimated from r_i and any of the a_{ij} that are observed in that study. If T_i, a_{1i}, a_{2i}, a_{3i}, and r_i (or suitable transformations of these variables) have approximately a multivariate normal distribution, then linear regregression provides a simple estimate $\hat{T}_i$ of T_i and the conditional variance $\sigma^2(\hat{T}_i)$ is just the square of the usual standard error of the estimate $\hat{T}_i$. The estimate $\hat{T}_i$ and its variance $\sigma^2(\hat{T}_i)$ are then used in place of T_i and $\sigma^2(T_i|\theta_i)$ in the EM algorithm. The most profound effect of missing data is that the estimate $\hat{T}_i$ of T_i typically has a larger conditional variance than does T_i, which reduces the weight of the information from that study in calculating θ_i. It will usually be the case, however, that T_i and r_i are highly correlated. Consequently, the loss of information resulting from estimation of T_i may not be as profound as might be imagined.

Note that this method for handling missing data on the a_{ij} does not completely eliminate problems of bias due to missing data, but it involves much less restrictive assumptions than do methods in the tradition of Hunter and Schmidt. The methods of Hunter and Schmidt involve the implicit assumption that the distribution of the artifact corrections (a_{ij}'s) that are observed are identical to those that are not observed, a very strong assumption. The method proposed in this chapter involves the much weaker assumption that the regression of T_i on r_i and the a_{ij} is the same for the studies in which the a_{ij} are observed as it is for those in which some of the a_{ij} are not observed.

Note that the implementation of this procedure is facilitated by grouping cases that have the same pattern of missing data, so that a different procedure (regression equation) for estimating T_i can be performed for each pattern.

EXAMPLE OF EMPIRICAL BAYES METHODS

The results of 18 separate validation studies of an algebra readiness test are summarized in Table 12.2 Each study was conducted at a different school and involved administering the test to a sample of eighth-grade algebra students at the beginning of the school year. The scores on the algebra readiness test were then correlated with scores on a test of algebra achievement administered at the end of the year.

The proportion of students taking algebra in each school differed and consequently the ranges of scores on the algebra readiness test and the algebra achievement test differed as well. Therefore differences in the restriction of range are expected to produce some variability in the test validities. The reliabilities of the tests were not believed to vary substantially across sites. Consequently the analysis of situational specificity was concerned with the effects of restriction of range on test validity.

In 14 of the validity studies the ratio u of the standard deviation of the algebra readiness test scores for the students taking the test to that of a national sample were estimated by using other test scores (from a nationally normed mathematics achievement test). In 4 of the sites the estimate could not be made because scores on nationally normed mathematics achievement tests were not available. Thus the correction factor α_{3i} was missing for these studies.

TABLE 12.2
Results of 18 Studies of the Validity of an Algebra
Readiness Test

Study	n_i	r_i	T_i	$\hat{\theta}$ Complete data	$\hat{\theta}$ All data
1	85	.57	1.19	1.09	1.10
2	67	.49	0.84	0.83	0.84
3	37	.44	0.61	0.68	0.68
4	46	.31	0.55	0.67	0.68
5	43	.45	0.65	0.71	0.71
6	61	.67	1.31	1.17	1.18
7	43	.25	0.27	0.42	0.42
8	61	.33	0.42	0.52	0.52
9	62	.47	0.83	0.82	0.83
10	68	.41	0.52	0.58	0.59
11	43	.48	1.28	1.03	1.05
12	42	.60	1.26	1.07	1.08
13	39	.46	0.74	0.77	0.78
14	39	.64	0.99	0.92	0.93
15	35	.58	——	——	1.02
16	24	.28	——	——	0.49
17	41	.60	——	——	1.05
18	33	.55	——	——	0.96

Estimation from Studies with Complete Data

First we consider the analysis of the 14 validity studies which yielded complete information. The mean and variance (in z score units) of the underlying validities estimated from these 14 studies are $\hat{\mu}_* = 0.805$ and $\hat{\sigma}^2_* = 0.074$. Examination of the improved estimators given in the table shows exactly the effect expected, namely that the improved estimates are pulled toward the grand mean.

To examine the question of the effects of σ^2_* on the improved estimators, we plot the five studies that are most influenced by σ^2_*. Fig. 12.1 shows the empirical Bayes estimates of θ_i with the likelihood superimposed. Note that the estimates all converge to the value .805 (the value of $\hat{\mu}_*$) if $\sigma^2_* = 0$, that is, when there is perfect validity generalization. The likelihood function, however, suggests that this value of σ^2_* is highly unlikely given the data. In the range of more likely values of σ^2_* (e.g., 0.02 to 0.22) the values of the θ_i are separated to considerable degree, indicating a nonnegligible degree of situational specificity. Similar plots could be constructed to show the effects of θ_i on the standard error of estimates of θ_i.

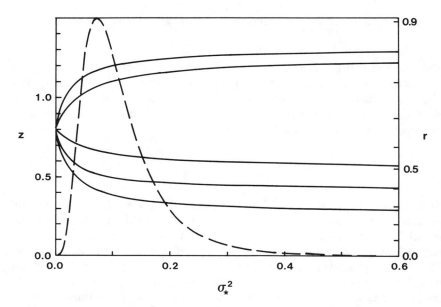

FIG. 12.1. Empirical Bayes estimates of θ_i as a function of σ_*^2 for the five studies most influenced by σ_*^2 (solid curves) with the likelihood function of σ_*^2 superimposed (broken curve).

Estimation Including Studies with Missing Data

Continuing with the example of the validity studies of the algebra readiness test, we now examine the effect of including the 4 studies with missing data on the range restriction correction. The idea of the procedure is to use the information that is available in the data on r to correct the estimate T. The regression equation for estimating T from r derived from the 14 studies with complete data is

$$\hat{T} = -.312 + 2.413r.$$

The correlation coefficient between T and r in these data is $r = .87$, and the variance of the observed T_i values is .116, so the estimated conditional variance of the estimated T_i is

$$\sigma^2(\hat{T}_i) = S_T^2(1 - r^2) = .116(1 - .763) = .028.$$

Because r and T are highly correlated, the estimates of T based on r have only a slightly larger variance than would the T values themselves (if they were observed). Consequently, in this example, the missing data on the restriction-of-range correction result in less loss of information than might be expected.

The estimates given in the last column of Table 12.2 show the estimates of the θ_i values based on an analysis of all 18 studies. The estimates of the mean and variance of the distribution of validities based on all 18 studies are

$$\hat{\mu}_* = 0.828, \text{ and } \hat{\sigma}_*^2 = 0.075.$$

The sensitivity of estimates of the θ_i to variations in σ_*^2 could be examined by generating plots analogous to Fig. 12.1. Such plots in the case of incomplete data show essentially the same features as does Fig. 12.1, namely that the estimates of the θ_i converge to $\hat{\mu}_*$ when $\sigma_*^2 = 0$, but that the $\hat{\theta}_i$ appear distinct for values of σ_*^2 that appear to be likely given the observed data.

CONCLUSION

The empirical Bayes approach to the meta-analysis of test validities has several advantages over conventional approaches. First, it provides a compromise approach between the extreme positions of perfect situational specificity and perfect validity generalization when the data support such an intermediate position. The data analysis reveals the degree of validity generalization that is consistent with the observed data. Second, estimates of the validity in particular situations are provided that strengthen the estimates based on data from a single study by combining information from other studies. Finally, the empirical Bayes methods provide improved procedures for handling missing data—procedures which involve much less restrictive assumptions than those of other methods.

ACKNOWLEDGMENT

I thank Henry Braun for useful comments on an earlier draft of this chapter. Research was conducted while the author was at the College of Education, Michigan State University.

REFERENCES

Albright, L. E., Glennon, J. R., & Smith, W. J. (1963). *The use of psychological tests in industry.* Cleveland: Howard Allen.

Anderson, T. W. (1958). *An introduction to multivariate statistical analysis.* New York: Wiley.

Box, G. E. P., & Tiao, G. (1973). *Bayesian inference in statistical analysis.* Reading, MA: Addison–Wesley.

Callender, J. C., & Osburn, H. G. (1980). Development and test of a new model for validity generalization. *Journal of Applied Psychology, 65,* 543–558.

Callender, J. C., & Osburn, H. G. (1982). Another view of progress in validity generalization: Reply to Schmidt, Hunter and Pearlman. *Journal of Applied Psychology, 67,* 848–852.

Callender, J. C., Osburn, H. G., Greener, J. M., & Ashworth, S. (1982). Multiplicative validity generalization model: Accuracy of estimates as a function of sample size, mean, variance, and shape of the distribution of true validities. *Journal of Applied Psychology, 67,* 859–867.

Cohen, P. A. (1981). Student ratings of instruction and student achievement: A meta-analysis of multisection validity studies. *Review of Educational Research, 51*, 281–309.

Cohen, P. A. (1983). Comment on: A selective review of the validity of student ratings of teaching. *Journal of Higher Education, 54*, 448–458.

Cramer, H. (1946). *Mathematical methods of statistics*. Princeton, NJ: Princeton University Press.

Deeley, J. J., & Lindley, D. V. (1981). Bayes empirical Bayes. *Journal of the American Statistical Association, 76*, 833–841.

Dempster, A. P., Laird, N. M., & Rubin, D. B. (1977). Maximum likelihood estimation from incomplete data via the EM algorithm. *Journal of the Royal Statistical Society, Series B, 39*, 1–38.

Der Simonian, R. & Laird, N. M. (1983). Evaluating the effectiveness of coaching on SAT scores: A meta-analysis. *Harvard Education Review, 53*, 1–15.

Efron, B., & Morris, C. (1975). Data analysis using Stein's estimator and its generalizations. *Journal of the American Statistical Association, 74*, 311–319.

Efron, B., & Morris, C. (1977). Stein's paradox in statistics. *Scientific American, 236(5)*, 119–127.

Ghiselli, E. E. (1966). *The validity of occupational aptitude tests*. New York: Wiley.

Guion, R. M. (1965). *Personnel testing*. New York: McGraw–Hill.

Hedges, L. V. (1982). Fitting continuous models to effect size data. *Journal of Educational Statistics, 7*, 245–270.

Hedges, L. V. (1983). A random effects model for effect sizes. *Psychological Bulletin, 93*, 388–395.

Hedges, L. V., & Olkin, I. (1985). *Statistical methods for meta-analysis*. New York: Academic Press.

Hunter, J. E., Schmidt, F. L., & Jackson, G. B. (1982). *Meta-analysis: Cumulating research findings across studies*. Beverly Hills: Sage.

James, W., & Stein, C. (1961). Estimation with quadratic loss. *Proceedings of the Fourth Berkeley Symposium on Mathematical Statistics and Probability*. Berkeley and Los Angeles: University of California Press.

Morris, C. N. (1983). Parametric empirical Bayes inference: Theory and applications. *Journal of the American Statistical Association, 78*, 47–65.

Olkin, I. & Pratt, J. W. (1958). Unbiased estimation of certain correlation coefficients. *Annals of Mathematical Statistics, 29*, 201–211.

Pearlman, K., Schmidt, F. L., & Hunter, J. E. (1980). Validity generalization results for tests used to predict job proficiency and training success in clerical occupations. *Journal of Applied Psychology, 65*, 373–406.

Raju, N. S., & Burke, M. J. (1983). Two new methods for studying validity generalization. *Journal of Applied Psychology, 68*, 382–395.

Rao, C. R. (1973). *Linear statistical inference and its applications*. New York: Wiley.

Raudenbush, S. W., & Bryk, A. S. (1985). Empirical Bayes metaanalysis. *Journal of Educational Statistics, 10*, 75–98.

Rosenthal, R., & Rubin, D. B. (1982). Comparing effect sizes of independent studies. *Psychological Bulletin, 92*, 500–504.

Rubin, D. B. (1976). Inference and missing data. *Biometrika, 63*, 581–592.

Rubin, D. B. (1980). Using empirical Bayes techniques in the law school validity studies. *Journal of the American Statistical Association, 75*, 801–816.

Rubin, D. B. (1981). Estimation in parallel randomized experiments. *Journal of Educational Statistics, 6*, 377–400.

Schmidt, F. L., Gast–Rosenberg, I., & Hunter, J. (1980). Validity generalization results for computer programmers. *Journal of Applied Psychology, 65*, 643–661.

Schmidt, F. L., & Hunter, J. (1977). Development of a general solution to the problem of validity generalization. *Journal of Applied Psychology, 62*, 529–540.

Schmidt, F. L., Hunter, J., & Caplan, J. R. (1981). Validity generalization results for two jobs in the petroleum industry. *Journal of Applied Psychology, 66,* 261–273.

Schmidt, F. L., Hunter, J. E., & Pearlman, K. (1982). Progress in validity generalization: Comments on Callender and Osburn and future developments. *Journal of Applied Psychology, 67,* 835–845.

Searle, S. R. (1971). *Linear models.* New York: Wiley.

Chapter 13

Some Uses of Structural Equation Modeling in Validity Studies: Extending IRT to External Variables

Bengt Muthén
University of California

1. INTRODUCTION

The aim of this chapter is to propose the use of a new extension of standard Item Response Theory (IRT) modeling of dichotomous items to include external variables. External variables may appear both as categorical grouping variables and as continuous variables. This requires the formulation of a model for the relationships between the external variables and the response items. Given the availability of sufficiently rich data, such extensions can yield a more informative and powerful analysis of constructs and their measurements than what has so far been possible by standard IRT.

To make the discussion concrete, we will illustrate the methodology in the context of educational achievement test data, analyzing the eighth-grade U.S. sample from the Second International Mathematics Study, SIMS (Crosswhite, Dossey, Swafford, McKnight, & Cooney, 1985). The achievement testing covered topics in algebra, measurement, geometry, and arithmetic. The responses to a set of algebra items administered at the end of the eighth grade will be related to a set of external variables in the form of background variables measured at the beginning of the eighth grade. The background variables include scores on mathematics tests, family background variables, information on the student's attitude toward math, and type of math class attended in the eighth grade. This information will be brought together in a single model.

The new general feature of this model is that it simultaneously addresses four important issues in item analysis:

1. Estimation of IRT-type item measurement parameters.

2. Assessment of the strengths of hypothesized antecedents to the student's latent trait level.

3. Detection of item bias (differential item performance).

4. Testing and relaxation of the IRT requirements of unidimensionality and conditional independence.

While the major novelty is the inclusion of external variables, there are several new specific features of the analyses to be presented. One feature is the relaxation of the conditional independence requirement for certain items that by virtue of the question format have an association that cannot be described solely by their common dependence on the single trait. Another feature concerns the handling of items that have been deemed "biased," e.g., items that are sensitive to instructional coverage, but still contain valuable measurement information. Such items can be retained in the model by explicitly including parameters that describe the differential item performance. A third feature is the potential for explaining item bias by the influence of background variables. A fourth feature is a stronger test of unidimensionality obtained by checking the homogeneity of the items in relation to the background variables, not only by considering inter-item associations, as is customary. Finally, the modeling is capable of including several sets of items of differing content in a simultaneous analysis of several traits.

To prepare for a discussion of the general modeling approach of Section 3 and the data analysis in Section 5, Section 2 briefly outlines relevant latent variable measurement modeling theory for dichotomous and continuous response variables. Section 3 outlines theory for the structural equation modeling that we propose for data of this kind. Section 4 describes the response items and a set of interesting additional variables that are available in the SIMS data. Section 5 uses this modeling approach to analyze the relationship between some of the response variables of the SIMS data and a set of external variables. Section 6 concludes.

The statistically less sophisticated reader may wish to skip Sections 2 and 3 and go straight to the description of the data in Section 4. Before doing so, such a reader may wish to note that the modeling framework is given in Fig. 13.1, where the relationships between the dichotomously scored ys and the latent trait η are described in an IRT fashion by two-parameter normal ogive item characteristic curves, while the relationship between η and the background variables of x is described by a standard linear regression (although values for η need not be estimated to obtain these regression coefficients).

2.   LATENT VARIABLE MEASUREMENT MODELING

Let us consider dichotomous and continuous response variable models. Assume a vector of p continuous latent response variables y^* that follow a standard linear measurement model in each of G groups of students (the student subscript i and the group subscript g will be deleted),

$$y^* = \nu + \Lambda\eta + \epsilon, \qquad (1)$$

where η is the latent variable vector, ϵ is the vector of measurement errors, ν and Λ contain intercept and slope (loading) measurement parameters, so that

$$E(y^*) = \nu + \Lambda\kappa, \qquad (2)$$

$$V(y^*) = \Lambda\Psi\Lambda' + \Theta, \qquad (3)$$

where κ is the mean vector of η, Ψ is the covariance matrix of η, and Θ is the covariance matrix of the measurement errors, usually assumed to be diagonal.

When modeling dichotomous response variables we have for variable j

$$\begin{aligned} y_j &= 1, \text{ if } y_j^* \geq \tau_j \\ &\ 0, \text{ otherwise} \end{aligned} \qquad (4)$$

When working with aggregates of items in the form of subscores or item parcels, we assume a continuous response variable,

$$y_j = y_j^*. \qquad (5)$$

This is the standard confirmatory factor analysis measurement framework of Jöreskog (1969), extended to a comparative multiple-group analysis in Jöreskog (1971) and Sörbom (1974, 1978), extended to a multiple-factor, dichotomous response model by Christoffersson (1975), Muthén (1978), and Bock and Aitkin (1981), and further extended to dichotomous multiple-group analysis in Muthén and Christoffersson (1981) (see also Muthén & Lehman, 1985). For an overview, see Mislevy (1986).

The generality of the above type of covariance/correlation structure framework makes it suitable for a wide range of analyses involving validity issues, see Jöreskog (1977) and, for instance, Bohrnstedt (1983). One specific example concerns the analysis of multitrait-multimethod matrices by covariance structure methods; for a recent overview, see Schmitt and Stults (1986).

Let us consider factor analytical modeling of achievement variables of the SIMS type. Our interest may be in assessing the dimensionality and strength of relation between each observed variable and the construct(s). The observed variables may represent the subscores for the different content areas of algebra, measurement, geometry, and arithmetic. The subscores may be broken down in suitable item parcels so that there are several observed scores for each area. We may entertain the simplistic hypothesis of a four-factor structure, assuming that the responses within each content area are unidimensional and that the correlations between the scores from different areas can be fully explained by their dependencies on the correlated constructs. We may also study the measurement qualities and relationships among the constructs across subgroups of students. By multiple-group approaches we may then test hypotheses of invariant measurement parameters in the G groups, such as

$$\nu_1 = \nu_2 = \ldots = \nu_G = \nu, \tag{6}$$

$$\Lambda_1 = \Lambda_2 = \ldots = \Lambda_G = \Lambda. \tag{7}$$

If (6) and (7) are true we may next want to test the structural hypotheses

$$\kappa_1 = \kappa_2 = \ldots = \kappa_G = \kappa, \tag{8}$$

$$\Psi_1 = \Psi_2 = \ldots = \Psi_G = \Psi. \tag{9}$$

We may find that for different instructional exposure to the topics covered in the test items, invariance of ν, or Λ may not hold for certain of the item parcel scores related to certain constructs, while for other scores measurement invariance may be found. As noted by Miller and Linn (1986), the instructional coverage may be assumed to affect the construct in question homogenously across a set of test items, so that bias does not exist at the item level. To further scrutinize such issues of validity in educational achievement data, it is useful to be able to shift the analysis from the score level down to the "micro" item level. We will describe such an effort, although it should be kept in mind that the techniques to be discussed are equally applicable on the aggregated continuous score level.

3. A STRUCTURAL MODEL

Let y^* be as in (1) and let the vector of latent constructs follow the linear structural equation system

$$\eta = \alpha + B\eta + \Gamma x + \zeta, \tag{10}$$

where α is an intercept parameter vector, B is a matrix of slopes for regressions among the ηs (the diagonal elements of B are zero and $I - B$ is nonsingular), Γ is a matrix of slopes for regressions of the ηs on the set of q exogenous observed x variables, while ζ is a vector of residuals. With standard assumptions it follows that

$$E(y^*|x) = \nu + \Lambda(I - B)^{-1}\alpha + \Lambda(I - B)^{-1}\Gamma x, \tag{11}$$

$$V(y^*|x) = \Lambda(I - B)^{-1}\Psi(I - B)'^{-1}\Lambda' + \Theta, \tag{12}$$

This model framework was described in Muthén (1983, 1984), where it was pointed out that structural models with dichotomous, ordered categorical, and continuous latent variable indicators could be fitted into the following three-part structure:

$$\text{Part 1: } \sigma_1 = \Delta^* \{ K_\tau \tau - K_\nu [\nu + \Lambda (I - B)^{-1}\alpha] \}, \tag{13}$$

(mean/threshold/reduced-form regression intercept structure)

$$\text{Part 2: } \sigma_2 = \text{vec } \{\Delta \, \Lambda \, (I - B)^{-1} \Gamma]\}, \tag{14}$$

(reduced-form regression slope structure)

$$\text{Part 3: } \sigma_3 = K \text{ vec } \{\Delta \, [\Lambda \, (I - B)^{-1} \, \Psi \, (I - B)'^{-1} \, \Lambda' + \Theta] \, \Delta\}. \tag{15}$$

(covariance/correlation/reduced-form residual correlation structure)

Here, Δ represents a diagonal matrix of scaling factors related to the covariance matrix $V(y^*|x)$ and the K matrices are designed to select various elements. This model also encompasses the LISREL formulation of Jöreskog (1973, 1977) and Jöreskog and Sörbom (1984). For an overview of the various types of modeling that are possible (see Muthén, 1983).

The parameters of the model are estimated by minimization of the generalized least squares fitting function

$$F = \tfrac{1}{2} (s - \sigma)' W^{-1} (s - \sigma) \tag{16}$$

where s contains the sample quantities corresponding to σ, $\sigma' = (\sigma_1', \sigma_2', \sigma_3')$, and W is an estimate of the asymptotic covariance matrix of s. Twice the F value at the minimum gives an approximation to a large-sample chi-square test of model fit to the restrictions imposed on σ. Large sample standard errors of parameter estimates are readily available. For technical details, see Muthén (1984).

Extending IRT to External Variables: A MIMIC Structural Probit Model

Of particular interest in this chapter is the formulation of a special case of the general model, namely a model with a single construct underlying a set of dichotomous items (letting $\nu = 0$),

$$y^* = \lambda \eta + \epsilon. \tag{17}$$

It is well known that assuming a normal ϵ that is independent of η and has independent elements gives rise to the two-parameter normal ogive model of Item Response Theory (IRT) (see, e.g., Lord & Novick 1968). This specifies a probit regression of each y on η. We will now extend this IRT model to include a set of regressors x,

$$\eta = \alpha + \gamma' x + \zeta. \tag{18}$$

The model is schematically depicted in Fig. 13.1. The broken lines in Fig. 13.1 represent potential direct relationships between the xs and the ys. With the model of (17) and (18), such direct relationships are hypothesized to be absent. In the data analysis that follows, however, a major concern is to check and, if needed, relax this hypothesis.

The reduced form solution for y^* is

$$y^* = \lambda \alpha + \lambda \gamma' x + \lambda \zeta + \epsilon \tag{19}$$

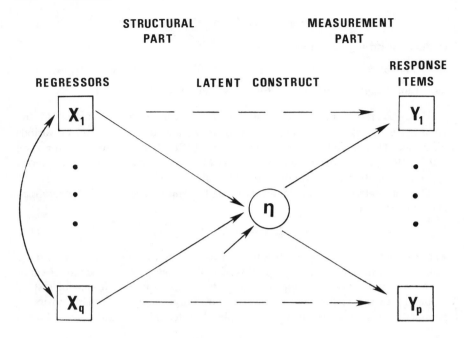

STRUCTURAL   MEASUREMENT
PART   PART

RESPONSE
REGRESSORS   LATENT CONSTRUCT   ITEMS

FIG. 13.1.   A MIMIC structural probit model.

The reduced form regression intercept vector is $\lambda\alpha$, the reduced form regression slope matrix is $\lambda\gamma'$ and has rank one, while the reduced form residual covariance matrix $\lambda\psi\lambda' + \Theta$ has a single-factor correlational structure. To standardize, we take $\mathbf{V}(y^*|x)$ to have unit diagonal elements. We will add the multivariate probit assumption that $y^*|x$ is multivariate normal. Note that this does not mean that we assume normality for the y^*s or for η, but normality is merely required for the residual ζ and for ϵ. The distribution of η and the y^*s is actually to some extent generated by the xs.

In its continuous response form, this is the traditional so called MIMIC (multiple indicators and multiple causes) structural equation model described (e.g., in Jöreskog & Goldberger, 1975; see also references therein). For dichotomous response variables, this type of model has been studied in Muthén (1979, 1981, 1983, 1985), and in Muthén and Speckart (1985), where it was termed a structural probit model.

A multiple-group version of the MIMIC model with dichotomous responses would seem to be particularly useful in analyzing the present set of achievement data, allowing a simultaneous analysis of several groups of students with respect to both measurement and structural properties in a single framework.

The generalized least-squares estimator becomes computationally heavy with a large number of elements in σ. Exceeding much beyond, say, 250 elements gives rise to unreasonable computing demands both in terms of storage and time. While an unweighted least squares estimator, using $W = I$, presumably can handle at least twice this number, it would not give a chi-square model test, nor would standard errors be provided. A simultaneous multiple-group analysis would normally involve all three parts of the model. However, in a single-group analysis the σ_2 and σ_3 part of the model need only be used, since such a model does not impose restrictions on σ_1. With p denoting the number of y variables and q denoting the number of x variables, there are pq elements in σ_2 and $p(p - 1)/2$ elements in σ_3. While problems with $p = 5$, $q = 30$ and $p = 10$, q = 15 could easily be handled by the generalized least-squares estimator, $p = 15$ would restrict q to less than 10. Larger models could be handled by ignoring the restrictions imposed on the σ_3 part, which would use less information in the estimation but would give all the results needed. Here, $p = 20$, $q = 10$ could be handled with somewhat heavy but not excessive computations. In the analyses of Section 5, a single-group analysis using σ_2 and σ_3 was carried out with $p = 8$ and $q = 24$ and a multiple-group analysis of two groups with $p = 8$ and $q = 14$. While the multiple-group analysis involved modest computing, the single-group analysis, using 224 σ elements, involved rather heavy but not excessive computing. Still, it is clear that the analyses proposed are best suited to the detailed scrutiny of a small set of items.

4. THE SIMS DATA

To illustrate the methodology in a realistic setting, we will use data from the Second International Mathematics Study (Crosswhite, Dossey, Swafford, McKnight, & Cooney, 1985). We will be concerned with a subset of data from the population of U.S. eighth-grade students enrolled in regular mathematics classes. A national probability sample of school districts was selected proportional to size; a probability sample of schools were selected proportional to size within school district; and two classes were randomly selected within each school yielding a total of about 280 schools and about 7,000 students measured at the end of spring 1982.

The achievement test contained 180 items in the areas of arithmetic, algebra, geometry, probability and statistics, and measurement distributed among five test forms. Each student responded to a core test (40 items) and one of four randomly assigned rotated forms (34 or 35 items). All items were presented in a five-category, multiple-choice format. In Section 6 our analysis will not include probability and statistics and will only use the core items within the other areas, 8 each for algebra, geometry, and measurement, and 16 for arithmetic. In this chapter, the responses to the 8 algebra items will be of particular interest.

The instructional coverage of algebra, and the mathematics curriculum in general, is rather varied for U.S. 13-year-olds. Hence, to complement the item response information for these algebra items, we will utilize a class-level variable which categorizes the mathematics classes into four types: basic or remedial arithmetic (REMEDIAL), general or typical mathematics (TYPICAL), pre-algebra or enriched (ENRICHED), and algebra (ALGEBRA). Furthermore, we will check the plausibility of our analyses by drawing from class-level, item-specific, information on teacher reports of opportunity to learn (OTL), where a student is regarded as having OTL if the teacher taught or reviewed the mathematics needed to answer the item correctly either during this year or prior school years.

The responses to the SIMS items that we have discussed were collected at the end of the eighth grade. The achievement level obtained by the student on the various aspects of the mathematics content has at that point of time been influenced by factors such as the type and amount of instruction given during the school year, initial aptitude, motivation, and interest in the topic, and a variety of socio-demographic and other variables. Regarding algebra achievement, the outcome should be strongly related to the type of class attended, since in the eighth grade the content of the algebra test would usually only be well covered in the enriched (pre-algebra) or algebra classes. To a certain extent, selection into such classes takes place based on the student's seventh-grade scholastic performance in mathematics, particularly the central topic of arithmetic. The participation in eighth-grade algebra classes may have important consequences since this allows students to take calculus in high school, which in turn opens up possibilities to study science and mathematics topics in colleges and universities (see also Kifer, 1984).

Much could be learned if student posttest performance could be related to the mathematics course taken and to student characteristics as they entered the course. With the SIMS data we are in the fortunate position of having available a set of such external measurements from the beginning of the eighth grade. Fall 1981 "pretest" data were gathered for a large portion of the "posttest" students measured in the spring of 1982. We will use this additional data to study both the algebra posttest item responses and a set of external variables in the framework of a model that relates the posttest algebra achievement to pretest predictors. These additional pieces of background data will now be briefly described.

The pretest data were gathered in the same way as the posttest data. The new set of variables to be used in our model in addition to the posttest algebra items includes pretest scores on the core items of algebra, measurement, geometry, and arithmetic, measurements of father's and mother's education, father's occupation, ethnicity, gender, attitude measurements describing the student's interest in more education, how useful he or she thinks mathematics knowledge will be, his or her attraction to mathematics, and finally information on class type. The measurement and scoring of these background variables is described in Table 13.1. The abbreviations of Table 13.1 will be used from now on. It is important to note that some of the variables were measured only at the posttest occasion,

TABLE 13.1
Description of External Variables

PREALG	Proportion of correct responses on seven pretest core items.
PREMEAS	Proportion of correct responses on seven pretest core items.
PREGEOM	Proportion of correct responses on eight pretest core items.
PREARITH	Estimated pretest theta based on the three-parameter logistic model using 16 items.
FAED	The highest type school attended by father or male guardian.
	1 = very little schooling, or no schooling at all
	2 = primary school
	3 = secondary school
	4 = college, university or some form of tertiary education
MOED	As in FAED, but for respondent's mother or female guardian.
MORED	Responses to the question "After this year, how many more years of full-time (including university, college, etc.) education do you exect or plan to complete?"
	1 = none at all (0 years)
	2 = up to 2 years
	3 = more than 2 years—up to 5 years
	4 = more than 5 years—up to 8 years
	5 = more than 8 years
USEFUL	Average score of four attitude items scored: Strongly disagree (1), Disagree (2), Undecided (3), Agree (4), and Strongly agree (5). These items are:
	1. I can get along well in everyday life without using mathematics (Reversed).
	2. A knowledge of mathematics is not necessary in most of occupations (Reversed).
	3. Mathematics is not need in everyday living (Reversed).
	4. Most people do not use mathematics in their jobs (Reversed).
ATTRACT	Average score of five attitude items. Scoring is as for USEFUL and the items are:
	1. I would like to work at a job that lets me use mathematics.
	2. I think mathematics is fun.
	3. Working with numbers makes me happy.
	4. I am looking forward to taking more mathematics.
	5. I refuse to spend a lot of my own time doing mathematics (Reversed).

Ethnicity dummy coding (0 = White)[a]:	NONWHITE
Class-type dummy coding (0 = Typical class):	REMEDIAL
	ENRICHED
	ALGEBRA
Gender dummy coding (0 = Male):	FEMALE
Father's occupation dummy coding (0 = Middle)[b]:	
	LOWOCC
	HIGHOCC
	MISSOCC

[a]The nonwhite category consists of American Indian, Black, Chicano, Latin, Oriental, and Other.

[b]The LOWOCC category of Father's occupation consists of the classifications unskilled and semi-skilled worker; the Middle category consists of skilled worker, clerical, sales and related; the HIGHOCC category consists of professional and managerial; and the MISSOCC category consists of no response and unclassifiable response.

particularly MORED, USEFUL, ATTRACT. These three measures were taken from Delandshere (1986).

The wording of the eight posttest algebra core items is given in Table 13.2.

The sample used for analysis is the match between post- and pretest students who have complete data on all variables except father's occupation. For this variable there was unfortunately a large portion of missing data and it was decided to retain such observations by including missing data as a special category, in addition to the dummy coded categories Low, Middle, and High. The analysis sample is, however, only a subset of the two pretest and posttest data

TABLE 13.2
Wording for Eight Posttest Algebra Core Items

1. If $5x + 4 = 4x - 31$, then x is equal to
   A -35
   B -27
   C   3
   D   27
   E   35
2. If $P = LW$ and if $P = 12$ and $L = 3$, then W is equal to
   A   3/4
   B   3
   C   4
   D   12
   E   36
3. $(-2) \times (-3)$ is equal to
   A -6
   B -5
   C -1
   D   5
   E   6
4. If $4x/12 = 0$, then x is equal to
   A   0
   B   3
   C   8
   D   12
   E   16
5. The air temperature at foot of a mountain is 31 degrees. On top of the mountain the temperature is -7 degrees. How much warmer is the air at the foot of the mountain?
   A -38 degrees
   B -24 degrees
   C   7 degrees
   D   24 degrees
   E   38 degrees

6. A shopkeeper has x kg of tea in stock. He sells 15 kg and then receives a new lot weighing $2y$ kg. What weight of tea does he now have?
   A $x - 15 - 2y$
   B $x + 15 + 2y$
   C $x - 15 + 2y$
   D $x + 15 - 2y$
   E   None of these
7. The table below compares the height from which a ball is dropped (d) and the height to which it bounces (b).

d	50	80	100	150
b	25	40	50	75

   Which formula describes this relationship?
   A $b = d^2$
   B $b = 2d$
   C $b = d/2$
   D $b = d + 25$
   E $b = d - 25$
8. The sentence "a number x decreased by 6 is less than 12" can be written as the inequality
   A $x - 6 > 12$
   B $x - 6 \geq 12$
   C $x - 6 < 12$
   D $6 - x \geq 12$
   E $6 - x < 12$

TABLE 13.3
Descriptive Statistics for the Different SIMS Samples

	Pretest Sample (N = 6517)			Posttest Sample (N = 7248)			Analysis Sample (N = 4320)		
	Mean	S.D.	N	Mean	S.D.	N	Mean	S.D.	N
PREALG	0.40	0.25	6353	——	——	——	0.43	0.26	4320
PREMEAS	0.49	0.25	6353	——	——	——	0.51	0.24	4320
PREGEOM	0.33	0.23	6353	——	——	——	0.35	0.23	4320
PREARITH (Obs. Score)	0.39	0.23	6353	——	——	——	0.52	0.26	4320
PREARITH (Theta Score)	——	——	——	——	——	——	0.40	0.18	4320
FAED	——	——	——	0.80	0.24	6831	0.82	0.23	4320
MOED	——	——	——	0.79	0.22	6879	0.80	0.21	4320
MORED	——	——	——	0.75	0.20	6931	0.77	0.19	4320
USEFUL	——	——	——	0.71	0.19	6878	0.72	0.19	4320
ATTRACT	——	——	——	0.54	0.20	6856	0.54	0.20	4320
NONWHITE	——	——	——	0.26	0.44	6694	0.22	0.41	4320
REMEDIAL	——	——	——	0.08	0.27	7248	0.07	0.25	4320
ENRICHED	——	——	——	0.22	0.41	7248	0.25	0.43	4320
ALGEBRA	——	——	——	0.13	0.34	7248	0.13	0.33	4320
FEMALE	——	——	——	0.52	0.50	7024	0.53	0.50	4320
LOWOCC	——	——	——	0.18	0.38	7248	0.18	0.39	4320
HIGHOCC	——	——	——	0.11	0.32	7248	0.13	0.33	4320
MISSOCC	——	——	——	0.42	0.49	7248	0.39	0.49	4320
POSTALG1	——	——	——	0.21	0.41	7013	0.22	0.41	4320
POSTALG2	——	——	——	0.69	0.46	7013	0.72	0.45	4320
POSTALG3	——	——	——	0.57	0.50	7013	0.58	0.49	4320
POSTALG4	——	——	——	0.49	0.50	7013	0.51	0.50	4320
POSTALG5	——	——	——	0.45	0.50	7013	0.47	0.50	4320
POSTALG6	——	——	——	0.55	0.50	7013	0.57	0.49	4320
POSTALG7	——	——	——	0.39	0.49	7013	0.40	0.49	4320
POSTALG8	——	——	——	0.56	0.50	7013	0.59	0.49	4320
ALG OTL%	——	——	——	0.71	0.26	6914	0.72	0.26	4224

sets and in order to judge the effects of the missing data, Table 13.3 gives descriptive statistics for relevant variables from each of the three data sets. For purposes of simplifying the analyses, the variables have all been transformed to a 0 - 1 range. The analysis sample has somewhat higher means than the other samples both on variables thought to be positively correlated with achievement and on posttest algebra performance.

Although not included directly in our analysis in Section 6, we will also utilize the item-specific OTL measurements on the posttest algebra items in order to enhance our understanding of the analysis. The upper panel of Table 13.4 gives the percentage correct on each item, broken down by class type, while the bottom panel gives the corresponding OTL means.

TABLE 13.4
Proportion Correct and Opportunity to Learn (OTL) Proportions
for the Eight Posttest Algebra Core Items by Class Type

				Item				
	1	2	3	4	5	6	7	8
Class type				Proportion correct				
Remedial	0.09	0.44	0.14	0.22	0.14	0.30	0.22	0.31
Typical	0.14	0.67	0.50	0.43	0.42	0.52	0.36	0.53
Enriched	0.22	0.81	0.73	0.63	0.55	0.63	0.46	0.68
Algebra	0.65	0.90	0.90	0.81	0.71	0.85	0.58	0.84
Total	0.22	0.72	0.58	0.51	0.47	0.57	0.40	0.59
				OTL Proportion				
Remedial	0.21	0.61	0.43	0.41	0.65	0.09	0.16	0.20
Typical	0.50	0.85	0.97	0.76	0.93	0.40	0.38	0.64
Enriched	0.78	0.96	0.94	0.94	0.95	0.47	0.58	0.83
Algebra	0.95	0.95	1.00	0.95	1.00	0.95	0.81	1.00
Total	0.61	0.87	0.93	0.80	0.92	0.46	0.47	0.70

		Sample Size		
Remedial	Typical	Enriched	Algebra	Total
299	2417	1061	543	4320

5.   ANALYSIS BY A STRUCTURAL MODEL

Let us now analyze the SIMS data using the modeling framework presented in Sections 2 and 3. It may be noted that the proposed analyses cannot be handled by present IRT software, nor by present standard structural equation modeling software, such as LISREL. The estimation and testing of the models to be presented was carried out by an experimental version of the LISCOMP computer program (Analysis of Linear Structural Equations by a Comprehensive Measurement model), developed by the author, Muthén (1987). (The program is now available to general users in an IBM mainframe version through Scientific Software, Chicago, IL, 317/831-6296.) LISCOMP provides limited information generalized least-squares estimation of the model parameters as they appear in the three-part structure of Section 3. Standard errors of estimates and a large-sample chi-square test of fit to the restrictions on the three model parts are also provided.

We consider the MIMIC model of Fig. 13.1. The response items of the y

vector correspond to the eight items of Table 13.4. The **x** vector of regressors consists of the 17 background variables given in Table 13.1: PREALG, PRE-MEAS, PREGEOM, PREARITH, FAED, MOED, MORED, USEFUL, AT-TRACT, NONWHITE, REMEDIAL, ENRICHED, ALGEBRA, FEMALE, LOWOCC, HIGHOCC, MISSOCC, and seven interaction terms, between NONWHITE and the three class-type dummies, between PREARITH and the class type dummies, and between NONWHITE and PREARITH. In a preliminary analysis we also included interactions between sex, PREALG, and the class-type dummies, but these were not found significant. The latent variable construct, posttest algebra achievement as measured by the core items, is viewed as an intervening variable in the regressions of the ys on the xs.

We have attempted to use a large set of regressors which also contains some variables that may not have a direct substantive influence on the latent variable construct. This was done for two reasons. One reason relates to the fact that our analysis sample was obtained by "list-wise deletion" of incomplete cases where judging from Table 13.3 the missingness appeared to be somewhat selective. If the missingness on the ys can be largely predicted by the included xs, the bias that could potentially have resulted in the parameters of the regressions may be small (cf. Marini, Olsen, & Rubin, 1980). A second reason is related to the fact that we will also study subgroups of students in certain class types, which will involve the analysis of selected samples. For instance, Kifer (1984) noted that whites are overrepresented in algebra courses, and also that ". . . almost $\frac{2}{3}$ of the students in algebra classes have pretest arithmetic scores in the top quarter of the distribution," while ". . . almost $\frac{2}{3}$ of the students whose pretest arithmetic scores are in the top quarter are not in algebra classes." Hence, we have included various interaction terms among the xs involving ethnicity, class type, and pretest arithmetic score, again to reduce potential bias. Furthermore, Muthén (1986) found that in addition to pretest scores and demographic variables, class-type membership was also strongly related to the attitude variables ATTRACT and MORED.

Section 5.1 deal with certain weaknesses in the actual data analysis. The reader who merely wants to view the analyses as illustrations of the potential of the new type of modeling may want to skip to Section 5.2.

5.1 Analysis Caveats

We may recognize some weaknesses in the forthcoming analyses related to the sampling, the temporal ordering of the variables, and the potential of measurement error and omitted variables in the set of xs, problems which may cause bias in the regressions. First of all, our analyses ignore the complications of stratified sampling and multilevel, hierarchical observations. Although we realize that these features may have nonnegligible consequences, the proper methods for handling them are not available in this context. Second, the attitudinal measurements MORED, USEFUL, and ATTRACT were obtained only at the posttest occasion, causing a possible problem if attempting to view these regressors as both predictors of entrance into advanced eighth-grade classes and posttest achievement. These scores presumably reflect attitudes built up both before and during the eighth grade, although they are most likely not a direct reflection of the posttest performance. Furthermore, the pretest scores are created from a small number of items, giving rise to low reliability. Although the rotated form items could have been used, this was avoided since it would have either involved equating of observed scores or using IRT techniques with sets of items many of which may have low validity at the pretest due to rather limited OTL. For the 16 pretest arithmetic items, an attempt was made to avoid the influence of measurement error by instead using factor scores. These were obtained in the form of estimated θ values from a marginal maximum likelihood estimation (see Bock & Aitkin, 1981) of the 16 items with a three-parameter logistic model using the computer program BILOG (Mislevy & Bock, 1984). Although reduction of measurement error would have been even more desirable for the other subtests, which involve fewer items, it was judged that the small number of items and the heterogeneous OTL measures for these subtests might not yield reliable results by IRT methods. For algebra and measurement, one item each was rejected as invalid in relation to the total 40-item score. This results in "favoring" the variable PREARITH in the search for influential regressors. However, it was thought to be important to try to measure this variable well since it may be viewed as a proxy for final seventh-grade mathematics achievement, which is an important factor in deciding eighth-grade curriculum.

A further measurement flaw includes a 40% missingness on father's occupation. We should also note that the ethnicity category NONWHITE is a very heterogeneous group consisting of 741 students, broken down as 8% American Indians, 41% Blacks, 17% Chicano, 6% Latin, 9% Oriental, and 19% other. In terms of omitted variables, parental income may be a predictor of class type but was not measured, and it would have been very valuable if more general ability measures had been available before entrance into the eighth grade instead of merely fall pretest scores. Also, measures of reading comprehension and vocabulary would have been of interest since they might play a role in "word problems."

Preliminary analyses were carried out on the posttest response items in order to investigate the presence of guessing (or nonzero lower item characteristic curve asymptote) and/or violations of unidimensionality in the algebra items. Marginal maximum likelihood estimation of the two- and three-parameter logistic IRT models was carried out in BILOG and unidimensionality was tested both via LISCOMP's limited information GLS procedure and via the full information estimation procedure of TESTFACT (Wilson, Wood, & Gibbons, 1984; see also Bock, Gibbons, & Muraki, 1985), in both cases assuming zero lower asymptotes. While unidimensionality could not be rejected using these approaches, the likelihood ratio chi-square test of zero lower asymptotes obtained a value of 46 with 8 degrees of freedom. Although the large sample size of 4,320 yields a strong power for rejection and lower asymptotes may not be well estimated from such small number of items, there seems to be a possibility of some nonzero asymptotes. The influence of this on our two-parameter model would presumably be a slight underestimation of the corresponding slope (loading) and a biasing of the threshold, while structural parameters may be relatively unchanged. Anticipating the subsequent analysis discussion, it is interesting to note that neither the difficult item 1 nor item 5 exhibits significant asymptotes, either when analyzing the 8 algebra items alone or together with the other core items in a 40-item analysis (39 items were actually used due to one flawed item).

5.2   A Structural Model for All Students: Model I

In the first step of the analysis we will consider the strongest and most restrictive model, where achievement is viewed as a unidimensional construct, so that a single latent variable intervenes in the regressions of the ys on the xs, without any direct regression paths from xs to ys. This model will be called Model I. It should be noted that in this first step of the analysis, the categorical grouping variables of class type, gender, and ethnicity are included as dummy coded variables among the set of xs. Our intention is to let the analysis of Model I, and modifications thereof, assist in generating ideas for subsequent simultaneous multiple-group analyses, where the grouping is based on such categorical variables, and where a more detailed analysis is possible. For our first analysis of the whole analysis sample of 4,320 students, the complete set of assumptions in Model I may not be entirely realistic, since we include all the different types of eighth grade classes, while Table 13.4 clearly shows that percentage correct and OTL varies greatly and in different patterns for different items over these classes. Nevertheless, this may be a useful starting point for our analysis.

   Model I is an overidentified model, which imposes 188 restrictions on the reduced form regression slopes and residual correlations. The standard IRT unidimensionality assumption with conditional independence contributes 20 restrictions; since 28 reduced form residual correlations are described by 8 parameters related to the measurement part. The concept of an intervening latent variable construct in the regressions of the ys on the xs contributes the remaining 168 restrictions, since 192 reduced form regression slopes are described by merely 24 structural regression slope parameters. Hence, in terms of restrictions imposed, the content of the model is largely a result of using the external variables of *x* and imposing MIMIC restrictions on the regression slopes for *y* on *x*. Utilizing external variables in this way gives a more powerful assessment of measurement qualities for the *y*s than would be obtained by considering responses to the *y*s alone as in standard IRT.

The large-sample chi-square test to fit to the 188 restrictions of Model I obtained a value of 681. This represents a significantly misfitting model. However, given the power resulting from the large sample size of 4,320, the value is, in our opinion, small enough to warrant attempts to modifying details of this first approximation rather than rejecting it in its entirety. Throughout, we will use the chi-square test results more as descriptive measures of overall fit for a sequence of models fitted to the same data than as a rigorous hypothesis-testing instrument. In terms of such a descriptive usage, some experience with structural models for dichotomous response data leads us to judge as reasonable fit a chi-square to degrees of freedom ratio scaled to a sample size of 2,000 that is less than say 1.5 (this ratio is 1.7 for Model I). We know that there may be clear substantive reasons for lack of fit in parts of Model I and we will not be satisfied with the model as it stands, but investigate the possible reasons for misfit in an attempt to arrive at a modified Model II.

The fact that Model I is strongly overidentified offers the opportunity to check the appropriateness of the various assumptions involved and to relax some restrictions if judged necessary. This would not be possible in a straightforward multivariate regression of the *y*s on the *x*s, but is the result of our notion of a single latent construct. To aid in attempts to check the fit of the various restrictions, so called modification indexes will be used. They are similar to what is provided in the LISREL structural equation modeling program (Jöreskog & Sörbom, 1984). Such an index reflects the expected improvement in fit if a restricted parameter, such as one set to zero, is allowed to be freely estimated. The indexes to be used in this version of LISCOMP are not scaled to represent the chi-square metric as in LISREL, but are merely the first-order derivatives of the parameters. It should be noted that the use of these modification indexes as a data exploration device may be dangerous. The information from the various indexes for a certain model can be misleading since they may be highly correlated, the information really only pertains to freeing up one parameter at a time, the indexes are only good approximations for models that are close to a well-fitting one, and we may capitalize on chance in our data. We will try to use these indexes with care in conjunction with substantive considerations.

The modification indexes for Model I are given in Table 13.5. The indexes in the top part of the table gives information on which direct paths from *x*s to *y*s may need to be freed from their restriction to zero. These paths correspond to the broken line arrows of Fig. 13.1. The indexes in the bottom part of the table gives information on potential violations of the conditional independence assumption of zero correlations among the residuals. In this table, the first-order derivative

TABLE 13.5
Modification Indexes for a Structural Model
(All Students, Model I, N = 4320)

	Item 1	Item 2	Item 3	Item 4	Item 5	Item 6	Item 7	Item 8
	Direct relationships between items and regressors							
PREALG	2	-1	-1	2	0	-1	0	-1
PREMEAS	-1	2	-2	-1	4	-2	1	-2
PREGEOM	1	0	-1	-3	1	-1	0	2
PREARITH	-1	1	-1	-1	3	-1	0	-1
FAED	-3	0	2	1	3	-3	-1	0
MOED	-1	0	1	1	3	0	-1	-3
MORED	0	-1	1	0	-1	1	0	-2
USEFUL	-1	1	0	0	-2	1	-1	1
ATTRACT	3	1	-1	0	-2	1	0	-1
NONWHITE	3	-4	1	5	-8	3	2	-1
REMEDIAL	3	1	-5	0	-1	2	2	0
ENRICHED	-9	3	8	5	-4	-7	-1	2
ALGEBRA	17*	-4	1	0	-6	-2	-4	0
FEMALE	0	5	3	4	-19*	0	-5	10
LOWOCC	1	0	1	-1	-2	1	0	1
HIGHOCC	-1	1	-1	2	-2	-1	3	0
MISSOCC	1	-2	-1	3	1	0	-2	-1
NONW × REM	2	0	-3	1	0	0	0	0
NONW × ENR	0	-1	0	2	-3	0	1	2
NONW × ALG	2	-1	0	1	0	0	0	-1
PREARITH × REM	1	0	-1	0	0	0	0	0
PREARITH × ENR	-4	1	3	2	0	-3	0	0
PREARITH × ALG	9	-3	0	0	-3	-1	-2	0
NONW × PREARITH	1	-1	1	2	-2	1	0	0
	Measurement error correlations							
Item 2	5							
Item 3	2	-1						
Item 4	3	0	7					
Item 5	6	-12	7	-11				
Item 6	4	10	-4	4	5			
Item 7	1	2	-6	-5	13	2		
Item 8	4	-3	-8	2	-7	21*	9	

*Freed parameter in Model II.

modification indexes have reversed signs so that the present sign describes the expected direction of change from zero in a parameter. The derivative values have also been divided by 10 and rounded.

Scrutinizing Table 13.5 in conjunction with other substantive information will lead us to Model II. Let us only consider the three largest modification indices for Model I, marked by asterisks in Table 13.5. Starting with Item 1's index of 17 for the ALGEBRA class dummy (comparing with the category of Typical classes), we have an indication of a positive direct "effect" of membership in algebra classes on the performance on Item 1 (cf. Muthén, 1986). It should be kept in mind that this direct influence occurs over and above the influence of the latent achievement construct on Item 1. This implies that students with the same algebra achievement level, but belonging to different class types, may perform differently on Item 1; algebra class membership gives an advantage. Hence, we have a suggestion of "item bias," or rather instructional sensitivity in Item 1. This empirical suggestion makes substantive sense when we consider our auxiliary information. This is the only one of the algebra items that deals explicitly with "solving for x." Table 13.4 shows that this is the hardest of the eight items, with a large difference in proportion correct between students of typical and algebra classes, and with the largest difference in OTL between typical and algebra classes. From Table 13.4 we see that Items 6 and 7 have somewhat similar features, but none of these items exhibit large ALGEBRA modification indexes in Table 13.4. It seems as if in this set of items the lack of instrumentional coverage in typical classes has a particularly detrimental effect on the response to Item 1.

The largest modification index for direct x to y paths in Table 13.5 occurs for Item 5 on the dummy variable FEMALE. This suggests a gender item bias. The negative sign would imply that, for given achievement level, females perform worse on Item 5 than males. We may note that this item involves a "word problem" in a way the other items do not. This potential gender difference will be further analyzed. The largest modification index in Table 5 occurs for a correlation between the measurement error of Item 6 and 8, suggesting a violation of the conditional independence for these two items in the form of a positive correlation. From the item wording of Table 13.2 we do in fact note that both items, and none of the others, involve a direct translation of a word problem into a mathematical formula. Hence it is possible that the correlation may indicate the presence of a specific skill, in addition to the algebra achievement construct, required for such a translation.

5.3   A Structural Model for All Students: Model II

Let us now free up the three parameters that were fixed to zero in Model I and consider the modified Model II. This model obtained a chi-square value of 441.59 with 185 degrees of freedom. The difference in chi-square from Model I is 240 with 3 degrees of freedom. Given the sample size we regard this outcome as an indication of a reasonable overall fit in the major parts of the model, although further adjustments could be made. Some interesting details may be noted before we consider the estimates of Model II. First, in this case the freeing up one of the three parameters at a time did by use of the largest modification indexes lead to the same final result, irrespective of the order in which this was done. Second, the major results in terms of general magnitude and significance of structural coefficients remain largely unchanged when going from Model I to Model II. Third, for Model II the modification index for PREARITH × ALG has been reduced to almost zero from the Model I value of 9, the Model I value of 10 for Item 8 on FEMALE has only been reduced to 8, the Model I value of 8 for Item 3 on ENRICH remains the same, and the Model I value of −8 for Item 5 on NONWHITE also remains the same. The remaining major modification indexes now appear among the error correlations with a few values of about 10.

The parameter estimates estimates for Model II are given in Table 13.6, where the first part of the table gives measurement parameter results and the second part gives results on structural parameters. For the measurement part we also give estimated reliabilities for each item.

The estimated reliabilities are in some cases rather low, although we must bear in mind that these are item-level responses. Since Items 1 and 5 are directly related to both the latent construct to be measured and one of the regressors, these two items, in relation to the other items in the set, are not homogeneous with respect to the set of regressors (cf. Muthén, 1985).

Regarding the structural parameter estimates, we find expected strong, significant influences on achievement from PREARITH and PREALG, and the other pretest scores, but also from USEFUL, ALGEBRA, FEMALE, and HIGHOCC. The significance of the last three dummy variables implies that other regressor values being equal, membership in advanced classes rather than typical ones,

TABLE 13.6
Parameter Estimates for a Structural Model
(All Students, Model II N = 4320)

| Response | Measurement Parameter Estimates | | | | |
| | Thresholds | | Loadings | | |
Item	Est.	Est./S.E.	Est.	Est./S.E.	Reliabilities
Item 1	2.19	27	0.54	16	0.19
Item 2	1.23	14	0.88	22	0.41
Item 3	1.91	20	1.00[a]	——	0.49
Item 4	1.76	20	0.82	23	0.37
Item 5	1.85	20	0.89	23	0.42
Item 6	1.59	19	0.82	22	0.37
Item 7	1.57	21	0.59	19	0.22
Item 8	1.34	17	0.73	21	0.32
Error correlation for Items 6 and 8					
			0.12	5	

(Continued)

TABLE 13.6 (*Continued*)

	Structural Parameters with the Latent Construct as Dependent Variable	
Regressor	Estimate	Estimate/S.E.
PREALG	0.68	11
PREMEAS	0.45	7
PREGEOM	0.33	5
PREARITH	2.09	16
FAED	0.07	1
MOED	0.02	0
MORED	0.18	3
USEFUL	0.45	7
ATTRACT	0.04	1
NONWHITE	−0.02	0
REMEDIAL	0.07	1
ENRICHED	0.22	3
ALGEBRA	0.56	4
FEMALE	0.14	6
LOWOCC	0.02	1
HIGHOCC	0.12	3
MISSOCC	0.05	2
NONW × REM	0.10	1
NONW × ENR	0.19	3
NONW × ALG	−0.18	−1
PREARITH × REM	−1.45	−3
PREARITH × ENR	−0.10	−1
PREARITH × ALG	−0.54	−2
NONW × PREARITH	−0.19	−1
Item - Regressor Relations not Mediated by Latent Construct		
Item 1 on ALGEBRA	0.86	13
Item 5 on FEMALE	−0.35	
Latent Construct Residual Variance	0.20	13

*a*Parameter is fixed to set the metric of the latent variable construct.

being female, and having a father in the high occupation category rather than the middle one, are conditions associated with a higher level of algebra achievement as represented by the latent variable construct.

In addition to this, we find from the bottom of Table 13.6 that for a given value of the achievement construct, membership in algebra classes and being female, respectively, is associated with a higher level of performance on Item 1 and a lower performance on Item 5, respectively. From the estimated parameters and the sample mean vector and covariance matrix for *x*, we may also calculate the mean and variance of the latent variable construct and the proportion of variation in this construct that is accounted for by the set of regressors. We obtained a mean 2.20, a standard deviation of 0.87, and 73% of the variation was accounted for. Using the mean and standard deviation we can translate the measurement parameter estimates to standard IRT *a* and *b* values on a 0,1 θ scale (see below in relation with Table 13.8).

5.4 A Simultaneous Structural Analysis by Gender in Typical Classes

In Muthén (1986), the above analysis is taken further by considering class-type differences. Hence, we will instead study in more detail the differences and similarities in measurement and structural parameters across gender. A simultaneous, two-group analysis will be carried out for students of typical classes. In these models, 14 *x* variables from the original set remain after eliminating class-type and gender-related dummies. Table 13.7 gives descriptive statistics for these regressors. We note that males have slightly higher means on variables associated with high achievement, except for USEFUL. The proportion correct for the posttest algebra items in typical classes were for Males: 0.14, 0.65, 0.50, 0.40, 0.47, 0.51, 0.37, 0.50, and for Females: 0.14, 0.69, 0.50, 0.46, 0.38, 0.53, 0.35, 0.56. The OTL values are given in Table 13.4 and do not vary appreciably over gender.

TABLE 13.7
Means and Standard Deviations for Males and Females
in Typical Classes

Regressors	Male (N = 1150)		Female (N = 1267)	
	Mean	S.D.	Mean	S.D.
PREALG	0.38	0.23	0.37	0.23
PREMEAS	0.50	0.23	0.45	0.23
PREGEOM	0.33	0.22	0.29	0.19
PREARITH	0.37	0.17	0.36	0.15
FAED	0.81	0.23	0.79	0.23
MOED	0.80	0.20	0.78	0.21
MORED	0.74	0.20	0.74	0.19
USEFUL	0.69	0.19	0.73	0.17
ATTRACT	0.52	0.20	0.54	0.20
NONWHITE	0.21	0.41	0.23	0.42
LOWOCC	0.21	0.41	0.20	0.40
HIGHOCC	0.11	0.31	0.11	0.31
MISSOCC	0.37	0.48	0.40	0.49
NONW × PREARITH	0.06	0.13	0.07	0.14

In the multiple-group analysis the effect of gender can be studied in more detail than was possible in the single-group analysis of Model II. In Model II, gender differences were only captured in the intercepts of the achievement and the latent response variable regressions. Although interaction terms between gender and other regressors in Model II could have been accommodated in the achievement construct relation, the dummy variable approach would not for instance be able to handle gender differences in measurement slopes (loadings). Also, in a multiple-group analyses it is easier to deal separately with tests of invariance in the measurement and the structural part.

In this analysis we will apply a multiple-group version of the Fig. 13.1 MIMIC model. Since the same measurement instrument was used for the two sexes, we will test the notion of invariance in the measurement thresholds and slopes (loadings) for the eight response items, allowing all other parameters to differ across the two groups. Based on the previous analysis results for all students, we will however allow the threshold and slope of Item 5 to vary. As a baseline model we will first consider a multiple group analyses of males and females where no parameters are invariant, in order to assess the appropriateness of the MIMIC model itself. With 236 degrees of freedom, this resulted in a chi-square value of model fit of 366. This fit is judged to be satisfactory. The total sample size is 2,417 broken down as 1,150 males and 1,267 females.

The addition of invariance of measurement intercepts and slopes, except for Item 5, resulted in a chi-square value of 381 with 248 degrees of freedom, yielding a nonsignificant chi-square increase of 15 with 12 degrees of freedom compared with the baseline model. Also adding invariance for Item 5, however, resulted in a chi-square difference test value of 33 with 2 degrees of freedom. This strong rejection of the invariance notion for Item 5 is in line with our single-group results for Model II in all class types. The parameter estimates for the multiple-group model of invariance measurement thresholds and slopes, except for Item 5, is given in Table 13.8.

From the measurement part of Table 13.8 we see that Item 1 has the lowest correlation with the latent achievement construct. This is in line with the low OTL value of 50% in Table 13.4. For Item 5, the gender difference in thresholds and loadings translates into (see Muthén & Christoffersson, 1981, Equations 28 and 29) a two-parameter normal ogive a (discrimination) and b (difficulty) value on a 0,1 θ-metric of 0.81 and 0.09 for males and 0.65 and 0.51 for females. Hence, the male item characteristic curve is shifted to the left from the female curve and is steeper, thereby favoring males. The reason for this gender difference is, however, unclear. The availability of further external variables, such as a reading comprehension test, might possibly have been able to shed light on this matter (cf. Muthén, 1985).

Regarding the structural slopes, the results are rather similar to those for all students in Model II of Table 13.6. In the present model the intercept difference in the structural relation for the latent variable construct is not significantly

TABLE 13.8
Parameter Estimates for a Simultaneous Structural Model Analysis
of Males and Females in Typical Classes

Measurement Parameter Estimates
(Thresholds and loadings invariant over gender, except for Item 5)

Response Item	Thresholds		Loadings		Reliabilities	
	Est.	Est./S.E.	Est.	Est./S.E.	Males	Females
Item 1	2.16	18.79	0.55	10.07	0.13	0.11
Item 2	1.50	9.58	1.09	14.66	0.39	0.36
Item 3	1.83	12.61	1.00[a]	——	0.35	0.31
Item 4	1.83	13.54	0.90	14.25	0.29	0.26
Item 5					0.40	0.30
Males	2.06	11.91	1.10	12.51		
Females	2.13	11.72	0.97	11.69		
Item 6	1.74	12.59	0.98	14.43	0.33	0.30
Item 7	1.71	14.45	0.72	12.22	0.20	0.18
Item 8	1.52	11.65	0.88	14.00	0.28	0.26

Structural Parameter Estimates

Regressors	Males (N = 1150)		Females (N = 1267)	
	Est.	Est./S.E.	Est.	Est./S.E.
PREALG	0.46	9	0.61	7
PREMEAS	0.51	5	0.46	5
PREGEOM	0.43	4	0.23	2
PREARITH	1.67	9	2.01	10
FAED	−0.12	−1	0.14	2
MOED	0.19	2	0.00	0
MORED	0.14	1	0.20	2
USEFUL	0.62	6	0.34	3
ATTRACT	−0.01	0	0.11	1
NONWHITE	0.10	1	0.02	0
LOWOCC	0.02	0	−0.03	−1
HIGHOCC	0.12	2	0.06	1
MISSOCC	0.12	3	−0.07	−2
NONW × PREARITH	−0.76	−3	−0.17	−1
Latent Construct Intercept	0.00[a]	——	0.12	1
Latent Construct Residual	0.15	7	0.13	7

[a]Fixed parameter.

different from zero. However, estimating the construct mean from the estimated coefficients and the sample mean vector for the xs, we find a value of 1.81 for males while females obtain 1.88. This difference should be viewed in relation to the male standard deviation of 0.67 and the female standard deviation of 0.63. Although males seemed to have slightly higher means on important regressors in Table 13.7, females end up with a slightly higher posttest achievement level. The proportion of variation in the construct accounted for by the xs is 66% for males and 68% for females.

In addition to imposing restrictions of measurement parameter invariance, it is also of interest to study the differences in the structural parameters across gender. For instance, are the possibly higher levels of the achievement construct for females due to the fact that females have higher slopes on important regressors (the important variable USEFUL would however be an important exception)? Adding the restriction of invariant structural slopes, yields a chi-square difference of 29 with 14 degrees of freedom, while restricting only the slopes for PREARITH to be equal across sex yields a chi-square difference value of 2 with 1 degree of freedom. There seems to be some evidence of differences in some of the slopes, although PREARITH seems to have equal predictive strength for the two sexes.

6. CONCLUSIONS

The MIMIC structural modeling approach was found to be quite useful with the present data where there was a particular interest in posttest responses and where pretest data were available. Using a single model framework that extends the boundaries of IRT, we were able to deal simultaneously not only with issues of measurement qualities, but also differential item performance in different subgroups and differential prediction of achievement.

Other versions of the general model of Section 3 would be relevant in other situations. The external x variables need not only appear as background variables, predicting the dichotomous ys. For instance, we may be interested in the differential predictive validity in different groups of a set of items or subtest scores for which certain constructs are hypothesized. Here, careful measurement modeling carried out on the exogenous side may lead to better predictions of a certain y criterion. The use of structural modeling in such situations does not seem to have been fully explored.

ACKNOWLEDGMENTS

This research was partly supported by grant OERI–G–86–003 from the Office of Educational Research and Improvement, Department of Education and by grant SES–8312583 from the National Science Foundation. The opinions expressed herein do not necessarily reflect the position or policy of these agencies. I would like to thank Leigh Burstein, Lee J. Cronbach, Ginette Delandshere, David Kaplan, and Linda K. Muthen for helpful advice and Chih–Fen Kao, Jahja Umar, and Shinn–Tzong Wu for valuable research assistance. I thank Margie Franco for drawing the figure.

REFERENCES

Bock, R. D., & Aitkin, M. (1981). Marginal maximum likelihood estimation of item parameters: Application of an EM algorithm. *Psychometrika, 46,* 443–459.

Bock, R. D., Gibbons, R., & Muraki, E. (1985). *Full-information item factor analysis. Final report to the ONR.* National Opinion Research Center, MRC Report No. 85–1.

Bohrnstedt, G. W. (1983). Measurement. *Handbook of survey research* (pp. 69–121). New York: Academic Press.

Christoffersson, A. (1975). Factor analysis of dichotomized variables. *Psychometrika, 40,* 5–32.

Crosswhite, F. J., Dossey, J. A., Swafford, J. O., McKnight, C. C., & Cooney, T. J. (1985). *Second international mathematics study summary report for the United States.* Champaign, IL: Stipes.

Delandshere, G. (1986). *The effect of teaching practices on math achievement in the eighth grade.* Unpublished doctoral disseration, University of California, Los Angeles, in progress.

Jöreskog, K. G. (1969). A general approach to confirmatory maximum likelihood factor analysis. *Psychometrika, 34,* 183–202.

Jöreskog, K. G. (1971). Simultaneous factor analysis in several populations. *Psychometrika, 36,* 409–426.

Jöreskog, K. G. (1973). A general method for estimating a linear structural equation system. In A. S. Goldberger & O. D. Duncan (Eds.), *Structural equation models in the social sciences* (pp. 85–112). New York: Seminar Press.

Jöreskog, K. G. (1977). Structural equation models in the social sciences: Specification, estimation and testing. In P. R. Krishnaiah (Ed.), *Applications of statistics.* Amsterdam: North–Holland.

Jöreskog, K. G., & Goldberger, A. S. (1975). Estimation of a model with multiple indicators and multiple causes of a single latent variable. *Journal of the American Statistical Association, 70,* 631–639.

Jöreskog, K. G., & Sörbom, D. (1984). LISREL VI: Analysis of linear structural relationships by maximum likelihood and least squares methods. Mooresville, IN: Scientific Software.

Kifer, E. (1984). Issues and implications of differentiated curriculum in the eighth grade. National Conference on the Teaching and Learning of Mathematics in the United States. University of Kentucky.

Lord, F. M., & Novick, M. R. (1968). *Statistical theories of mental test scores.* Addison–Wesley: Reading, MA.

Marini, M. M., Olsen, A. R., & Rubin, D. B. (1980). Maximum likelihood estimation in panel studies with missing data. In *Sociological Methodology.* San Francisco: Jossey–Bass.

Miller, M. D., & Linn, R. L. (1986). Invariance of item parameters with variations in instructional coverage. *Journal of Educational Measurement,* forthcoming.

Mislevy, R. J. (1986). Recent developments in the factor analysis of categorical variables. *Journal of Educational Statistics, 11*(1), 3–31.

Mislevy, R. J., & Bock, R. D. (1984). *BILOG: Marginal estimation of item parameters and subject ability under binary logistic models.* Chicago: International Educational Services.

Muthén, B. (1978). Contributions to factor analysis of dichotomous variables. *Psychometrika, 43,* 551–560.

Muthén, B. (1979). A structural probit model with latent variables, *Journal of the American Statistical Association, 74*, 807–811.

Muthén, B. (1981). Factor analysis of dichotomous variables: American attitudes toward abortion. In D. J. Jackson & E. F. Borgatta (Eds.), *Factor analysis and measurement in sociological research: A multi-dimensional perspective* (pp. 201–214). London: Sage.

Muthén, B. (1983). Latent variable structural equation modeling with categorical data. *Journal of Econometrics, 22*, 43–65.

Muthén, B. (1984). A general structural equation model with dichotomous, ordered categorical, and continuous latent variable indicators. *Psychometrika, 49*, 115–132.

Muthén, B. (1985). A method for studying the homogeneity of test items with respect to other relevant variables. *Journal of Educational Statistics, 10*(2), 121–132.

Muthén, B. (1986). *Instructionally sensitive psychometrics: Applying structural models to educational achievement data.* In preparation.

Muthén, B. LISCOMP. Analysis of linear structural equations using a comprehensive measurement model. *User's Guide.* Mooresville, IN: Scientific Software, Inc.

Muthén, B., & Christoffersson, A. (1981). Simultaneous factor analysis of dichotomous variables in several groups. *Psychometrika, 46*, 485–500.

Muthén, B., & Lehman, J. (1985). Multiple group IRT modeling: Applications to item bias analysis. *Journal of Educational Statistics, 10*(2), 133–142.

Muthén, B., & Speckart, G. (1985). Latent variable probit ANCOVA: Treatment effects in the California civil addict programme. University of California, Los Angeles. *British Journal of Mathematical and Statistical Psychology, 38*, 161–170.

Schmitt, N., & Stults, D. M. (1986). Methodology Review: Analysis of Multitrait-Multimethod Matrices. *Applied Psychological Measurement, 10*(1), 1–22.

Sörbom, D. (1974). A general method for studying differences in factor means and factor structure between groups. *British Journal of Mathematical and Statistical Psychology, 27*, 229–239.

Sörbom, D. (1978). An alternative to the methodology for analyses of covariance. *Psychometrika, 43*, 381–396.

Sörbom, D. (1982). Structural equation models with structured means. In K. G. Jöreskog & H. Wold (Eds.), *Systems under indirect observation: Causality, structure, prediction.* Amsterdam: North–Holland.

Wilson, D., Wood, R., & Gibbons, R. (1984). TESTFACT: Test scoring and item factor analysis. Mooresville, IN: Scientific Software, Inc.

Editors' Introduction to the Discussion

The conference from which this volume was developed had the good fortune to have Professor Donald B. Rubin in attendance. His insightful and provocative discussions of the papers enlightened and enlivened the exchange of ideas. We have decided to try to convey some of the spirit of that discussion to the readers of this volume by including an edited transcription of his remarks. These tend not to be confined strictly to the papers presented, but rather to be wide ranging, reaching out to provide a broader perspective. Furthermore, we decided not to balkanize Rubin's discussion by putting various pieces of it after each associated chapter; instead we left it intact. We believe that this provides a useful synthesis. We hope that this does not deter the reader who may want to refer to the appropriate section of these discussions after reading a particular chapter; it merely reflects our predilection to think of it as an ensemble.

Chapter 14

Discussion

Donald B. Rubin
Harvard University

Well, it's certainly nice to be back and see all my many friends from ETS and the Princeton area. Howard arranged for my discussion to deal with any of the talks that preceded me. He arranged it to begin at 4 o'clock. I assume that I have until 11 tonight. I think that's probably just about adequate time. We may have to cycle through coffee and doughnuts to keep people awake.

ON CRONBACH AND MODELING SELF-SELECTION

Lee Cronbach commented that one of the important issues in validity studies is the effect of selected populations. That is, how to handle restriction of range and the general extrapolation issues that arise. He alluded to the fact that we really aren't very rich in models right now to do that. I think that's a fair assessment. But I also think that we're well positioned to make good progress on those problems right now. Part of the reason we're in a good position is that in the last 10 or so years there's been a substantial amount of work on problems of handling missing data, such as from nonresponse in surveys. A lot of this work can be applied—not directly, but at least it's a leg up—to these problems of restriction of range and adjusting for selection effects. As Lee knows, all of these adjustments require extrapolation and so rely on models. Consequently, modern statistics cannot perform magic for you and get rid of this necessary reliance on models. But at least the existing technology for specifying models that may be realistic, and for working from those models toward answers, seems to be much better than it was 10 years ago.

ON MESSICK AND THE VALIDITY OF INFERENCES

A second point is one that Sam Messick brought up and I agree with very strongly. Inferences are the things that are to be validated and not the tests. I think that's a very important idea. How can a test by itself be valid if one doesn't describe what the test is to be used for? It's the *use* of the test (in the full sense of the inference from the test) that is the thing to be validated; not just the test itself. Maybe everybody knows that, but when I heard Sam say it, it rang a true chord. Even though everybody may say "Well, we already knew that stuff," it seems to me that it is not stated often enough. Maybe it's just that jargon tends to be sloppy, but I think that the validation of inferences using tests rather than just tests is a very important idea.[1]

ON THE REPRESENTATIVENESS OF TESTS

Related to the idea that what one is validating are inferences on the whole ensemble of actions that are taken based on tests is the idea of "representative tests." The phrases "representing the domain of tests," "of items," or "representing the domain," in some sense were commented on by Pellegrino, Messick, and Bill Angoff. Bill made a comment that this idea of "being representative of a domain" is only important when you actually randomly sample items from a domain in some formal sense. If that's what he meant, I believe that it's probably too restrictive. I think that "representing a domain" does not mean just that there is a process of random sampling, but refers again to the inference. A test represents a domain if you can draw inferences from the test items back to the domain.

"Representativeness" doesn't mean that the sampling is simple random sampling or stratified random sampling or cluster sampling that draws items so that the sample looks like the population. That's not the issue. The issue is: Does the model that you're willing to place on reality (the mapping that you make from the test items back to the domain of interest) allow you to draw valid inferences back to the domain? Thus, for example, you can take a highly stratified sample of items that oversamples difficult items (or undersamples easy items) and because you know the sampling process you can draw inferences back to any weighting of those items in the domain. You're not restricted to only drawing inferences to domains that weight difficult items more heavily than easier items. So it's the

---

[1]Messick references Cronbach (1971) for the genesis of that idea. (Ed.)

fact that you're willing to conceptualize the test as being drawn with some known probabilities (or some structure like that) from the domain, that allows you to draw inferences. You can then draw inferences to any weighting of the items in the domain.

There are a variety of contexts where I have been in discussions with people about the word "representativeness." I think it is a word that creates confusion because it tends to create the image that a sample is only representative when it looks like a a simple random sample from that population. That's just not true. The right definition is that the sample is representative if it allows you to draw valid inferences back to the domain (the population). This really ties in quite closely with Sam's comment and evidently was something Lee said 15 years ago.

ON CHECKING ON THE VALIDITY OF MODELS
AND APPROPRIATENESS MEASUREMENT

Another point that's related to some extent to this ability to "represent," is the fact that there's usually some implicit model of reality that allows you to make the generalization. When we use models, we should use diagnostic information about how good those models are. The phrase "diagnostic information" came up in Richard Durán's talk. It was also implicit in Paul Holland's talk and Dave Thissen's talk about which items are appropriate for different subgroups and differential item functioning.

The one thing that I want to point out is that there is some literature on this that wasn't mentioned by any of the speakers, which I think is fairly relevent. There is work that Mike Levine and I did jointly (but Mike is the prime instigator of the work and has continued to develop it at Illinois) called "appropriateness measurement." The idea is to measure whether an item or test is appropriate for any particular individual or subgroup. The essential idea is a very easy one. If a person takes a test (on which we have calculated item difficulties based on some population) and gets all the hard items right and the easy items wrong, something is inappropriate somewhere. Maybe English was not the examinee's native language and the easy items require a particular knowledge of English that wasn't true of the other items. Or perhaps there's something strange about the items per se. But there are ways of getting information at either the item level or at the person level to say whether there's a match-up; whether things are appropriate. Mike and I used a collection of fairly naïve models, at least by current statistical standards. But Mike has continued to develop the ideas. Thus Dave Thissen's comment that Fred Lord's work is the only principled attempt at this is a bit overstated.

ON HOLLAND AND THISSEN
AND THE MEANING OF "ROBUST"

The next comment relates to the Mantel–Haenszel procedure that Paul Holland suggested and the work that Dave Thissen reported that compares the Mantel–Haenszel test statistic with the likelihood ratio (or the Wald statistic version of the test). This test is for the cross-product ratio, for the odds ratio being one in a group. The work that Thissen reported indicated that the Mantel–Haenszel test statistic is really quite robust in the sense that it gives the same sort of answers, at least the same sorts of conclusions, as the more computationally expensive likelihood ratio test statistic (the Wald statistic test). The usual way of summarizing that, in fact, the way I did just now was to say, "That makes the Wald statistic robust." But that's a phrase that I don't like at all. It's not the word "robust" that I dislike, I dislike the idea that it's the statistic that's robust. That's really not true. It is really that the question you're asking is robust. That is, it's a simple question to address and, therefore, different procedures for getting answers give you about the same answer.

Let me give an example. People often say that the median is a robust statistic and the mean is not. I think that's a misguided way of stating what's going on. The statistics are not robust. What's robust is the quantity being estimated, the estimand. The median is an easy parameter to estimate under most reasonable models. In contrast, the mean is a very difficult parameter to estimate. I can specify the "middle" of the distribution as far as I want, up to the .01 and 99.99th percentiles, and I still don't know how to estimate the mean. I have to know what the tails of the distribution are like. Thus, if I only give you the middle of the distribution (however you want to define the middle, t and $100 - t$ percentiles for any $t > 0$), you still don't know whether that distribution has a finite mean. However, you know the median exactly. In fact, you don't need to know very much at all to know the median. So, it's the quantity being estimated that defines the robustness. There are lots of ways of estimating a robust estimand and the values of the statistics tend to be the same: The estimates of a robust estimand tend to be the same.

So I think that the right way of describing the phenomenon that Thissen saw in the design is that this odds ratio is an easy quantity to estimate for the class of models that were investigated. I wish Dave had a little bit more time to describe the simulation study that he did. From what was presented, I had the feeling that he was picking and choosing a few points. Maybe this isn't true, but if it is, I encourage some work on a more systematic experimental design. First look at what factors might be involved in making the odds ratio difficult to estimate and then systematically vary them in a 2^4 or 2^5 or 3×2^2 design: a real experimental design from which you can draw inferences and build a response surface model. A response surface shown as a function of these factors can tell us when the odds ratio becomes difficult to estimate. When this occurs, these different estimators ought to start varying because they are optimal under different assumptions about the underlying model. Of course, the full design may not be necessary if after having chosen extreme points, you do not find much variability.

ON THISSEN AND DETECTING DIFFERENCES IN SMALL SAMPLES USING LARGE SAMPLE TEST STATISTICS

I believe that Dave commented that in order to detect differences, he would probably have to increase sample size in the simulation. I'm not so sure about that. Maybe yes, maybe no, but I don't think you've done quite enough yet to say whether you need larger samples. The reason, as you know, is that all the methods discussed were the standard large-sample methods. To tie the large-sample ideas to standard terminology—and you did this, Dave—there's a likelihood ratio test that compares the heights of the likelihoods at different points. There's also a likelihood-based test statistic, using the curvature near the maximum. I've been calling this test statistic the Wald statistic, you called it the Mahalanobis distance statistic. It's been called the Wald statistic for 30 or 40 years, but by whatever name, it still relies on some normal approximation. The way the normal approximation was described here was actually very Bayesian. It had to do with the shape of the likelihood function itself. These statistics have perfectly valid Bayesian interpretations as do the p values that arise from these statistics. But the assumptions that drive them under the frequentist model really have to do with the sampling distributions of the statistics; that is, the sampling distributions of the statistics are normal and not the likelihood function per se.

So from a frequentist point of view, one can look at a likelihood function and see it drastically nonnormal and say, "I don't care. This likelihood function is not normal, but I know in repeated samples that this statistic will be normally distributed." A frequentist is happy with that. So there are differences there between the Bayesian's and frequentist's view of large-sample statistics in small samples.

If we are going to study small samples, we have to worry a bit about what might be the small-sample analogs of these large-sample statistics. It used to be a hard problem—it still is not conceptually easy—but at least we have a tool now that we can use very easily: computing. We can get a lot of these answers by simulation, for example, by simulating posterior distributions. This should be done before we give up and say that we've squeezed all of the information out of the data that's there. In small samples, sometimes just the skewness in likelihoods can convey information. I don't think you squeezed quite hard enough. But maybe the sample sizes are such that the appropriate normality is always attained, and then I'm talking about a mathematical/statistical point that's not worth pursuing.

ON HOLLAND AND EXTENDING THE DIF MODEL

Now on Paul Holland's work. One issue certainly is how to define the subgroups. I'm not going to worry about that. I found that a bit woolly, but I think Paul feels the same way: exactly how to define the subgroups *is* a bit woolly.

I'd like to suggest that, in some cases, it may be important to extend the model that Paul described to include one more parameter. This takes it beyond the Mantel–Haenszel statistic, I'm afraid. But, the extra parameter may be worth it in some cases. Just to review, the model that Holland proposed has a constant odds ratio (or a constant log-odds ratio) across all the different groups. The null value of this log-odds is zero (or the null value of the odds ratio is one). This null value states that there is no *dif*—no difference between the groups. When there are a fair number of groups, it might be informative to enrich the model. Suppose we think of these log-odds ratios, these deltas, as having a normal distribution with say mean μ and variance σ^2. In that context, Holland's null model says the variance is zero. I'll consider Paul's null hypothesis to be that the common log-odds is zero versus the alternative hypothesis that it is not zero.

The model that I'm suggesting says that, these log-odds may vary across the different groups, but on average might be zero. Why do I think that might be useful? Well, suppose that we fit the expanded model where these log-odds have a normal distribution and found out that the average log-odds was zero, but the variance was large. I'm not sure how powerful the Mantel–Haenszel would be to reject that null. I may be wrong, but I suspect it wouldn't be very powerful. But, in fact, finding a situation with deltas having zero mean and large variance may be an important discovery. It would say that these groups of people that have been created, if taken as an ensemble, show no overall indication of *dif* because they balance each other—some favor one, some favor the other one. That might be okay in some contexts if you're always going to be dealing with this group intact. On the other hand, if for some reason, you're going to start chipping away at parts of this group, then you can severely unbalance the situation.

Also it gives you a way of addressing whether any *dif* is important in size. For example, suppose that in my larger model, with both a mean and a variance, that the mean was small and the variance was small. That indicates you're probably okay, as opposed to the case where the mean was small and the variance was large. I'm not saying how to fit that model, but merely pointing a worthwhile way to spend one more parameter.

This idea of using one more parameter wisely is one of the games statisticians often play. What Paul said implicitly was that giving a different parameter for each group is a silly way to use parameters, and that this common log-odds is a good parameter. I agree, but if there is one more parameter to spend, I think it may be the variance of the log-odds. It seems that there may be something more to be teased out of the data, at least in certain contexts.

In addition it would be nice to handle all items at once. Then the same kinds of comments can be made about the ensemble of items. Log-odds for the items that average to zero say that this test, as an ensemble, is sort of fair—at least it averages out. However, if you start selecting items, you're in trouble if the variance is large, even if the average log-odds is zero. Thus there is another context in which worrying about the variability of these log-odds seems to be potentially important.

ON WILLINGHAM AND USING LOW DOSE TECHNOLOGY TO TEST HANDICAPPED PEOPLE

My final comments on this first collection of talks have to do with Warren Willingham's paper on trying to calibrate tests for handicapped people. It seems to me it's a very hard problem and needs a framework pretty badly. While Warren gave an excellent outline of the problems, I'm less enthusiastic about his outline of the solutions. I suspect that's because he didn't really try terribly hard to outline many kinds of solutions. I tried to think a bit about what a framework would be. I couldn't come up with much except one little proposal, which I'll describe. Maybe this is old hat, or wrong.

There are factors that we can define that can be altered from a standard test to create a test for handicapped people. For example, one factor would be the time allotted to take it. Another factor would be size of type, and so forth. There might be lots of these factors. Factors like "Braille vs. written" I'm not quite sure how to handle within this framework, so I'll focus more on the factors that are like "time" and "type size."

Suppose we define values of these factors such that a priori we believe that handicapped people are *not* disadvantaged for those values. That is, if we gave this test based on extended time and enlarged type size to all test takers, the handicapped person would not be disadvantaged with respect to the nonhandicapped person. Now it also seems clear, though, that nonhandicapped persons with the extra time might do better than they would have done in the usual testing environment. But eventually you would reach a point where if you made the type even bigger and gave them even more time, it wouldn't make any difference—so the format of the test is no longer a barrier. Now because of the chosen values on these factors, the factors are no longer a barrier to good performance on the test. All examinees are performing at their best on the test.

Suppose we view this problem as being analogous to the low-dose extrapolation problems for possible carcinogens. Low-dose extrapolation, for those of you who don't know about it, is used to structure experiments on doses of potential carcinogens. While we really care about the dose levels that people actually get if they're drinking five Diet Rites or Diet Cokes a day, experiments on rats or mice with those dosages would have to run for many years or on millions of rats before anything is detected. So instead what's done is to pump rats full of huge doses;

some at the equivalent of 12 cases of Diet Coke a day, some at 6 cases of Diet Coke a day, and some at 2 cases of Diet Coke a day. Next a response surface is calculated and *extrapolated* down to the normal region to determine elevated cancer risk at low doses. So if you read in the paper about a really stupid study at EPA in which they pumped these rats full of 12 cases of Diet Coke a day, you shouldn't dismiss it as being irrelevent because you'll never drink 12 cases of Diet Coke a day. The experiments are designed to draw inferences about a question that's very hard to address directly by doing something relevant in a reasonable amount of time.

Now let's return to the handicapped testing situation where factors like time-to-take-a-test are analogous to dosage. What you could do is obtain a response surface for nonhandicapped people as a function of these manipulable factors like time. Thus you give these tests, with extended factors, to a collection of nonhandicapped people and find a response surface, which would tell you what their average performance is as a function of these factors. Presumably their performance would improve as you made these factors more liberal (larger type probably won't do much but more time should help). Such a response surface would have at one extreme the actual operational test, and at the other extreme of the factor space, a test with the values of these factors that you're contemplating using with handicapped people. This is a lot of information.

Next, you assume that this surface also represents handicapped people, so you can extrapolate scores back. You take the score that a handicapped person has on the test and use the normal response function to extrapolate back to the score that he would have received had he not taken special administration. It's a sub-junctive outcome. It's hypothetical. The person has a handicap. But given his performance on a test that does not hinder him by its format, you can compare him to nonhandicapped people taking the same test. To repeat, this is accomplished by using this response surface idea to extrapolate back and say how he would have performed in a regular testing situation. Now, you could just do this in a prediction format, but I think the idea of the response surface for both nonhandicapped and handicapped individuals is a way to verify whether the underlying assumptions are at all realistic. At least it gives you some insight as to what you might mean by doing the calibration.

This is as close as I could get to answering, "What does it mean to give a test that's different, with respect to these factors, but obtaining a score that's comparable?" I did this by trying to create a score that somehow is comparable to the scores that were given to nonhandicapped people. It's certainly not a perfect idea, and I haven't spent much time thinking about it. But, something like this may be a way to obtain agreement on how to calculate scores for handicapped people on those tests. That's the way people get agreement on low dose extrapolation and thus satisfy the Delaney clause[2] for what is a carcinogen and what is not.

---

[2]The Delaney clause specifies that one cannot add anything to any food or drug that is carcinogenic.

I'd be interested in any comments that Warren or anyone else might have about whether this perspective makes any sense at all. I think that the handi-capped calibration problem is probably the hardest one that we heard today. It's very difficult to make progress, especially if we don't come up with some framework within which we can get agreement.

ON BERT GREEN AND COMPUTER-AIDED TESTING

It's nice to see that computer-aided testing is a not being viewed as a panacea and that there is careful thought being conducted concerning the host of new prob-lems that may be associated with its use. Years ago, my naïve understanding of what was going on with computer-aided testing suggested that many people felt that all the hard problems had been solved. It's quite clear from Bert's descrip-tion that now a lot of careful thought is going into the new problems that have arisen.

ON MUTHÉN AND STRUCTURAL MODELING

First, I was pleased to see a balanced presentation of the uses of structural equation models. I'm also pleased to see the avoidance of the causal language that seems to swirl around the use of such models. Lots of people have made the point that the use of the word "cause" in such models usually has nothing to do with the use of "cause" that we know in the English language (e.g., "I took two aspirins and that "caused" my headache to go away.") These are "causal" statements with different meanings of the word "cause" that have nothing to do with the meaning "I performed a manipulation and therefore something changed." My conversations with the sophisticated people who do such model-ing show that they know that this is true. It's only the casual causal modelers who run the danger of believing that it has something to do with cause and effect. To repeat: We're not talking about cause and effect when we apply such models, and so I'm happy to see Bengt avoiding that jargon. Also, I think that it important that he pointed out that there are lots of poor applications of such causal models.

Certainly there are lots of poor applications of structural equation modeling. I think the area leaves itself open to a lot of criticism. Some of the criticism has come from mathematical statisticians. While I'm sympathetic to some of the points being made, I'm not generally sympathetic with the general attitude ex-pressed in these criticisms. Structural modeling is a pretty easy target in the sense that it's a giant program in which you stuff inputs and it spews outputs. The danger is that nobody thinks very hard about what is put in or what comes out. On the other hand, people use it a lot. Social scientists use it because it appears to address the kinds of questions that they have and for which they want solutions. A hardline critic sounds like a' naysayer, saying, "You can't do it, it's bad science.'' But, he doesn't offer much in return; he doesn't provide any alternatives. I think that serious researchers in the field aren't going to give something up that appears to help them unless something is offered in its place. This kind of hardline criticism characterizes a lot of mathematical/statistical criticism that evolves from a purist point of view stating that if your data don't satisfy all the constraints, you shouldn't use the method. I don't think that's fair. I think researchers are going to use the tools that are available. If we say that those tools aren't so good, they are going to continue to use them unless we show that they're really making drastic mistakes or give them something that does the job better. I think that statisticians haven't been particularly good at coming up with alternatives, although they have been pretty good at making criticisms.

One of these criticisms is that because structural equation modeling is a gigantic machine that works like a black box (and very few users understand what's inside the black box), it tends to make the user very distant from the data. You don't really know what's going on; this giant thing churns away and out comes an answer. Being distant from the data means it's tough to create diagnostics that indicate whether the data really fit the model. There are all these assumptions about very high-dimensional normal structures with complicated constraints, and so verifying that the model assumptions are plausible is a tough job.

I think the models can be very useful if thought of as exploratory (the same way that factor analysis can be thought of as exploratory). At the end, however, you should try to return and explain what is learned in terms of the things that are observable. If you learn something from fooling around with a big data set and building all these models, it should tell you something that's pretty simple in terms of the variables that were collected. Furthermore, you should be able to explain it in a simple way, so that the man on the street can understand. If the only way conclusions can be understood is within some giant multivariate model, then you probably don't really understand your data. I'm a fan of using complicated models for the purposes of understanding what's going on in the data. But for the goal of being able to display the results in a simple way, users often stop much too high up in the analysis, too removed from the data. Bengt made it clear that he does not do that very often. He didn't really believe the p-values. He understands that the p-values really aren't p-values (uniform on $[0,1]$ under the null). They are merely used as guides as to which models fit better. That's important.

There are three additional limitations of the structural modeling approach to the world, that is in addition to removing you far from the data.

1. They are not particularly suited to dichotomous outcomes (although I'd be interested in what Bengt says about them in this context). It's not that the linear model can't be used with dichotomous outcomes or categorical data, but the meaning of ''no interaction'' is different when you're using linear models than

log-linear models. It converts no interaction to probabilities that add up. In log-linear models, no interaction means the probabilities are multiplicative, which corresponds to independence in the distributional sense of independence.

Simple structures for describing the world usually use models with independence in the usual sense of distributional independence. The experience I have with such things is that if you use linear models on dichotomous data, you tend to find far more complicated stories (more high-order interactions, more parameters) than you would if you use a more natural model (e.g., log-linear), where no interaction corresponds to distributional independence.

2. The second criticism is that structural models really don't handle data in the way they are collected in the real world. We collect data as clustered, stratified, probability proportional to size (PPS) samples. In fact, the data that were used for illustration may have been from a clustered, stratified, PPS sample. The data structure is complicated, but then we dump it into one of these programs and the model underlying the program only *really* works perfectly when there is simple, random sampling with no clustering, no stratification, and no PPS. The consequences are unclear. Certainly, standard errors and p-values are grossly optimistic in a lot of cases because the algorithm doesn't account for the clustering or the disproportionate sampling. In cases where there are interactions with variables that define the clusters, the estimates can be *way* off, even if the underlying model is, in fact, essentially correct. That's a real limitation, I think, of the way the structural modeling programs are applied to data bases. Thus if this technology is applied to large data bases that have been taken from public use files that come from highly structured samples, the programs don't match the data structures very well, and as a result the inferences aren't necessarily valid, even if the models are O.K. However, if the programs are used in an exploratory way, that is not a severe criticism. If you do it just to figure out what sort of structure might be there and then do a later analysis that is much simpler and more down to earth, I think it can be useful.

3. The third general criticism of the structural modeling approach, as it is used, is that it doesn't handle missing data. For example, in the data set that was used as an illustration, one of the variables, father's occupation, was 40% missing. The right way to handle that isn't currently available within the structural modeling approach. I think that this is an issue that gets pushed under the rug, the same way other more subtle issues do when researchers, who have a large research agenda, become so interested in turning the crank to get output from this big machine that they abuse the data in various ways to make it fit.

So, the general tone of those comments is negative because I believe structural equation modeling is overused, but I want to emphasize again that I'm not negative about the presentation that was given. Of course, Bengt focused more on the positive aspects of structural modeling so I tried to balance the picture for general users with the warnings contained in my criticisms.

ON LARRY HEDGES, TEST VALIDITY
AND META-ANALYSIS

I find Larry's formulation right on target. That's not surprising. I think that the clear stating of the assumptions is critical as is the attempt to try to stay relatively close to the data. For those who haven't previously seen the algebra that Larry put up, it may seem like you're quite far from the data. In fact, you're not. Each of those little parameters is really closely tied to things that are observable. Even the algorithm that Larry talked about, the EM algorithm, produces output at each step that has a very clear interpretation in terms of things that you wish you could observe. So, it's not Newton–Raphson where you're talking about the first and second derivatives of some log-likelihood function. It works simply. Suppose there is a value you wished you had observed. What the EM algorithm does is iteratively estimate the missing values and then reestimate the parameters. So it does what you would do if you had complete data. With each new estimate of the parameters, it reestimates the missing values and just cycles around. Each iteration of the algorithm produces these two steps. The output of these steps is something that you can stare at and make sense of. The output is very statistical and very close to the data. It's estimating what were the missing values. Thus if there are crazy values being estimated, then you shouldn't believe what is going on—you shouldn't believe the underlying model.

One slight correction to Larry's description of the EM algorithm, which also applies to the way I just described the E-step, is that EM doesn't really estimate the missing values, except in certain cases, like contingency table models, where the statistics that you thought that you needed were linear in the data values. So in the case that Larry was talking about, when he wished that he had the true values, the θ_i, he said in the E-step he had estimated the θ_i. Well, that wasn't quite right. He had to estimate the variance of the θ_i as well. The variance of the θ_i depends upon θ_i^2. So, you actually have to estimate both the θ_i and θ_i^2. That's just a little warning on the use of EM. You can't just estimate the missing values, stuff them in, do a complete data analysis and cycle. That's not quite right. But it's close. It's close in spirit but you have to be a little more careful.

Two points of caution on the use of empirical Bayes and the EM algorithm approach that Larry described are as follows:

1. You have to worry a bit about the exchangeability assumption. If you have no way of distinguishing among any of the studies out there, if the studies are exchangeable, then there's no order to them. If they're exchangeable, you don't know how to group them in any way. If this is really the case, then the particular method that Larry described is fine and it makes a lot of sense.

On the other hand, if there are subgroups of the studies that should hang together, then you do not want to be shrinking to a point (which is what the empirical Bayes procedure that Larry was describing does—shrinking toward the

252

grand mean in some sense). You want to be shrinking toward some other surface, maybe a local mean for this type of study, and another local mean for another type of study and then maybe shrink those local means toward the grand mean. So, there's a hierarchy of models that can be fit, sometimes shrinking toward a regression plane, sometimes shrinking toward a mixture model. The rule can be more complicated than the one that Larry described. The algorithms still work but they get harder, and so sometimes you have to do more work. The point here is that there is a danger in thinking, "I have a hundred studies. I can shrink them all toward a common value and I'll have a great estimate." Well, be careful. Some of the studies may lie in some region defined by observed factors where different things are going on. I'll come back to that point in the context of the Schmidt presentation.

2. My second concern with the general empirical Bayes approach is that sometimes you can shrink too much by using a point estimate. The empirical Bayes approach that Larry described yielded a point estimate of the between variance. Even if the best point estimate of the between variance is zero, you may not want to use it. Consider the plot that Larry showed which had the likelihood function that looked like a gamma or a chi-square distribution. It was somewhat positive, but then came down rapidly. Even if the graph for the likelihood of the between variance had peaked at zero, so that the best single estimate of the between variability was zero, that doesn't mean that you should use zero. There's still a lot of evidence that there is variability. The likelihood function doesn't come dropping down like a cliff. There's still a lot of probability for positive values. In fact, that sort of plot appeared in the data analysis I did of eight coaching studies at ETS several years ago. In that case, the plot actually was maximized at zero. The standard empirical Bayes approach would shrink everything to zero, saying there was no variability in these coefficients. My paper tried to point out that that's a bad answer—that the validity coefficients do differ and you don't want to shrink them all, even though in that case the F-test for different effects was less than one. So just because the data are consistent with the hypothesis that there's no variability, that does not mean you always want to act as if there is none.

ON SCHMIDT AND VALIDITY GENERALIZATION

That brings me to the last paper by Schmidt. One of his underlying themes is that if there is only weak evidence that something is not zero, you should treat it as zero. That may be something of an overstatement, in which case Frank certainly can respond. However, one can demonstrate, in a lot of cases, that this attitude doesn't give you good answers; at least *as* good answers.

If you try to summarize the world in a simple way, certainly it's easy to say there's no evidence to contradict the model that there is no variability in these validity coefficients. That's a useful summary, which I'm not going to argue with at all. But, to go from that to say, "I now can make my best predictions using this simple summary" is just wrong. I think a simple example can demonstrate that.

Suppose we had a lot of validity studies, say one from each of a hundred environments done with the same amount of restriction of range and other sorts of noise with observed correlations that vary between .8 and .2. Further suppose that we wouldn't reject the hypothesis that all had the same underlying population correlation coefficient with P-value .7; thus the evidence seems to be very much supporting the null hypothesis of constant coefficient.

Well, now let's say I propose a bet, and we're going to go back into two of these environments and redo those validity studies with much larger sample sizes and really nail down the validity coefficients. The two environments that we will choose are the ones with the *highest* observed validity coefficient and with the *lowest* observed validity coefficient. Well, out of the hundred, we would have gone with the one with an observed validity coefficient of .8 and the other with an observed validity coefficient of .2. The Schmidt hypothesis is that in these new validity studies in the two environments it will be equally likely that the .2 environment will have a higher validity coefficient than the .8 environment. The hypothesis (the simple one that has been accepted for purposes of description) is that the population validity coefficients are identical, and so the only difference between the .2 and the .8 is the sampling variability. Therefore, Frank should be happy to take either side of that bet. If you are happy to take either side of that bet, I'd be very happy to gamble with you—especially if there's a lot of money at risk.

Notwithstanding the evidence supporting the null hypothesis, there's some evidence that the .8 is higher than the .2. Such evidence won't go away with a hypothesis test, and it won't go away with any amount of data that you're likely to see. The point is that although it is often useful to think about the validity coefficients as being essentially the same when the evidence is like this, such a null hypothesis is not a statement of fact. It's not something that you'd bet the mortgage on; it's just a summary to make life simpler for you.

Now I'd like to return to the question of subgroups and shrinking toward planes or shrinking toward mixture models or other kinds of models, in addition to the common method of shrinking toward the grand mean. There are a lot of descriptors of these various validity studies, and I think that a careful analysis really would be concerned with differences that might occur if we built in these possible descriptors of what these validity studies really are. I didn't see very much about such possibilities in the Schmidt presentation.

I had a hard time figuring out how to discuss much of the Schmidt presentation because a lot of it was a position paper on validity generalization and a documentation of its broad use. To this statistician, the presentation seemed to be documenting the broad use of mixed model analysis of variance. It's nice to see modern statistical ideas finding their way into applications. I'm positive about that, but I have to say that I prefer seeing more of the kind of formulation that Hedges presented. It leaves more open ends. It leaves science more to do—reflecting the state of nature. It doesn't try to tie up all the loose ends by saying, "Well, we really know now what's going to happen in the future. There is no variability." The models that Larry was pointing out say, "There are other ways to model the world and you may find something out sometime later." I like that a bit more.

One other comment relates back to the structural equation modeling issue. One of the trends that Schmidt talked about was the emphasis on latent variables and LISREL in structural modeling. As I said before, I'm less enthusiastic about such models. I'm sympathetic to the desire to provide answers, but I'm unsympathetic to the black box use and the lack of understanding of how highly model-dependent the resultant answers really are. People can often fool themselves in dealing with latent variables. It's hard to know about things you never see and how invisible things might relate to each other.

You all know the tale about the guy who does a factor analysis, develops a wonderful story based on his interpretation of all the factors, and then his research assistant tells him that he put his matrix in upside down. He says, "Oh well, it doesn't matter. I'll do it again," and comes out with another wonderful story—completely different—but it still makes a completely wonderful wondrous story. I think that's very easy to do when there's nothing observed that you want to estimate. All these things are figments of your imagination. Theories are figments of the imagination and it's nice to have theories, but it's nicer to have theories that have behavioral consequences; things you can observe. People too often stop with the latent variables because they think they have discovered something simply when they can name it.

I'll make a final comment on something that did not appear in the talk that Schmidt gave, but did appear in his paper. It is related, again, to Hedges's formulation. In Hedges's formulation, the things that were being pulled toward each other were the validity coefficients—in fact the Fisher z-transform of the correlation. Schmidt didn't seem to like the z-transform very much. Frank didn't do anything that was technically wrong, but for uses like this where you're trying pull coefficients toward each other, the z-transform is the right thing to do. That comes from the fact that the sampling distribution of the correlation coefficient is clearly nonnormal and its variance depends on the underlying correlation coefficient. The whole idea behind the Fisher z-transformation is that its sampling distribution *is* nearly normal, even for relatively small sample sizes. Furthermore, its sampling variability is pretty much independent of the value of true correlation. So, you can treat them the way you treat usual normal measurements. That point seems to be missed in the Schmidt paper. Of course one gets different averages when you average Fisher zs and then transform to obtain a correlation than when you directly average the correlations.

The point is you're estimating two different quantities. Median income does not equal mean income. You have to decide which estimand you like. I think that very often it makes more sense to average up zs than to average up rs. The difference between a correlation of .90 and .98 is enormous in lots of ways — much larger than the difference between the correlations 0.0 and 0.08. The r-to-z transform takes that into account by stretching out the tails. The average of the zs is thus the more appropriate average than the simple average of the correlations.

SUMMARY

In summary, I thought that the talks yesterday and today really covered a very broad range of topics. This indicates that there's a lot of thinking and progress in the areas of test validity and validity generalization, both on the conceptual-psychological front and on the statistical front. As a statistician, I'm particularly glad to see some of the more modern statistical ideas finding their way into this important area.

Author Index

U.S. Equal Employment Opportunity Commission, 177, 182, *189*

V

van der Flier, H., 141, 143, *144,* 149, *168*
Van Lehn, K., *58, 59*
Vicino, F. L., 82, 84, *86*
Vojir, C., 96, *103*

W

Wainer, H., 80, *86,* 142, *145,* 149, 152, 162, *169*
Wald, A., 152, 153, *169*
Walker, D. F., 4, 7, *15*
Wanous, J. P., 177, *188*
Ward, W. C., *121*
Wardrop, J. L., 149, *168*
Warren, B. M., 112, *121*
Weil, E. M., 66, *75*
Weiner, S. S., 4, 7, *15*

Weiss, D. J., 82, *86*
Welsh, J. R., 10, *17*
West, S. G., 177, *187*
Wetzel, C. D., 82, *86*
Whetzel, D. L., 176, *189*
White, D. M., 78, *86*
Wigdor, A., 85, *86*
Wilfong, H. D., 82, *86*
Williams, D. M., 137, *145,* 149, *169*
Willingham, W., 92, 97, *103*
Wilson, D., 227, *238*
Wood, R., 227, *238*
Wunder, R. S., 182, *189*

Y

Yalow, E. S., 6, 7, *17,* 38, *45*
Yule, G., 118, *120*

Z

Zedeck, S., 179, *188*

Subject Index

U

Unidimensionality, 214, 226

V

Validity,
  concurrent, 21, 25, 28
  content, 22–23, 25, 27–28, 34–36, 38,
    106, 109
  convergent, 26–28

  criterion, 21, 25, 34–36, 51, 58, 86, 173
  predictive, 12, 20, 22, 25, 56, 83, 100, 116
Validity arguments, 1, 4, 7, 14
Validity assessment, 171, 173
Validity coefficients, 28, 53, 191–192, 199,
    201, 206, 254
Validity studies, 24, 192, 200, 254
Variance components, 195
Visual impairment, 90–94

W

Wald statistic, 244, 245